Not for Profit. All for Education.

Oxford University Press USA is a not-for-profit publisher dedicated to offering the highest quality textbooks at the best possible prices. We believe that it is important to provide everyone with access to superior textbooks at affordable prices. Oxford University Press textbooks are 30%–70% less expensive than comparable books from commercial publishers.

The press is a department of the University of Oxford, and our publishing proudly serves the university's mission: promoting excellence in research, scholarship, and education around the globe. We do not publish in order to generate revenue: we generate revenue in order to publish and also to fund scholarships, provide start-up grants to early-stage researchers, and refurbish libraries.

What does this mean to you?
It means that Oxford University Press USA published this book to best support your studies while also being mindful of your wallet.

Not for Profit. *All* for Education.
As a not-for-profit publisher, Oxford University Press USA is uniquely situated to offer the highest quality scholarship at the best possible prices.

OXFORD
UNIVERSITY PRESS

The Paradoxes of the American Presidency

The Paradoxes of the American Presidency

THOMAS E. CRONIN
Colorado College

MICHAEL A. GENOVESE
Loyola Marymount University

MEENA BOSE
Hofstra University

FIFTH EDITION

New York   Oxford
OXFORD UNIVERSITY PRESS

Oxford University Press is a department of the University of Oxford. It furthers the University's objective of excellence in research, scholarship, and education by publishing worldwide. Oxford is a registered trade mark of Oxford University Press in the UK and certain other countries.

Published in the United States of America by Oxford University Press
198 Madison Avenue, New York, NY 10016, United States of America.

© 2018, 2013, 2010, 1999 by Oxford University Press

Library of Congress Cataloging-in-Publication Data

Names: Cronin, Thomas E., author. | Genovese, Michael A., author. | Bose, Meenekshi, 1970- author.
Title: The paradoxes of the American presidency / Thomas E. Cronin, Colorado College, Michael A. Genovese, Loyola Marymount University, Meenekshi Bose, Hofstra University.
Description: Fifth edition. | New York : Oxford University Press, 2018.
Identifiers: LCCN 2017001164 | ISBN 9780190648503 (pbk.)
Subjects: LCSH: Presidents—United States.
Classification: LCC JK516 .C73 2018 | DDC 352.230973—dc23 LC record available at https://lccn.loc.gov/2017001164

TABLE OF CONTENTS

PREFACE

After his surprising election victory in 2016, President Donald J. Trump moved quickly in 2017 to reverse many of his predecessor's initiatives and advance instead the conservative policies and populist measures on which he had campaigned. Viewing his election as a new era or even a new order in American politics—in the tradition of the eras of Andrew Jackson, Lincoln, FDR, or Ronald Reagan—Trump indicated he wanted to be an activist and ambitious president, one who will test the traditional limits of presidential leadership.

Nearly 138 million Americans voted on November 8, 2016. Of the total votes cast, former Secretary of State and U.S. Senator Hillary Clinton won nearly three million more than Trump. But Trump succeeded in winning the Electoral College—304 Electoral College votes to Clinton's 227. And under our system specified in our Constitution, this is how the presidential election is decided.

That a popular vote winner can lose the presidential election is one of the paradoxes of our American democracy. The system that provides for the Electoral College is one of the federalist legacies left to us by our founders. How this works and why it was so designed is discussed in Chapter 3.

The 2016 election was also our fifth-eighth consecutive election, and on January 20, 2017, we witnessed for the twenty-second time the peaceful transfer of power from one political party to the other. No other country has achieved this political and constitutional record.

The 2016 campaign was one of the nastiest and most controversial in our history (with Russian hacking of the Democratic Party, last-minute intervention by the FBI, character smears, and fake news stories). Neither candidate enjoyed favorable public approval ratings. About 42 percent of those eligible to vote in the election chose not to vote at all, and almost eight million of those who did vote voted for one of third-party candidates.

Hillary Clinton's campaign appeared to embrace most of Barack Obama's policies, and although Obama had 60 percent positive job approval rating at the end of his second term, this was not enough in the Democratic ticket to win over the critically important rural and rust-belt vote. Trump, who had surprised most everyone again by winning the Republican nomination, again surprised everyone when he won the Electoral College vote. Pollsters, media pundits, political scientists, Democrats, and even many Republicans underestimated the appeal of Trump's populist, anti-Washington, and border security message. In many ways, too, Trump's message was his attitude.

Trump's campaign pronouncements were often strident and alarmist, yet he also presented himself as the candidate for change, for shaking things up, for "draining the swamp" of Washington, D.C. Like a rogue elephant in the Republican Party, he separated himself from the herd. "I refuse to be called a politician," he announced, funding much of his campaign from his own fortune. In today's media environment, Trump benefited from twelve years of experience as the star of his own reality TV show *The Apprentice*, which gave him celebrity status as well as plenty of stagecraft confidence.

Trump's simple campaign slogan, "Make America Great Again," evoked images of a past national glory that he alone might reclaim for the nation. And in a year in which 75 percent of Americans thought we were headed in the wrong direction, this strategy worked.

As we suggest in this book, Americans hold conflicting views about what they want in a president. While we want reasoned and reflective judgment and significant political experience in our political leaders, we also yearn for a fresh face, an outsider who will challenge the status quo and become an agent for change.

Trump capitalized on the fear of working-class Americans that they were losing ground economically, with manufacturing moving overseas and employers illegally hiring undocumented workers. He was probably also helped by the fact that 2016 was a relatively low-growth economic year for America. In this economic environment, Trump appeared as the ultimate paradoxical candidate—a privileged urban billionaire who became the voice of rural and working-class Americans. He overshadowed his rivals in the primary by dominating the news every day. He bragged about his successes, and his supporters perceived his unscripted political incorrectness, his passionate (if sometimes inaccurate) claims, and ad hoc speaking style as that of an authentic "non-politician."

As Trump began his presidency in early 2017, his rhetoric as president still reflected his ad hoc campaign style. He had come into office with a low job approval rating (44 percent) and protest marches occurring across the country the day after his inauguration, but he also had majorities in both the Senate and the House of Representatives. Ignoring the narrowness of his election margin (a shift of 78,000 votes in three states would have resulted in a Clinton victory), Trump acted as if he had a populist mandate across the country.

Appointing conservative business leaders and generals to his cabinet, Trump regularly rebuked mainstream media and worked hard to convert traditional Republicans to his more populist and "America First" agenda. He signed executive orders loosening regulations on businesses, banks, and local governments; investing in public works projects; and strengthening the military. He nominated conservative U.S. Appeals Court Judge Neil Gorsuch to the U.S. Supreme Court. And most Congressional Republicans climbed on board.

Many observers have suggested that the office and our constitutional system will change Trump more than Trump will change our system. But no one doubts that the Trump presidency will be a different one. He comes to the White House with no foreign policy or military experience and little political experience. He has a combative temperament and doesn't mind contradicting himself. Can an outsider and an outsized personality like Trump do what insiders have been unable to accomplish? Can he bypass the media and go directly to the people?

Trump's unilateralist approach ("America First!"; "Build the Wall and Make Mexico Pay for It!") has worried many observers. Whereas few economists or business leaders believe that protectionism and trade wars will benefit the United States, Trump has said that the United States is too involved in the rest of the world and hinted at trade wars and a lessened role in defending our European and Asian allies. Of one thing we can be sure—there will be continuing debates within the country about the proper role for the United States in its global relationships. The foreign policy challenges the president faces are discussed later in this book.

Dealmaker Trump knows that business deals involve compromise. Yet in his own business and in his campaign Trump has been used to getting his own way. His businesses were privately owned so he did not have to report to a board of directors. In the White House, however, Trump has to work within a three-branch system of government; deal with the federal bureaucracy, the media, and more than 200 foreign nations; and, most important, show that he is willing to be held accountable to the consent of the American people.

THE TRUMP PRESIDENCY: THE EARLY GOING

One of the central paradoxes of the American presidency is that what it takes to become president is not the same as what is needed to be a successful president. For Donald J. Trump, the only president to come to the White House with no political or military experience, this paradox was particularly evident in his first months in office.

Trump campaigned as a populist, promising to drain the "swamp" of Washington, D.C. As president, however, he surrounded himself with multi-millionaire cabinet appointees and generals, yet was slow to recruit people to lower administrative positions. The bravado and off-the-cuff style of his campaign rhetoric translated into questionable and conflicting presidential pronouncements. His simplistic campaign slogan ("Make America Great Again") has given way to his understanding that "nobody knew how complicated [health care] was." His first months served as an illustration of the paradox that succeeding in getting elected is not the same as succeeding in being president.

Indeed, Trump's first months read like a primer on the paradoxes of the American presidency.

On the campaign trail Trump had direct contact with large audiences; the format was one person—Trump—talking to the many. As president, however, he has had to deal with individuals who are leaders in their own institutions: with recalcitrant members of Congress, independently-minded judges and loud skeptical reporters.

These institutions, part of our checks-and-balances system of government, have made governing harder than expected for the new populist-elected president. Trump has revealed his frustrations at these checks-and-balances, blaming members of Congress for not passing a bill, castigating "so-called" judges for ruling against executive orders, labeling unfavorable press reports as "fake news."

This is another demonstration of the central paradox—the campaigner needs to offer a clear vision of what he or she sees for a future pathway for the nation. But the president needs to work with other institutions to persuade them that the changes he or she wants make sense. And so, Trump has backed away from some of his campaign pledges. With NATO, NAFTA, and dealing with China, he has become more conventional.

Why do we care about the first 100 days of a new presidency? Isn't that an artificial benchmark? The answer is yes, but ever since Franklin Delano Roosevelt, it has been a shorthand way to measure a president's likely success.

Roosevelt came to office amid the Great Depression of 1929. He was elected in a landslide along with Democratic majorities in both houses of Congress. In his first 100 days, Roosevelt succeeded in getting a series of sweeping reforms passed and that has become a benchmark for judging how well a president is doing.

As Donald Trump took office, economic conditions in the country were good: the economy was growing, unemployment was down and the upheavals of the Great Recession of 2008-2010 were slowly being improved. Yet President Trump offered a dark, dystopian view of the state of the nation in an address to Congress, describing our country's condition as "American carnage."

In the early days of his presidency, Trump signed a flurry of executive orders, including a ban on all immigration from seven majority-Muslim countries. Within days this order was overturned by a federal judge in Washington state and then by the Ninth Circuit Court of Appeals. Part of the reasoning offered by the judges was that Trump's campaign speeches clearly showed that the intent of his executive order was to discriminate against Muslims.

After this defeat Trump issued a new executive order, with minor changes, but still banning immigration from six predominantly Muslim countries. This new order was quickly blocked by federal judges in Hawaii and Maryland. Trump also signed executive orders giving local immigration officials more power to detain and deport illegal immigrants and limiting "sanctuary cities" from receiving federal funds. But the future of these executive orders remained uncertain.

As President Trump assumed office, a steady drip of possible scandal accompanied him, as the press carried a series of revelations about Russian influence on the 2016 presidential election. Clear evidence (presented to Congress by F.B.I. Director James Comey) showed that Russia had hacked into Democratic Party e-mails and saturated social media with fake news stories in an attempt to influence the election in Trump's favor. (Russian president Vladimir Putin, who was directly involved in ordering the Russian hacking, apparently had a strong personal antipathy to Secretary of State Hillary Clinton.)

Meanwhile, the press kept reporting about contacts between Trump advisors and Russian representatives. The big question—the possible scandal—was whether Trump officials knew about the Russian hacking, whether they tolerated it, or even encouraged it.

Such a charge would be serious. Even if there was no collusion between members of the Trump team and Russian officials, the idea that a foreign country could influence an American election was widely perceived as a threat to our national security. As reporters kept uncovering new connections between Trump advisors and Russia, the steady drip of news stories became a cloud of possible scandal hanging over the new president's head.

Frustrated by the relentless barrage of news stories, Trump complained that these reports were "fake news." He first issued blanket denials, then fired his newly-appointed national security advisor (retired Army General Michael Flynn). He banned unsympathetic reporters from White House press briefings and labeled the press "the enemy of the people." News analysts suggested Trump was trying to delegitimize the press.

In his first year in office, President Trump was definitely an activist. He regularly issued executive orders and called for lessened regulations on business. His biggest early victory was working with the U.S. Senate to win confirmation of the conservative judge Neil Gorsuch to the Supreme Court.

His top policy priorities of reforming the tax system, investing huge new funds in infrastructure, and overhauling the Affordable Care Act, however, proved difficult and frustratingly slow for Trump, to bring about.

Trump's first months were a classic example an inspired outsider maverick storming the nation's capital, only to find that our constitutional system of Madisonian checks-and-balances, as well as the generally moderate ideology of most Americans, make sharp policy shifts difficult to accomplish.

America is a powerful and rich country, but our political system is a multi-splintered one, with many different governing arrangements. Many factors influence a president's ability to make and execute policy decisions. The limitations a president faces are discussed later in this book.

In this second decade of the twenty-first century, Americans' trust in our national government is low. Economic anxieties are high. Many issues divide the nation. The American presidency can be a unifying influence, helping to articulate and encourage the search for the elusive common good. Yet this country has had at least as many failed presidencies as successful ones. As we discuss later in this book, strong presidents are undesirable unless their political objectives are fair and in service of the public good and unless their dealings are democratic and constitutional. We admire Hamiltonian energy in the White House, yet only if it is wisely used to encourage us live up to our Jeffersonian and Rooseveltian ideals. These conflicting goals for the presidency—and for the country—are the subject of this book.

ACKNOWLEDGEMENTS

Special thanks to our Oxford University Press editors Jennifer Carpenter, Matt Rohal, and Scott Bledsoe for guiding us through this fifth edition. Michael and Tom are grateful that distinguished Hofstra University presidential scholar Meena Bose has joined us as a co-author.

We thank Debbie Ruel for her excellent copy-editing, Jenelle Emmert at SPi for her supervision of the production process, and Ken Hassman, for his help in indexing.

Throughout this revision, we profited from thoughtful and thorough feedback reviews by the following political science professors: Nathaniel Birkhead, Kansas State University; Thomas W. Bonnett, Baruch College, CUNY; Christine L. Day, University of New Orleans; Jasmine Farrier, University of Louisville; Samuel B. Hoff, Delaware State University; Ambrus Price, California University of Pennsylvania; Adam L. Warber, Clemson University; and Darren Wheeler, Ball State University.

Tom Cronin thanks Jessica Pauls for typing and editing and Ansel Carpenter, Addis Goldman, Robert D. Loevy, Jared Russell, and Ray Barrie-Kivel for research assistance. Michael Genovese is grateful to Ashley Oshiro, Breanne Schneider, and Jeremy Selland for their assistance. Meena Bose thanks Lucy and Brian Barr and Hofstra University. We thank our incomparable students at Colorado College, Loyola Marymount Univsersity, and Hofstra University.

Finally, and importantly, we thank Tania Cronin, Gabriela Esteva, and Colin Barr, for their love, patience, and unfailing encouragement.

CHAPTER 1

Presidential Paradoxes

The American presidency can best be understood as a series of paradoxes, clashing expectations, and contradictions. We want presidents to share our common opinions, yet also have their own uncommon perspective and talents. Be consistent, yet also flexible. Listen to us, yet lead us. Celebrate and cherish our traditional values, yet be an innovative change-agent. Be above politics, yet be a master politician—and even a little bit Machiavellian, "working the dark side," if the nation's survival depends on it.

We admire presidential power, yet we fear its abuse. We yearn for inspiration, idealism, and optimism, yet we insist that presidents be honest and confront brutal realities. We yearn for the heroic yet remain suspicious of it.

We demand dynamic leadership, yet we grant only limited powers to a president. We want leaders to be bold and innovative, yet we allow presidents to take us mainly where we want to go. We want presidents to be representative of us, yet not too representative—we want to see ourselves in them, yet have confidence that presidents are better than us.

We are impressed with presidents who have fearless self-confidence, yet we dislike arrogance and respect those who can express reasonable self-doubt. We have learned, too, that qualities that prove successful in some circumstances can be harmful at other times.

Effective presidents necessarily embody and embrace the contradictions and paradoxes of America. They learn to navigate contrarian and divergent demands. They understand the presence of opposites and, much like a first-rate coach or conductor, know when to reformulate plays, bring in the right players or sections, when and how to turn the volume up or down, and learn to balance and manage amidst conflicting ideas, ideals, and constituencies.

One of the starkest realities about the American presidency is that Americans simultaneously want leadership, yet cherish freedom, liberty, and individualistic rights. It has always been a challenge, save in national crises, for presidents to try to exercise bold leadership in a nation that prizes individualism over obligations, and freedom over community. Yes, we want leadership, yet we also want freedom and limited government, with fewer regulations and taxes.

The American political system is grounded in three governing paradoxes. First, Americans may love their country, yet we are generally skeptical of big government and bold leadership. Second, Americans want presidents to "bring us together" and help unify the nation, yet we simultaneously believe in competing and sometimes contradictory "American Dreams." Third, a dominant strand of the American Dream privileges individualism over communitarian projects.

These realities have both empowered and constrained presidential leadership. Americans want a strong, resilient presidency with appropriate power to protect and advance American interests, yet American citizens also want a strong Congress, a vital, independent judiciary, a strong entrepreneurial private sector, a market-based economic system, a well-educated and questioning free press and citizenry—and safeguards and checks that will prevent arbitrary or imperial presidential leadership.

We generally exaggerate the capacity of presidents to shape events, granting them too much credit when things go well and too much blame when things go wrong. When things go well, we are inclined to attribute the success to leaders or a leader. This bias is sometimes called "the romance of at least some of leadership." What psychologists call the "fundamental attribution error" suggests that people have an understandable tendency to attribute what they see to something about the person performing the action, even when the behavior they believe they are seeing is likely caused by others or something else in the larger context of evolving events.[1]

Americans also tend to judge and evaluate current presidents through idealized memories of their favorite presidents, as well as through the filtering lens of their partisan loyalties.

The constitutional founders purposely left the presidency imprecisely defined. This was due in part to fears of both monarchy and the masses, and in part to hopes that future presidents would create a more powerful office than the framers were able to win ratification for at the time. They knew that, at times, the president would have to move swiftly and effectively, yet they avoided enumerating specific powers to calm the then-widespread fear of monarchy. After all, the nation had just fought a war against executive tyranny.

Thus the paradox of the invention of the presidency: To get the presidency approved in 1787 and 1788, the framers had to leave silences and ambiguities for fear of portraying the office as overly powerful. Yet, when we need central leadership, we turn to the president and read into Article II of the Constitution various prerogatives that permit a president to perform as national leader.

Today, the informal and symbolic powers of the presidency often account for as much as the formal, stated ones. Presidential power expands and contracts in response to varying situational and technological changes, as well as historical developments. The powers of the presidency are thus interpreted so differently that they sometimes seem to be those of different offices. In some ways, the modern presidency has virtually unlimited authority for almost anything its occupant chooses to do. In other ways, a president seems hopelessly ensnarled in a web of checks and balances.

We may not be able to resolve some of these clashing expectations. Still, we should develop a better understanding of what we ask of our presidents, thereby increasing our sensitivity to the limits and possibilities of what a president can achieve.

The following are some of the paradoxes of the presidency. Some are a function of confused expectations. Some are cases of our wanting one kind of presidential behavior at one time and another kind later. Some are cases in which positive characteristics of presidential leadership become negative because they are excessive. Still others stem from the contradiction inherent in the concept of democratic leadership, which, on the surface at least, appears to set up "democratic" and "leadership" as contending concepts. Whatever the source, each has implications for presidential performance and for how Americans judge presidential success.

> *Paradox #1.* Americans demand decisive presidential leadership that helps solve the nation's problems. Yet we are inherently suspicious of strong, centralized leadership and we fear the abuse of power.
>
> *Paradox #2.* We yearn for a democratic and authentic "common person" and, simultaneously, a leader who has uncommon genius, charisma, and star quality.
>
> *Paradox #3.* We want a decent, caring, and compassionate president, yet we also admire a cunning, guileful, and, on occasions that warrant it, even a ruthless, manipulative president. We might call this the "Mother Machiavelli paradox." For we yearn for a *good person* like a Mother Teresa who can be an exceptional role model and who helps unlock the caring, love, and goodness in all of us—and yet we know there is also a need for *tough love*, occasional pugnacious S.O.B. leadership to do the necessary things to make us an exceptional nation. Foreign policy experts sometimes refer to this as the soft power vs. hard power dilemma.
>
> *Paradox #4.* We admire an "above politics," nonpartisan, bipartisan, or "post-partisan" style of leadership, and yet the presidency is perhaps the most political office in the American political system, requiring an entrepreneurial master politician. Similarly, we want presidents who can both unify us and take the necessary bold and unpopular decisions that are likely to divide us.
>
> *Paradox #5.* We expect our presidents to provide creative, visionary, innovative, *programmatic* leadership, yet at the same time to respond *pragmatically* to public opinion. Thus, presidents must lead *and* follow, educate *and* listen. Presidents sometimes have to affirm existing values and traditions, yet sometimes must reframe an appropriate new vision for America.
>
> *Paradox #6.* Americans want self-confident, resolute presidential leadership. Yet we are inherently suspicious of leaders who view themselves as infallible or above criticism, and who don't learn from mistakes. We want presidents, in other words, with strong but not swollen egos.

> **Paradox #7.** What it takes to become president may not be what is needed to govern. To govern successfully, presidents must understand these paradoxes and embrace or balance a variety of competing demands and expectations.

We devote the rest of this chapter to explaining and giving examples of these seven paradoxes.

Paradox #1. We admire power but fear it. We love to unload responsibilities on our leaders, yet we intensely dislike being bossed around. We expect impressive leadership from presidents, yet we simultaneously impose constitutional, cultural, and political restrictions on them. These restrictions often prevent presidents from living up to our expectations.

Our ambivalence toward executive power is hardly new. The founders knew the new republic needed more leadership, yet they feared the development of a popular leadership institution that might incite the people and yield factious or demagogic government. Indeed, if there was one thing the framers of the Constitution did not want, it was a too-powerful presidency. Thus, the early conception of the American president was of an informed, virtuous statesman whose detached judgment and competence would enable him to work well with Congress and other leaders in making and implementing national public policy.

Popular leadership too grounded in the will of the people was viewed as a danger to be avoided. The founders' goal was to provide some distance between the public and national leaders, especially the president, and to use this distance to refine the popular view.

But the presidency of 1787 is not the presidency of today. The twenty-first century presidency is a larger office, structurally similar to the original design yet with a much expanded set of responsibilities and prerogatives (many of which devolve from precedents and the age of nuclear war and cyberwarfare). As the nation has evolved, so must the conceptions of the presidency evolve. Nowadays many people believe a president is the primary representative of the American people. New arrangements for nominating and electing presidents, including caucuses and primaries, have reinforced this conception, as have the role of television and the Internet.

The demand for a more immediately responsive president often conflicts with the demand for an informed, judicious statesman. The claims of politics and popular leadership have altered the early notions of presidential behavior. And as the presidency has become a lightning rod for much of society's discontent, so also have presidents sometimes sought to be all things to all people.

Still, while looking for strong, popular presidential leadership, Americans also remain profoundly cautious about concentrating power in any one person's hands.

It often seems that our presidency is simultaneously *too strong* and *too weak*: too powerful given our worst fears of tyranny and our ideals of a "government by the people"; too strong, as well, because it now possesses the capacity to wage nuclear or cyber wars or wage crisis leadership (a capacity that doesn't permit much in the way of checks and balances and deliberative, participatory government); yet too weak when addressing nuclear proliferation, the rising national debt, environmental challenges, inequality, racism, and other fundamental problems that must be confronted.

We often think the presidency is too strong when we dislike the incumbent, yet limitations are bemoaned when we believe the incumbent is striving valiantly to serve our definition of the public interest. The Lyndon Johnson presidency typified this paradox: Many who believed he was too imperial in Vietnam also believed he was too enfeebled to wage an effective War on Poverty. Others believed the opposite. The George W. Bush presidency suggested this as well. He exercised too much power, many think, in some aspects of his War on Terror, yet his powers and influence seemed inadequate when it came to needed Social Security and immigration reforms, and economic stimulus initiatives. Similarly, critics faulted Obama for overreaching on health care reform and banking or saw him as ineffective on border security or Middle East issues. Yet others praised him on these matters.

Since President Washington took office, we have multiplied the requirements for presidential leadership and made them increasingly difficult to fulfill. Students of the presidency often conclude that more power, not less, will be needed if presidents are to get the job done—especially in domestic and economic areas.

But if the presidency is to be given more power, should it not also be more accountable and transparent? Perhaps so. But what controls will curb the power of a president who abuses the public trust and, at the same time, not undermine the capacity of a fair-minded president to serve the public interest?

Presidents are supposed to follow the laws and respect the constitutional procedures that were designed to restrict their power; still, they must be powerful and effective when action is needed. We recognize the need for secrecy in certain government actions, yet we resent being deceived and left in the dark—again, especially when things go wrong or presidents lie to us.

Although we sometimes do not approve of the way a president acts, we approve of successful results. Thus, Lincoln was criticized for acting outside the limits of the Constitution, yet he was largely forgiven due to the apparent necessity for him to violate certain constitutional principles to preserve the Union. Franklin Delano Roosevelt was often flagrantly manipulative of his political opponents and sometimes of his allies as well. In the end, however, history generally endorses a victorious president as exercising leadership for the public good.

Political scientist Andrew Rudalevige wrote of the reemergence of the imperial presidency, and his decidedly paradoxical conclusion is that "strong executive leadership is at once unacceptable and unavoidable."[2] Presidents will continue to be aggressive in their claims to power just as Congress, more often than not, will defer to most, or at least many, of these claims.

We need government, yet we resist its power when we can, and we dislike admitting our growing dependence on it. We may want strong leadership, yet if such leadership comes in the wrong form, we resent it. This results in a

roller-coaster ride of support for the heroic presidency model, followed by con-
demnations of presidential power.

In sum, our constitutional order and its health depend on a paradox. "We need
a president who is both sufficiently strong to take those essential actions without
which we cannot be secure," writes political scientist Benjamin A. Kleinerman,
and yet "sufficiently circumscribed so that such actions do not become the norm."[3]

Paradox #2. We want our presidents to be like us, yet better than us. We like to
think America is the land where the common sense of the common person reigns.
Nourished on a diet of "common-person-as-hero" movies such as *Mr. Smith Goes
to Washington* (1939) and *Dave* (1993), and the literary celebration of the average citizen by authors such as Whitman and Twain, we prize the common touch.
The plain-speaking Harry Truman, the up-from-the-log-cabin "man or woman of
the people," is enticing. In practice, however, we want presidents to succeed and
we yearn for brilliant, uncommon, and semi-regal performances from presidents.

Although we fought a revolution to depose royalty, part of us yearns for genius
and mastery. Woodrow Wilson describes Lincoln's appeal: "Lincoln never ceased
to be a common man: that was his strength," writes Wilson. "But he was a common
man with a genius, a genius for things American, for insights into the common
thought, for mastery of the fundamental things of politics."[4]

We yearn for and demand both king *and* commoner. Our thirst for the heroic
is so enduring it is as if history is meaningless without heroes. At the same time, we
are told the hero is the individual the democratic nation must guard itself against.
"Pity the nation that needs heroes," a proverb attributed to German writer Bertolt
Brecht says. Why is this a haunting warning? Strong leaders, it is believed, can
sap, diminish, and possibly even destroy the very wellsprings of self-government.
Hence the notion: Strong leaders can make for a weak people.

Americans crave to be governed by a talented and self-confident president,
yet someone who is also down-to-earth and humble. If presidents get too special
they get roasted and leveled a peg or two. If they try to be too folksy, people get
bored. We cherish the myth that nearly anyone can grow up to be president, that
there are no barriers and no elite qualifications; still, we want smart, savvy, talented, uncommonly effective leaders.

Ronald Reagan illustrated another aspect of this paradox. He was a representative
all-American small-town Midwesterner, yet also a celebrity of stage, screen, and television. He boasted of having been a Democrat (which he was until the early 1960s),
yet he campaigned as a Republican. A veritable "Mr. Smith Goes to Washington,"
he had uncommon star quality. Candidate Bill Clinton portrayed himself as both a
Rhodes Scholar and an ordinary saxophone-playing member of the high school band
from Hope, Arkansas, as a "Jack Kennedy" and an "Elvis" figure. Donald Trump was
a privileged golf- and squash-playing private jet-setting New Yorker and developer's
son who became a debonair celebrity billionaire yet successfully portrayed himself as
a populist advocate of rust-belt and rural working-class voters.

Do we pay a price when we encourage heroic popular leadership in the White
House? Does it possibly dissipate citizen and civic participation and responsibility?

Many of the heroic, larger-than-life presidents have inadvertently weakened the office for their successors. The impressive and often bold performances of Jefferson, Jackson, Lincoln, and FDR may have complicated leadership prospects for their immediate successors.

There is another related problem with the notion of heroic presidential leadership. Most of the time, those who wait around for heroic leaders in the White House are disappointed. This is because presidents seldom provide sustained, galvanizing policy leadership. In practice, the people and policy movements make policy more often than presidents do; solutions usually percolate up rather than being imposed from the top down. Indeed, on many of the more important issues, the people generally have had to wait for presidents to catch up. In the overall scheme of the untidy policymaking process, the public is, in fact, sometimes out in front of the "leaders," as they were in the move to get out of Vietnam; and in women's rights, civil rights, gay rights, stem-cell research, and climate change.

Effective presidents, much of the time, are essentially shrewd followers; it is primarily in national emergencies such as Pearl Harbor or 9/11 that they sometimes can become consequential, pacesetting or ahead-of-their-times leaders.

In the end, we want our presidents to be special yet have the common touch. We don't want them to be average, just like us, or merely highly likable. Rather, we want someone who understands us, who can sympathize and empathize with our situations—someone we feel comfortable turning to in times of need.

Paradox #3. There is a fine line between boldness and recklessness, between strong self-confidence and what the ancient Greeks called "hubris," between dogged determination and pigheaded stubbornness. Opinion polls indicate that people want a just, decent, and intellectually honest individual as our chief executive. Yet the public also demands toughness.

We may admire modesty, humility, and a sense of proportion, yet most great leaders have been vain and crafty. You don't get to the White House by being a wallflower. Most have aggressively sought power.

Franklin Roosevelt's biographers, while emphasizing his compassion for the average American, also agree that he was narcissistic, devious, and secretive. These, they note, are often the companion flaws of great leaders. Significant social and political advances are made by those with drive, ambition, and a certain amount of brash self-confidence.

Americans insist that our country's leaders display moral judgment, yet they like decisiveness. George McGovern and Gerald Ford were criticized for being "too nice," "too decent." Being a "nice guy" is sometimes equated with being soft and afraid of power. The public likes strength and backbone. The Donald Trump campaign narrative of boasting, demagoguery, and unilateralism was an apparent response to Obama's preference for diplomacy, multilateralism, and reliance, when possible, on soft-power strategies.

Would-be presidents simultaneously have to win our trust by displays of integrity while possessing the calculation, single-mindedness, and pragmatism of a jungle fighter. Dwight Eisenhower reconciled these clashing expectations better than most presidents. Blessed with a wonderfully seductive, benign smile and a reserved, calming disposition, he was also the disciplined, strong, no-nonsense five-star general with all the medals and victories to prove it. His ultimate resource as president was this reconciliation of decency and proven toughness, likability alongside demonstrated valor. Biographers suggest that his success was at least partly due to his uncanny ability to appear guileless to the public, yet act with ample cunning in private.

Still, one of the ironies of the American presidency is that those characteristics we condemn in one president, we look for in another. A Jimmy Carter supporter once suggested that Sunday School teacher Carter wasn't "rotten enough," "a wheeler-dealer," "an S.O.B."—precisely the virtues (if they can be called that) for which Lyndon Johnson was most criticized a decade earlier.

We seem to demand a double-faced Janus personality. We demand the sinister as well as the sincere, the cunning and the compassionate, President Mean and President Nice, the president as Clint Eastwood or Frank Underwood and the president as Mr. "Won't You Be My Neighbor" Rogers. We want them tough enough to stand up to Vladimir Putin and North Korea, to terrorists and dictators, or perhaps to press the nuclear button, yet compassionate enough to fight on behalf of the ill fed, ill clad, and ill housed, and the vulnerable.

Former President Nixon, in writing about leaders he knew, said a modern-day leader has to employ a variety of unattractive qualities on occasion to be effective—or, at least, to appear effective. Nixon himself carried these practices too far.

We want decency and compassion at home, but we demand toughness and guile when presidents have to deal with our adversaries abroad. We want presidents to be fierce or compassionate, nice or mean, sensitive or ruthless, depending on what we want done, on the situation and, to some extent, on the role models of the recent past. Yet woe to a president who is too much or too little possessed of these characteristics.

In other words, leaders have to be uncommonly active, attentive listeners, yet along with listening we expect leaders to decide and make judgments. Leaders such as Hamlet wait too long. Others, like Shakespeare's King Lear or Othello and Sophocles' King Creon of Thebes, listen too little and act in haste.

Ambition is essential if a leader is to make a major difference. And, to gain power and retain it, one must have a love of power. Effective presidents must on occasion be manipulators, recognizing the necessity of deception and arm-twisting to manage a crisis or negotiate a deal.

Machiavelli, in his famous essay "The Prince" (1513), jolted us when he wrote that effective leaders must sometimes overcome their moral inhibitions and learn not to be good. He was not condoning evil, yet he advocated the necessity of fighting fire with fire where necessary and only when necessary. Thus, a leader may be doing exactly the right thing on behalf of the common good, yet be guilty of breaking the rules we usually want to live by.

This raises questions. Just as it is said that war can make a mockery of justice, so cyber wars and the age of terrorism may be making a mockery of traditional checks and balances envisioned in constitutionalism. So who judges on what are called these "dirty hands" or "moral paradox" leadership issues? What are the moral and constitutional standards?

The key, usually, is whether the leader is seeking self-aggrandizement, or whether he or she is truly serving the common good. Leadership divorced from worthy purposes is merely manipulation and deception and, in the extreme, repressive tyranny.

Still, a paradox remains: Power can be used to enslave people as well as liberate people.

It was said of the nineteenth-century statesman Henry Clay that he was so brilliant and capable and yet also so corrupt that "like a rotten mackerel in the moonlight, he both shines and stinks." That depiction lives on because it is clever and speaks to a moral ambiguity most Americans find hard to comprehend. "We look for heroes to represent us, although we rarely find them," writes journalist Alan Ehrenhalt. "We take certain perverse pleasure in unmasking hypocrites and dispatching blowhards who fail to deliver on their promises. The leaders we have trouble dealing with are those of obvious talent and genuine achievement who turn out to have displayed ethical insensitivity—or worse."[5]

Few things, Abraham Lincoln reminded us, are wholly good or wholly evil. Most public policies or ideological choices are an indivisible compound of the two. Lincoln, like other effective political operatives understood that sometimes hypocrisy or two-facedness, when creatively harnessed to advance negotiating or overt war, can be a necessity and a public good. The best presidents are balanced individuals; they are sure of themselves yet not dogmatic; they are self-confident yet willing to acknowledge and learn from their mistakes. They understand both the need for integrity and for craftiness.

Effective presidents understand that compassion and toughness are not inherently contradictory. There are times for compassion, yet equally there are times when one must be resolute. To be cunning does not necessarily mean one is unjust so much as one has a keen sense of timing. The specific context of the situation requires that presidents balance these two sides of their personality and character.

Paradox #4. The public yearns for a George Washington or a second "era of good feelings"—anything that might prevent partisanship or politics as usual in the White House. Former French President Charles de Gaulle once said, "I'm neither of the left nor of the right nor of the center, but above." Similarly, Jefferson once said, "We are all Federalists, we are all Republicans." The job of president demands that the officeholder be a gifted political broker, ever attentive to changing political moods and coalitions, and assiduously working to strengthen his or her political coalitions.

Several early presidents condemned parties while blatantly reaching out for party support when they needed to get their programs through Congress. It is another paradox of the presidency that presidents owe their party much of the credit for their getting there, yet once there, they can only be successful if they can build coalitions that transcend their party.

A president is expected at times to be the least political and most bipartisan of national figures, yet at other times the same president must act as the craftiest of politicians on the national stage. Presidents are not supposed to act with their eyes on the next election, yet their power position demands it. They are not supposed to favor any particular group or party, nor wheel and deal nor twist too many arms. Instead, a president is supposed to be "president of all the people," above politics, "a uniter, not a divider."

A president is also asked to lead a party; to help fellow party members get elected or re-elected; to deal firmly with party barons, interest-group chieftains, and congressional political brokers. A president's ability to gain legislative victories depends on his or her party leadership skills and on the size of his or her party's congressional membership.

To take the president out of politics is to assume, incorrectly, that a president will be generally right and the public generally wrong, that a president must be protected from the push and shove of political pressures. But what president has always been right? Over the years, public opinion has often been as sober a guide as anything else in our political culture. Having a president constrained and informed by public opinion is, after all, a defining characteristic of a democracy.

Politics, properly conceived, is the art of accommodating the diversity and variety of public opinion to meet commonly shared goals. Politics is the task of building durable coalitions and majorities. It isn't always pretty. A president must reward loyalty. No president can escape party politics. Presidents must first be nominated by their party to be a candidate for the general election. Presidents who are effective must work closely with party leaders in Congress and the states. A president, to be sure, must be much more than a party leader, yet if he or she is not at least this, he or she will fail.

In their attempts to be unifying leaders, presidents try to avoid polarizing conflicts. One of the lessons of history, however, is that early confrontation of controversial issues may avoid later violence. Further, sharpening conflict is often an important leadership responsibility. After he left the White House, Harry Truman said a president "who is any damn good at all makes enemies. I even made a few myself when I was in the White House, and I wouldn't have been without them."

Presidents try to portray themselves as unconcerned with their own political futures. Yet, the presidency is a highly political office; it cannot be otherwise. Moreover, its political character is, for the most part, desirable. A president separated from, or somehow above, politics might easily become a president who doesn't listen to the people, doesn't respond to majority sentiment or pay attention to views that may be diverse, intense, and at odds with his or her own. Presidents may not always wish to obey the will of the majority—in fact, leadership sometimes requires them to publicly argue against majority sentiment—but they cannot be unmindful of the will of the people.

A standard diagnosis of what's gone wrong with an administration will be that a presidency has become too politicized. Yet it is futile to try to take the president out of politics. A more useful approach is to realize that certain presidents try too hard to hold themselves above politics, or at least to give that appearance, rather than engage in it deeply, openly, and creatively. A democratic president has to be politically calculating regarding controversial issues if any semblance of government by consent is to be achieved, yet presidents at the same time need objective, professional, and multiple sources of expertise.

A president should be a national unifier and a harmonizer; at the same time the job requires priority-setting and advocacy leadership. Such tasks are nearly opposite.

The United States is one of the few nations that calls on its chief executive to serve as its symbolic, ceremonial head of state *and* as its political head of government. Elsewhere, these tasks are spread around. Some nations have a monarch and a prime minister; others have three visible national leaders: a head of state, a premier, and a powerful party chief.

In the absence of an alternative office or institution, we ask our president to act as a unifying force in our culture. It began with George Washington, who artfully performed this function. He was a unique symbol of our new nation. He was a healer and an extraordinary man for several seasons. Today, we ask no less of our presidents than that they should do as Washington did.

We have designed a presidential job description, however, that sometimes forces presidents to act as national dividers. Presidents must necessarily divide when they act as the leaders of their political parties, when they prioritize certain policy goals or groups at the expense of others, when they forge and lead political coalitions, when they move out ahead of public opinion and assume the role of national educators, when they choose one set of advisers over another, when they decide we should enter a military campaign. A president, as a creative executive leader, cannot help but offend certain interests. Those presidents who have proposed bold measures on civil rights, immigration, and health care, for example, eventually lost public support for themselves and their parties.

George W. Bush and Barack Obama paid a price for political boldness. Bush's decision to wage war in Iraq divided the country and ultimately hurt his party. But he was convinced he did the right thing. Similarly, Obama fought for comprehensive health insurance reform; he swung big and paid for it with major losses in his party in the next elections. These presidents divided, yet they believed they were providing leadership the nation needed.

The nation is torn between the view that a president should primarily preside over the nation and merely serve as a convener or referee among the various powerful interests that control who gets what, when, and how, and a second position, which contends a president should gain control of government processes and powers to use them instrumentally to impose coherent order and provide coherent policy in a nation where otherwise the parochialism of Congress undermines effective government.[6]

The president is sometimes seen as the great defender of the people, the ombudsman or advocate general of "public interest." But this should be viewed as merely a claim, for some presidents have acted otherwise, even antagonistically, to mass or popular preferences.

Paradox #5. We want both pragmatic and programmatic leadership. We want principled "conviction" leadership *and* flexible, adaptive leaders. *Lead us*, yet also *listen to us.* We want presidents with creative plans who will also respond to facts and be able to improvise according to varying contexts.

Most people can be led only where they want to go. "Authentic leadership," writes James MacGregor Burns, "is a collective process." It emerges from an appreciation of the mutually shared goals of both followers and leaders. The test of leadership, says Burns, "is the realization of intended, real change that meets people's enduring needs." Thus, a leader's key function is "to engage followers, not merely to activate them, to commingle needs and aspirations and goals in a common enterprise, and in the process to make better citizens of both leaders and followers."[7]

Leadership, at its best, unlocks the talent and energy of the nation. Strong presidential leadership can provide a vision that empowers us to rise above the routine and make significant contributions to our common purpose. Yet, Americans rebel against overly hierarchical authoritarian leadership, and we emphatically resist being led too far in any one direction.

We expect vigorous innovative leadership when crises occur. Once a crisis is past, however, we sometimes act as if we neither need nor want those leaders around. We expect presidents to provide bold initiatives "to move us ahead," yet we resist radical new changes and usually embrace "new" initiatives only after they have achieved some consensus.

Most of our presidents have been conservatives or "pragmatic liberals." They only cautiously venture much beyond the conventional consensus of the times. They follow public opinion more than shape it. John F. Kennedy, the author of the acclaimed book *Profiles in Courage*, was criticized for presenting more profile than courage. Kennedy responded to his critics by pointing out he had barely won election in 1960 and that great innovations should not be forced on the public by a leader with a slender mandate.

Leadership requires radiating hope, grounded in reality. Be visionary, yet be able to fight for the achievement of your visions. The challenge is how to bring about the doable and the desirable, while at the same time encouraging innovation. A constant balance, reconciling dreams and reality, intuition and logic, is needed.

Americans may admire consistency in the abstract, but in politics consistency has its costs. Everett Dirksen, a popular Republican U.S. senator from Illinois, liked to say, "I'm a man of fixed and unbending principles—but my first fixed and unbending principle is to be flexible at all times." President Trump, a more recent example, backed away from or switched his position on at least a dozen issues (e.g., the use of torture) on which candidate Trump had campaigned.

Franklin D. Roosevelt proclaimed that the presidency is preeminently a place for moral leadership. Yet, he was also an opportunist and pragmatist just as Lincoln and Theodore Roosevelt were before him and as Kennedy, Reagan, Clinton, and Obama later would be.

These men knew that political leadership responsibilities in America meant sometimes being detached, vague, and uncommitted, while at other times taking a stand and being passionately committed. They knew, too, that changing their minds—or what we often derisively call "flip-floppery"—was sometimes in order. Lincoln changed his mind on how to deal with slavery. FDR changed his mind on a balanced budget and on neutrality in World War II. Nixon changed his mind on dealing with China. Reagan was a "tax cutter" who actually raised taxes about nine times, and he evolved a lot on how best to relate to the Soviets.

Leaders sometimes change their minds because circumstances have changed. Sometimes, too, they change because they have learned new facts or understand new realities. Of course, they also change their minds because of political expediency. It is only the stubborn, overly self-confident and politically deaf leader who is unwilling to compromise and change course. We insist on consistency, yet creative compromising is sometimes appropriate.

Successful presidents radiated hope and stirred the hearts and minds of Americans with an almost demagogic ability to simplify and convince. "We need leaders of inspired idealism," said Theodore Roosevelt, "leaders to whom are granted great visions, who dream greatly and strive to make their dreams come true, who can kindle the people with the fire from their own burning souls."[8]

Presidents who do not raise hopes are criticized for letting events shape their presidency rather than making things happen. A president incapable of radiating optimism and confidence is rejected as un-American. For many people around the world, America has been the land of promise, of possibilities, of dreams—the world's indispensible nation. No president can stand in the way of this truth, regardless of the current dissatisfaction about the size of government in Washington and its incapacity to deliver the services and dreams it promises.

Do presidents overpromise because presidential aspirants are congenital optimists, or because they are pushed by a demanding public? Or are competing candidates engaged in an escalating spiral of promise heaped on promise as they try to outbid each other for votes? Surely the public demands it, yet only self-confident optimists need apply in the first place. Whatever the source, no president has been able to keep all promises.

Charlie Brown of "Peanuts" cartoon fame once said, "I have very strong opinions, but they don't last long." So also American public opinion shifts—sometimes quickly, sometimes slowly. There are times when we want presidents to be engaged actively as innovators, and on other occasions we would like to see them sit back and let things run their course.

Many people and, perhaps, media pundits especially, yearn for a president to respond to emergencies with bold new programs and militaristic bully pulpit rhetoric. Yet it may be more appropriate and prudent for presidents, on some such occasions, to carefully weigh their options and decide to do little or nothing in the face of a no-win or unsolvable problem.

Not every problem requires bully pulpit and massive spending responses. Yet a president who "leads from behind" or chooses not to act boldly invites critics to complain of "weak," "feckless," or "low-energy" leadership.

The script of what we expect from presidents includes expecting that presidents can send a man to the moon, tell the Soviets to "tear down that wall" in Berlin and send in the Navy Seals to capture and kill Osama bin Laden. Yet that script or narrative may, on many occasions, run counter to the course of actions that may be wisest. Choosing not to act, like President Eisenhower's decision not to go to war in Vietnam or maybe Obama's decision not to go to war in Syria, may be the right course of leadership. In these cases, presidents are faced with the paradoxical demands of choosing between what they believe may produce the best outcome for the long term and the public and media expectations for "High Noon," "Breaking News" dramatic leadership.[9]

President Obama said he was both an idealist and internationalist, yet confided he was, in a way, "a Hobbesian optimist." He believed that the "world is a tough, complicated, messy, mean place, and full of hardship and tragedy. And in order to advance both our security interests and those ideals and values we care about, we've got to be hardheaded at the same time as we're bighearted. . . ." Obama added, "There are going to be times where we can do something about innocent people being killed, but there are going to be times where we can't."[10]

Contexts are always changing. Presidents sometimes find themselves in a period when the yearning for affirmative government or defense buildup is quickly followed by calls for tax cuts and a general downsizing of government.

Effective presidents need to be able to read these changing contexts and develop a "contextual intelligence" to tack one way or the other. Leaders must learn how to integrate the obvious advantages of one possible approach without completely canceling out the advantages of alternative approaches.

Presidents celebrate traditional American values and the American way of doing things, yet an effective president often has to help us create a new order when, as Lincoln reminded us, the dogmas of the past become irrelevant to new challenges.

Presidents can serve as catalytic modernizers in the United States. No nation can stagnate and long endure. But political change is often resisted. Since we fear change, and a variety of political roadblocks stand in the way, how are needed reforms enacted? To promote change, presidents must simultaneously affirm and create order. They begin by affirming the past and they use that past to improve on the present and recreate it on the basis of past values.[11]

Abraham Lincoln understood this. In his Gettysburg Address and Second Inaugural Address, he affirmed the nation's commitment to past values, yet reinvented the future by reinterpreting those values to reflect modern necessity. He paid tribute to the framers of the Constitution while elevating the principles of the Declaration of Independence above the Constitution. In effect, he promoted a conservative revolution: conservative in that it grounded itself in the security of known values from the past, yet revolutionary in that it reordered those values to place political democracy and equality above all else. Lincoln affirmed the reordered traditional values of the collective past as a way to affirm a new vision for the future.

Franklin Roosevelt came to the White House in 1933 as a result of a major repudiating 1932 election. That election, in addition to vanquishing Herbert Hoover, led to a Democratic U.S. Senate with a 60 to 37 margin and a Democratic House with 310 Democrats to 117 Republicans.

Roosevelt had to promote economic security and develop job-creating programs. He, his cabinet, and Congress redefined the government agenda—both reaffirming traditional American values such as liberty and freedom, while also emphasizing economic opportunity and economic security.

Ronald Reagan, in his two election victories, helped redefine his era. He sought to slow the march to a welfare state and celebrate individual freedoms as conceived by the constitutional framers. "No one understood better than Reagan the transformative political effect of bringing the order-shattering and order-affirming elements of presidential action into alignment" writes political scientist Stephen Skowronek.[12] Reagan himself understood this: "They called it the Reagan Revolution. Well, I'll accept that, but for me it always seemed more like the great rediscovery, a rediscovery of our values and our common sense."[13]

In a way, all presidents are compelled to couch reform and modernization in the comforting, familiar clothing of past values. To be forward-looking, we must affirm the past. Change, to be acceptable, must be grounded in deeply rooted American values. Great presidents "have been the most wrenching in their assault on the system." They have, in effect, shaken things up and been disrupters or disturbers of peace. "All told, the relationship between the presidency and the American political system is not at all a comforting one. It is always paradoxical and often perverse."[14]

Another point: People yearn for courage and the heroic, but few presidents provide the policy purity or coherence or the ideological consistency many want. Lincoln didn't like slavery, yet he knew that any embrace by him of full political equality for black Americans was incompatible to his being elected president and maintaining the fragile collection of Northern and border states he needed to win the war. So he was pragmatic and incremental at the time, even if we retrospectively view him as visionary.

Paradox #6. We cherish our three branches of government with checks and balances, countervalence and dispersed and separated powers. We want presidents to be successful and share their power with Congress and other responsible national leaders. Likewise, we oppose the concentration of power, dislike secrecy, and resent depending on any one person to provide all of our leadership.

Yet Americans, at least on occasion, also yearn for dynamic, heroic presidents—even if they do cut some corners. We celebrate gutsy presidents who made a practice of pushing Congress. We perceive the great presidents to be those who stretched their legal authority and challenged, if not dominated, the other branches of government. It is still Jefferson, Jackson, Lincoln, and the Roosevelts who get top billing. Whatever may have been the framers' intentions for the three branches, most experts believe that most of the time, especially in crises, our system works best when we have a self-confident, assertive president.

Although we want presidents to be open-minded, we also admire the occasional "profile in courage" type of decision. One of the most fondly remembered Lincoln stories underscores this point. President Lincoln supposedly took a vote at a cabinet meeting and it went entirely against him. He announced it this way: "Seven nays and one aye, the ayes have it." Much of the time, however, Lincoln followed the leadership of Congress, his advisers, and the general public.

Critics faulted George W. Bush for overreaching when he called for "regime change" in Iraq in 2003. He believed he acted in good faith and with appropriate CIA and military intelligence. But years later many critics, including some in his own party, like Trump, fault him for reckless decision-making.[15]

Critics faulted Barack Obama for overreaching on his controversial Affordable Care Act of 2010. The American public was obviously divided, and Republicans vigorously opposed Obama's proposals. Even Obama and his advisers wondered, in retrospect, whether they had done the right thing. But the Supreme Court upheld it and Obama stalwartly campaigned in 2012, saying, "We did the right thing. We have to move forward not backward," adding that no American should go broke because of bad health. His attitude was somewhat similar to what LBJ said when some of his political advisers recommended waiting until later to aggressively push for the Civil Rights Act of 1964. A president, aides advised, shouldn't spend time and power on lost causes, no matter how worthy these causes. "Well," replied LBJ, "what the hell's the presidency for?"[16]

Humility is admirable, yet excessive humility paralyzes. Significant advances in the world have generally been made by confident innovators. "Any self-doubts the leader may have, especially in the battlefield, must be concealed at all costs," wrote military historian John Keegan. "The leader of men in warfare can show himself to his followers only through a mask . . . made in such form as will mark him to men of his time and place as the leader they want and need."[17]

Rare is the great commander, the truly successful executive or the politician who is not self-centered and conceited. It takes great courage to get up on the public stage and do what is needed to win the office. A leader must be self-confident enough to believe he or she is consequential. Untempered confidence, however, is dangerous. Hitler oozed it. So did Herman Melville's mad Captain Ahab. Both had vision, purpose, and enormous drive, and yet were toxic leaders.

The question is whether leaders with large egos are subject to reasonable self-control. Self-discipline is key. An unrestrained ego that constantly needs to be fed and isn't placed in disciplined service to worthy public purposes invariably corrupts.

Former Secretary of Defense Robert S. McNamara (who served JFK and LBJ) believed that major mistakes were made in starting and conducting the Vietnam War due to hubris and a failure to fully understand our alleged enemy and their motivation. We misjudged the nationalistic intentions of the Vietnamese and we had a profound ignorance of their history and culture, McNamara said. He also said the decision-making process was flawed in several ways. Finally, "Where our own security is not directly at stake," McNamara writes, "our judgment of what is in another people's or country's best interests should be put to the test of open discussion in international forums. We do not have the God-given right to shape every nation in our image and as we choose."[18]

Leaders must believe in themselves, yet they cannot afford to discredit the ideas, plans, counsel or criticism of others. Leaders who encourage thoughtful dissent in their organizations are, according to most studies, likely to produce better organizational decision-making. Effective presidents encourage and reward criticism without retaliating against the critics. Hitler eliminated his critics. Ahab, in *Moby Dick*, ignored his. In *Antigone*, Sophocles' King Creon listened almost entirely to himself, which proved fatal. His son, Haemon, chided him in vain, saying, "Let not your first thought be your only thought. Think if there cannot be some other way. Surely, to think your own the only wisdom and yours the only word, the only will, betrays a shallow spirit, an empty heart."

But Creon dismissed his son's advice, saying, "Indeed, am I to take lessons at my time of life from a fellow of his age?" He ignored everyone else as well until it was too late.

A fine line separates self-confidence from conceit, boldness from recklessness, positive and entrepreneurial ambition from narcissistic personality disorder, mindless adherence to the course from reevaluation and redirection. The challenge is how to blend the competing impulses and combine them effectively.

Life and history are complicated and paradoxical. That's why we have constitutionalism and regular elections. "The reason we have democracy is that no one side is right all the time," writes David Brooks. "The only people who are dangerous are those who can't admit, even to themselves, that obvious fact."[19]

In sum, Americans want exceptionally vigorous presidents who will use without hesitation every power the Constitution and the office grant them but, paradoxically enough, this is why every president should be held strictly accountable to the Constitution, the Congress, and the people.

We know we need Hamiltonian energy in our Madisonian system of separated powers to achieve lofty Jeffersonian ideals but, as the framers at Philadelphia stressed: Make a president too weak, and the Congress will usurp powers. Make the president too strong, and the president will usurp the Congress.[20]

Paradox #7. Winning a presidential election takes ambition, money, years of hard work, masterful public relations strategies and egotistical self-promotion, as well as good luck. It requires making promises and forming an electoral coalition. To govern a democracy requires much more. It requires the formation of a *governing* coalition, and the ability to compromise and bargain on a much more expansive field.

A former Reagan White House chief of staff sums up part of this paradox by noting that presidential campaigns are all about "destroying your adversary," while governing requires the art of "making love with your adversary."[21] Obama spent much of his transition period emphasizing that there was a time for campaigning, yet the time had now come for governing.

"People who win primaries may become good presidents—but 'it ain't necessarily so," wrote *Washington Post* columnist David Broder. "Organizing well is important in governing just as it is in winning primaries. But the Nixon years should teach us that good advance men do not necessarily make trustworthy White House aides. Establishing a government is a little more complicated than having the motorcade run on time."[22]

Ambition and determination are essential for a presidential candidate, yet too much of either can be dangerous. A candidate must be bold and energetic, but in excess these characteristics can produce a cold, frenetic and perhaps driven candidate. To win the presidency obviously requires a laser-like single-mindedness, yet our presidents must also have a sense of proportion, be well rounded, have a sense of humor, and have hobbies and interests outside the realm of politics.

To win the presidency, many of our candidates (Kennedy, Clinton, Obama, and Trump, to cite a few) had to pose as being more progressive or populist than they actually were; yet, to be effective in the job they were compelled to appear more cautious and conservative than they often wanted to be.

Another aspect of campaigning for the White House is the ambiguous position candidates take on issues to increase their appeal, first to their party caucus and primary voting base and then to the centrist and independent voters in the general election. A typical example of this paradox: "I want my presidential candidate to have clear-cut policies, to be as clear and precise as possible on positions, not hazy and ambiguous—to run a campaign that educates people and persuades them to adopt the candidate's position. But I also want my candidate to win."[23]

Policy positions are seldom comprehensively outlined; bumper sticker slogans and entertaining TV ads are designed to please people and offend few. Presidential pledges such as LBJ's "We will not send American boys to fight the war that Asian boys should be fighting," George W. Bush's "I'm a uniter, not a divider," Obama's upbeat but vacuous "change we can believe in" and Trump's nativist appeal "Make American Great Again" to American exceptionalism are illustrative.

One of the challenges of campaigning is to win without proving you are unworthy of the job you are seeking. A common temptation is for candidates, including some incumbents, to run a "bureaucrats-are-bums," "anti-Washington," outsider kind of campaign. There is something more than a little deceitful, and certainly a lot that is ironic, in presidential candidates who are trying to get to Washington by saying that they are running "against Washington," and one hoping to be elected to the most powerful office in the world by proclaiming that they are against big government. An irony is that both Ronald Reagan and George W. Bush campaigned against big government yet left bloated deficits, a proliferation of defense programs, and a vastly bigger government than anyone ever would have imagined back in 1980 and 2000.

We expect a president to be able to work effectively with Congress and civil servants. Candidates who bad-mouth Washington officials invariably breed resentment; if they get to the White House they will have a difficult time winning sustained cooperation from those same officials.

We would like both a "fresh-faced" outsider as a presidential candidate *and* a seasoned, mature, experienced veteran who knows the corridors of power and the back alleyways of Washington. Frustration with past presidential performances leads us to turn to a "fresh new face" that is uncorrupted or at least less corrupted by Washington politics and its "buddy system." But inexperience, especially in foreign affairs, has sometimes led to blunders by outsider presidents.

New nominating rules combined with the requirements of the media and high-tech campaign age sharpen the clash between what is required of a successful candidate and a successful president.

To be a winning candidate, a would-be president must put together an electoral coalition involving a majority of voters advantageously distributed across the country, especially in ten or so "battleground states." The candidate must thus appeal to all regions and interest groups and cultivate the appearance of honesty, relaxed sincerity, and experience. This is fine. It's good to travel around the country, meeting people, learning about their problems and testing ideas on diverse audiences. Once elected, however, the electoral coalition has served much of its purpose, and a governing coalition is the order of the day.

Recent presidents have found it difficult to abandon or transcend what is now called the permanent campaign. This is the case, in part, because our presidential campaigns are so long and so highly professionalized. There are other factors at play, yet the campaigning mode of operation readily carries over to the White House.

Campaigning to win the White House is less about deliberation than it is a fight, a contest, a marketing and an adversarial contest to win needed electoral votes. On the other hand, governing involves "deliberation, cooperation, negotiation, and compromise over an extended period" as opposed to waging an either/or short-term primary competition.[24]

Producing legislation acceptable to a broad public is usually much harder than destroying political rivals. The former is the work of governance; the latter is the work of polarizing, partisan political campaigning—and we have seen a lot of that over the past generation.

To become president takes a determined, and even a driven person, a master fundraiser (unless you happen to be a billionaire), a person who is glib, dynamic, charming on television, and somewhat calculating on the issues. But, once president, we want that person to be well-rounded, careful in reasoning, more transparent, and more specific in communications.

CONCLUSION

Effective leaders understand their jobs as embracing and resolving paradoxes and managing the contradictions of public life.

Presidents need to be optimists, yet realists. Sunny Ronald Reagan made optimism a seemingly indispensable ingredient for presidential leadership. Presidential candidates and presidents all say they are optimistic and accuse their opponents of being pessimistic. But we don't want presidents who are merely Pollyannaish. We want leaders who help us confront reality with prudent objectivity.

Political leaders with mature emotional intelligence recognize the moods and needs of the moment and fashion their leadership style to respond accordingly. This requires leaders capable of discerning the requirements of the moment as they shape policies and deal with both the context of the times and the mutually shared aspirations of their countrymen. This requires "style-flexing"—something few leaders can do. You first need to recognize the contradictions and then devise strategies to deal with problems.

A key element of leadership is to identify the needs of the times and to solve the problem at hand. Leaders cannot be passive observers; they must improvise, synthesize, facilitate, and recontextualize. Psychologist Howard Gardner suggests that effective leaders learn to knit together information and ideas from competing sources into a coherent strategy. "As synthesizers, they will need to be able to gather together information in ways that work for themselves and can be communicated to other persons."[25]

Effective presidential leadership involves infusing vision, purpose, and energy into an administration. It also involves the ability to reinvent new strategies to deal with a myriad of exacting challenges such as the much more partisanized Washington, trade and cyberwars, and technological change.

This requires a multidimensional leader. Lincoln was such a leader. He was arguably the most "complete" person ever to serve in the White House. He had good judgment, empathy, political skill, cunning, wit, intellect, resilience, and determination. He managed the vast contradictions of the Civil War with skill, imagination, ruthlessness, compassion, and disciplined focus. Lincoln was usually the master of contradictions, not their victim.

The formal and informal powers of the presidency are impressive if both are used skillfully. Yet, they are of little consequence unless exercised in accord with constitutional principles and in service to the nation's mutually shared aspirations.

Leading amid paradoxes requires presidents to (1) read the signs; (2) adapt strategy to the demands and needs of the context; (3) work to persuade followers; (4) understand the importance of balance and mediation; (5) understand the importance of timing; (6) devise a governing strategy; (7) manage the machinery of government; (8) reevaluate, reexamine, and improvise, and continually re-imagine a more just, more generous vibrant constitutional republic. Effective presidents are smart diagnosticians, artful teachers, effective agreement builders, and masterful jugglers of life's paradoxes.

FURTHER READINGS

Cheney, Dick, and Liz Cheney. *Exceptional: Why the World Needs a Powerful America*. New York: Threshold Editions, 2015.

Goldsmith, Jack. *Power and Constraint: The Accountable Presidency After 9/11*. New York: Norton, 2013.

Hacker, Jacob S., and Paul Pierson. *American Amnesia: How the War on Government Led Us to Forget What Made America Prosper*. New York: Simon and Schuster, 2016.

Howell, William G., and Terry M. Moe. *Relic: How Our Constitution Undermines Effective Government, and Why We Need a More Effective Presidency*. New York: Basic Books, 2016.

Meacham, Jon. *Destiny and Power: The American Odyssey of George Herbert Walker Bush*. New York: Random House, 2015.

CHAPTER 2

Evaluating Presidents

Americans were tough on King George III, and we continue to be exacting in how we treat our own governing elites. We love our country, yet we often talk as if we hate our government. Presidents as symbols of government are regularly scrutinized and blamed for many ills of society. That presidential approval is often a function of national *and* global economic cycles or foreign policy events that are largely beyond a president's influence doesn't matter. Presidents have to appear prepared, informed, and "in charge" as much as is possible or pay a heavy penalty.

The average American doesn't have a strong grasp of American history. Americans like certain presidents whom they know or at least about whom they have heard positive stories. Thus recent Gallup poll popular favorites are John F. Kennedy, Ronald Reagan, Bill Clinton, Franklin D. Roosevelt, as well as Abraham Lincoln.

American historians and biographers generally agree that Lincoln, Washington, and Franklin D. Roosevelt were our best presidents. Runners-up include Jefferson, Jackson, Teddy Roosevelt, Wilson, Truman, and Eisenhower.

A paradox in how we evaluate presidents is the confused standards by which we judge leaders. While we are "results oriented," we are also rightly concerned about means. We demand that presidents succeed, and we criticize them if they do not. But they must not demand too much of us, push the system too far, call for too many sacrifices, or trample on our rights and liberties. It is one of the paradoxes that we want heroic leaders with soaring visions yet we also want presidents who pay close attention to our views. We want presidents to lead, yet also to be responsive to us, and what we think matters. We demand that presidents think and act constitutionally, yet we also expect them to do "whatever it takes," especially in national security matters. We yearn for effective leaders to become president, yet only sometimes do we want them to have the powers and resources necessary to do the job.

Virtually all our paradoxes apply to this chapter. We want strong, decisive leaders, yet we are deeply suspicious of the abuses of power. We want a common person who is extraordinary. We want a kind, caring president on one day, and a guileful, sometimes ruthless president the next. Our presidents should be above politics and unify our nation, yet the presidency is a supremely political position and their decisions must occasionally divide us.

We have come to understand that presidential power can be used to achieve both noble and ignoble ends. Limited tenure, as required by the Twenty-Second Amendment, and additional statutory checks and accountability procedures such as special prosecutors and ethics codes, are some of the devices we use to try to keep strong power from becoming irresponsible power.

The growth of presidential power came in fits and starts over our first 140 years. But since Franklin D. Roosevelt, the office and its power have steadily grown. We may have modified or even abandoned some earlier constitutional principles. In addition, times have changed, popular expectations have changed, and Congress has passed laws and delegated increased responsibilities to presidents, especially during crisis periods.[1]

One of the obvious paradoxes is that the office, as created, has stayed constitutionally the same over time, and yet the demands we have placed on the office have grown dramatically. We expect our presidents to do more, yet we fear too much power in one person's hand.

What follows is a discussion of how what we want from presidents has changed over time.

WHAT THE FRAMERS EXPECTED

The framers of the Constitution were paradoxically torn between their fears of executive tyranny and the urgent need for executive power. They feared the possibility of an arbitrary and ruthless leader. However, even the most vigorous champions of a strong executive insisted that the president not become a monarch. Alexander Hamilton in *Federalist # 69* compared the powers of a president with those of a king, and he argued persuasively that presidents would possess much less power than the English monarch.

The framers were deliberately vague about the precise character of presidential powers, thereby providing the office with a potential for growth. Over the short run, they wished a president to be no more than a partner in a triumvirate, to be restrained by the judicial and especially by the legislative branch. They took care in drafting the Constitution to construct a governmental system that did not depend on a strong, popular leader. Even to admit the need for strong leadership was to leave open the possibility for the exercise of discretion and thus power. Unchecked power was considered dangerous.

Alexander Hamilton optimistically argued in 1788 that the office of president would seldom fall to anyone not in an eminent degree endowed with the requisite qualifications. Indeed, he predicted that the office would be regularly filled by individuals noted for ability and virtue. In fact, however, presidents have varied dramatically in skill and character. A more realistic James Madison wrote that "enlightened statesmen will not always be at the helm" (thus the need for all the Madisonian checks and balances).

The framers of the Constitution were not of one mind, and the final constitutional provisions were compromises, sometimes guesses. They left much to be worked out.

One expectation, however, has remained constant. We want prudent and intellectually wise leaders who exercise their powers to the fullest when emergencies arise. We want presidents who will place the country and the Constitution ahead of their own personal or partisan interests. At the same time, both framers and citizens worried that a president capable of exercising robust executive power in a crisis could also become the worst kind of tyrant. The tension between energetic executive power and popular control is an enduring one. Hence, checks, both formal and informal, would always be needed to safeguard liberty.

The framers, in a burst of intellectual cleverness, devised a constitutional system that made dynamic presidential leadership exceedingly difficult, except in times of crisis. Alexander Hamilton, however, believed effective government would be realized not from the absence of power but from the presence of decisive executive power and leadership.

The framers obviously hoped for wise and virtuous statesmen to be presidents, individuals who would work closely with Congress and respond to the "sense of the community." Implicit, if not explicit, in their early expectations was the notion that each president, as well as members of Congress, would be preoccupied with what ought to be done rather than with what shortsighted temporary majorities might desire. They thus sought to insulate the president from the pressures of popular whim, and likewise to protect the other branches from the dangers inherent in a president armed with the support of masses and a large military.

The reason for providing distance between the people and the presidency is clear. It was to allow ample scope for leadership and statesmanship. In a constitutional democracy, or republic, public opinion would not always be identical with the public interest. There is at least the hint in Hamilton's conception of national leadership that sometimes a president would have to have the power "to do what the laws would do if the laws could foresee what should be done, as well as the power to make exceptions in the execution of the laws, exceptions governed by a judgment as to whether it would be good to apply them or not."[2]

Hamilton's prediction came true more quickly than he may have imagined. President George Washington set some precedents for unilateral executive action not exactly envisioned by the framers. He saw to it that he alone would lead the executive branch of government. In foreign affairs he issued the Neutrality Proclamation of 1793 without the consent of Congress. He withheld information from Congress he thought should not be disclosed for reasons of national security. Congress conceded to Washington most of the executive powers he exercised, especially those in foreign policy matters. By making the president commander-in-chief and allowing him to appoint ambassadors and to negotiate treaties, the framers provided important foreign policy and symbolic roles for the newly invented presidency.

Once Washington established these early practices, however, executive assertiveness was limited. Monarchial fears of the anti-federalist opponents of the Constitution were not realized. With few exceptions, Adams, Jefferson, Madison, and Monroe regularly deferred to Congress. The framers, and the American voters of the day, did not expect extensive domestic and economic policymaking leadership as much as administrative efficiency. Washington, in taking executive action yet always acknowledging the power, partnership, and centrality of Congress, set the prudent example.

What was expected of our early presidents was an executive role with neither tyrannical nor hereditary powers, restrained by representatives of the people and the Constitution, yet able to protect the people, at least on occasion, from their own representatives. Under George Washington, Americans in the 1790s got what they wanted.

WHAT WAS EXPECTED IN THE NINETEENTH CENTURY

Early presidents did not have to conduct presidential campaigns as we know them today. Due to the natural restrictions of travel and the absence of modern media tools, they remained distant from the average citizen. To be sure, presidents traveled about the country for occasional ceremonial visits. The early presidents also held weekly social gatherings and were accessible even to casual visitors in the nation's capital. Many presidents deemed it a requirement of the job to take an occasional "bath in public opinion," to paraphrase Lincoln.

Still, presidents in this period were not expected to provide popular leadership. Elected representatives, it was believed, would be better able to make important decisions than the average citizen. Being physically removed from the workings of government, the public had fewer—or at least more general—expectations of their representatives, and of the president. Moreover, the impact of the national government on the average citizen was decidedly less than it is today.

The typical nineteenth-century president was expected to be a "constitutional executive," a dignified presider over the administrative branch who would not tread on the responsibilities of the other branches. Although the nineteenth century eventually witnessed remarkable industrial growth based on individual initiative, much of that growth operated independently from any governmental regulation. Freedom *from* government seemed to permeate most aspects of economic and social life.

General Andrew Jackson, the seventh president and the first real "outsider" to win the presidency (in 1828), unquestionably altered prevailing conceptions of the office. In common with George Washington, Jackson was charismatic, imposing, and a national celebrity because of several military ventures, most notably because of his much celebrated military triumph over the British in the 1815 Battle of New Orleans.

"Old Hickory" (it was said he was as tough as a hickory branch), or "The Hero of New Orleans," was an irascible duelist, gunslinger, Indian-slaying Westerner from Tennessee. He owned 150 or more slaves, lived well on a vast estate of thousands of acres, and was not especially known for populist political views prior to his presidency. But he and his followers believed he was "robbed of the presidency" in 1824 when, his supporters believed, Henry Clay and John Quincy Adams rigged the election in the House of Representatives for Adams, denying the presidency to the election's popular plurality winner, Jackson.

Jackson became the "people's candidate"—the champion and representative of the farmers and workers—and railed against the establishment made up of the well-born, the bankers, and the privileged classes so exemplified by its Harvard-educated son of a president, John Quincy Adams.

As president, Jackson called for the popular election of presidents and portrayed the presidency as an office that could represent the general public's views better than the other branches of government. Biographer Jon Meacham writes: "His larger argument was that a president should not simply defer to the will and wishes of the Congress or the judiciary. Instead, Jackson was saying, the president ought to take his own stand on important issues, giving voice as best he could to the interests of the people at large."[3] More activist than his predecessors, Jackson fought South Carolina's nullification efforts, vetoed the rechartering of what he considered the elitist privilege-serving Second Bank of the United States, waged a preemptive military strike in Sumatra, and much more.

To say that nineteenth-century presidents had less to do than contemporary presidents does not mean emergencies did not arise. The Civil War was the greatest challenge the nation and our constitutional system ever faced. Rather, it means that the public seldom viewed presidents the way we do today.

With the exception of Jackson's experience and Lincoln's crisis leadership, the presidency was rarely a dominant and often not an especially visible leadership institution in America. For much of the first half of the century, government was shaped by congressional leaders such as Daniel Webster, Henry Clay, and John Calhoun. Andrew Jackson, forceful executive though he was, did not approve of a forceful national government prior to taking office. Abraham Lincoln, before he was elected president, counseled against a strong presidency. And save in matters of war or security, Lincoln regularly deferred to Congress and his cabinet.[4]

Not until Theodore Roosevelt did the general public consciously expect a president to provide sustained assertive leadership. Populist manifestoes of the late nineteenth century began to change attitudes, as people turned to mass movements, popular political figures, and the central government as possible remedies for their economic problems. The populist crusade to elect Democrat William Jennings Bryan in 1896, 1900, and again in 1908 was illustrative of this new development. Attitudes toward presidential leadership had begun to change.

Teddy Roosevelt used the "bully pulpit" of the presidency to set the nation's programmatic agenda, and in doing so over time he also expanded expectations for the office. Woodrow Wilson echoed and extended Roosevelt's conception.

Wilson wrote that the presidency should respond to and help enact the progressive sentiments of the people. Since the country had expanded in so many ways, so too the government and the presidency must expand. The people, Wilson suggested, should look to their presidents to serve as a spokesman and conscience of the nation.

PUBLIC EXPECTATIONS IN RECENT TIMES

Public attitudes toward the presidency are subject to certain cycles. After strong presidents, who are often crisis or war presidents or who helped enact especially bold, controversial politics, the public yearns for a lessened presidential role, a return to normalcy. After a weak leader, and especially after a series of weak leaders, we yearn for strength. Presidents live in the shadows of their predecessors, and presidents often pay for the "sins" of a predecessor. After the presidencies of Theodore Roosevelt and Woodrow Wilson, the Harding, Coolidge, and Hoover administrations assumed a more passive posture. After the more modest presidencies of Ford and Carter came the more assertive Reagan presidency. After the boldness of George W. Bush came the more cautious Barack Obama.

Coolidge once said that nine out of ten problems brought to his office could be safely ignored and did not require his attention. Franklin Roosevelt, who came to office in the depths of the Great Depression, had a different conception and acted accordingly. After Franklin Roosevelt, however, there was a backlash; the public supported the Twenty-Second Amendment in an apparent effort to punish the institution (as well as reaffirm the two-term tradition). After the Johnson and Nixon administrations there was another backlash to presidential power, as Ford and Carter provided a return to normalcy and rectitude in the White House. However, Ford and Carter paid for the political excesses of Nixon by being more constrained by an energized Congress.

Seldom does a president actually relinquish any formal powers associated with the office. The more passive ones may not use the powers in a vigorous way, but even the three Republican presidents of the 1920s (Harding, Coolidge, Hoover) attempted to protect the powers of the office they inherited.

President Franklin D. Roosevelt set a precedent for executive leadership that became a benchmark as the national government became more and more involved in everyday life. Roosevelt established a pattern that most chief executives would inevitably follow: proposing legislation, lobbying to get proposals enacted, rallying public opinion in support of his measures, creatively using radio, and inserting himself into ongoing international diplomatic negotiations.

In the beginning of the Republic there was at best a grudging acceptance that a president would intervene in the affairs of the Congress. Now it is taken for granted that presidents regularly initiate and seek to win support for their measures. The FDR performance irretrievably altered people's views of presidents and the presidency. General Dwight Eisenhower added the reputation of a national hero to the luster of the office. Then, partly due to the glamour of the Kennedy administration, people and scholars were captivated by the potential magic of the office.

Lyndon Johnson won a landslide election in 1964 and enjoyed an almost two-year honeymoon with Congress. He sponsored vital civil rights legislation and initiated the Great Society programs. The power of the modern presidency appeared robust. Public and scholarly celebration of the presidency reached a peak.

Then came Vietnam, increased secrecy and duplicity, school busing and affirmative action, more rights for the accused, the Nixon Watergate scandals, obstruction of justice, and an increasingly frustrated American public. This dissatisfaction was reflected by an increasing anti-Washington sentiment. Public approval of presidents declined, and expectations of presidents were temporarily lowered.

Presidents Johnson, Nixon, Ford, and Carter were criticized and found wanting. Yet, after a brief infatuation with the idea of turning to Congress for national leadership (notably in the 1973–1980 period), Americans revived their demand for more assertive presidential leadership. Ronald Reagan won election in part because he played upon this yearning. Reagan's self-assurance, charm, optimism, wit, and decisiveness struck a responsive chord among a demoralized public. Reagan's likeability, his talent for speaking plainly, his ability to convey his love of the country, and his ability to give the people he was talking to, whether an individual or the public at large, the impression of liking them made him a rare political phenomenon. Reagan called for and promised a more powerful presidency, and he charmed and often entertained the nation.

Here are a few factors that affect how we evaluate and understand presidents and public opinion:

- The American public has rewarded presidents who "provided," or at least presided over, periods of peace and prosperity, and who displayed courage and leadership.
- Presidents go to great lengths to win public support for themselves and their initiatives for the simple reason that public support is viewed as a strategic resource in winning support in Congress, in the bureaucracy, in diplomatic endeavors, as well as, occasionally, in the courts.
- Public approval of presidents is less shaped by charisma or election results than by the times, the economy, the context of the challenges presidents have to face, and their success in dealing with these challenges.
- A president can be popular and a splendid communicator yet also ineffective. What the public thinks about presidents is not always what historians and political biographers will conclude. Thus Kennedy, Reagan, and Clinton were often popular with the public yet are viewed as average or even "overrated" presidents by many students of the presidency.
- Finally, presidential leadership involves more than becoming popular; Americans expect presidents on occasion to rise above doing what might be conventionally popular in favor of doing the right thing—that is, to lead us, to educate us, and to bring out our better, more idealistic selves. Thus, we may

ask a president to serve or even pander to our short-term or selfish interests, yet we define leadership as more than this.

QUALITIES AMERICANS LOOK FOR IN
PRESIDENTS TODAY

We have a tough, unwritten code of conduct for our nation's chief executive. We demand much, and many of our expectations—lower my taxes but give me more services—are quite paradoxical. Part of this is because many Americans nowadays cherish the idea of American Exceptionalism—the idea that America is somehow a superior, exemplary nation, perhaps even blessed by God to point the way for other nations. Part of this also comes from our inflated image of what "the great" presidents did. Our selective memories about the past glories and victories under our favorite presidents result in our holding incumbents to unusually high standards.

Many Americans favor an increased concentration of power in the American presidency and argue that in an age of terrorism, the country is in better hands when executive branch power is left unfettered by intrusive legislative, judicial, or international constraints. Such views both exaggerate the integrity and competence of most presidential administrations and do a serious injustice to our separation-of-powers, shared governance system.

When looking for a new president, Americans search for a leader who is honest and bright and who can bring us together and bring out the best in us. This is an especially tough assignment in a country shaped by stalwart individualism, embedded partisanship, polarized media outlets, and an abiding irreverence for politics and centralized government.

Most of us yearn for so many talents and qualities in our prospective presidents that it comes close to wanting "God—on a good day"—or at least a pleasant amalgam of Lincoln, the Roosevelts, Churchill, Mandela, Mother Teresa, Rambo, and the Terminator. Remember the "Mother Machiavelli" paradox.

However much we may expect of presidents, we are highly unlikely to ease up on them.

Experts usually rate experience, judgment, ability, vision, and intellectual capacity over honesty. But this is not the case with the average person. *Honesty, credibility, consistency, and good moral character* are the qualities people generally want in presidential candidates. Voters say they want a leader whose words they can both understand and believe, and someone they can trust and who will fight for the people (see Figure 2.1).[5]

It also helps if they are likable, "real," and understanding of the challenges facing average people.

When George H. W. Bush enjoined the public to "Read my lips: no new taxes," and later felt compelled to break that vow, the public was unforgiving. When candidate Bill Clinton promised a middle-class tax cut but broke that vow, and when he acknowledged lying under oath, he lost political capital as well as credibility. Similarly, the general public was highly critical of George W. Bush's misleading

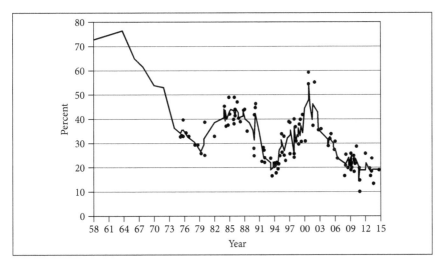

Figure 2.1 Decline of Trust in Government

justification for going to war in Iraq when no weapons of mass destruction were found, as well as his tepid response to the victims of hurricane Katrina.

The public consistently rates honesty as the top quality a president should have but they also want their president to have compassion, intelligence, empathy, sincerity, decisiveness, and decision-making ability. Strength and perceived leadership ability also rank high. Knowledge of economic issues and international affairs are also cited frequently.

The public as well as pollsters ask the following tough questions of presidents: Is the president willing to make tough, gutsy decisions? Can the president get things done? Is the president an effective manager of the government? Can the president deal effectively with Congress? Does the president share our values and relate to average Americans? Is the president an effective leader?

The Gallup Poll organization finds that about 75 percent of Americans think the country would be better off if their leaders followed the public's view more closely. This finding holds true for at least the past three decades regardless of party affiliation. Those with more college and graduate education are somewhat less supportive of this idea.

These and related public opinion findings, reflecting the heightened distrust in the national government, plainly suggest that Americans have more confidence in themselves when it comes to making important public policy judgments than they do in their national legislative or executive branch elected officials.

The problem with this sentiment is that Americans are deeply divided on many important issues, from health care to immigration. Moreover, the general public seldom has well developed, not to mention well informed, views on a whole host of national security and international relations issues. Thus, what exactly should our foreign policy be toward Pakistan, China, Somalia, or Iran? On such issues the people understandably look for guidance to leaders in both our elected branches as well as in the State and Defense departments, more than to their neighbors for informed leadership.

President Lincoln said that public support is indispensable for a president to succeed. Lincoln, who lived through the most trying of times without Gallup and CNN polls reporting his considerable public disfavor, would warn us today that in evaluating presidents we should be careful not to take polls too seriously, for the sources of positive or negative evaluations are often superficial. He would doubtless also say the influence between a people and their president is reciprocal: Presidents, paradoxically, must be both leaders and followers of public opinion.

The Gallup organization, since the late 1930s, has been asking random samples of adult Americans, "Do you approve or disapprove of the way [the incumbent president] is handling his job as president?"

This question allows us to learn, at least in part, whether presidents meet public expectations or not and whether or not a president seems responsive and accountable to citizens.

Over the past seventy years we can discern at least a few patterns:

- Presidents tend to be more popular in their first year than they are later in their terms.
- Presidential approval ratings often rise during the "honeymoon" early months in office.
- Over time approval ratings usually drop, with a number of zigs and zags caused by specific events, conditions, or crises.
- Presidents typically lose popularity during midterm elections, when the "guns" of the opposition party are aimed directly at the White House.
- Domestic crises, especially recessions, typically cause approval evaluations to drop.
- Increased polarization has led to partisans judging presidents of the opposing party harshly.
- International or terrorist crises, regardless of what a president does, typically cause us to rally around our president in the short run.
- Presidents often enjoy a rebound late in the first term—especially when they begin to be evaluated in comparison with likely opponents.
- If a president is reelected, the pattern often repeats itself, although approval ratings drop more quickly and tend to be lower in second terms.
- Polls do not necessarily accurately reflect how well a president is doing the job. And at least a good part of poll fluctuations concern issues beyond the influence or control of a president.

As political scientist Lyn Ragsdale has noted, "The course of presidential popularity proceeds up and down in varying sequences of intensity and duration, yet always more inevitably downward. . . . The one obvious difference between the presidential ride and the amusement park ride is that presidents do not finish where they began. Instead they start higher, finish lower, and presumably have less fun."[6]

While these patterns are persistent, they are not inevitable. Moreover, it is premature to be definitive when we are examining just a dozen or so presidencies.

The American people find it convenient to blame presidents for a whole range of problems, regardless of whether the problems are subject to presidential influence and solution or not. Presidents are the focus of attention and receive blame, and sometimes praise, for events over which they have little or no control. As noted earlier, psychologists refer to this as the "attribution fallacy."

Another paradox for a president stems from the public's desire to want contradictory things from government. The public wants budget cuts yet not service cuts (for themselves, at least); we want tax cuts yet also demand that entitlement programs such as Social Security and Medicare be fully funded.

Presidents want to unite and lead the nation as well as to maintain high public opinion and approval; but each of them confronts the dilemmas and paradoxes of a plural democratic presidency in the era of twenty-four-hour instant news cycles. They have to listen to myriad groups on myriad issues—"many of which are contradictory, while appearing to devise solutions to the problems in such a way as to maintain the nation's unity and to retain their presidential images as natural leaders of all the people."[7]

Presidential resources tend to wane as the years roll by. Every presidential honeymoon comes to an end. Prominent politicians who are rivals for the office begin, after a short grace period, to criticize a president's positions; partisan followings crystallize, and the ranks of those who disapprove of the president begin to swell. Presidential promises, at least some of them, go unachieved. Presidential achievements often fail to get acknowledged. Factions in a president's own party inevitably develop. Press criticism increases. (See Figure 2.2.)

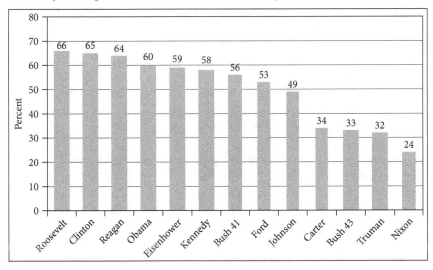

Figure 2.2 Presidential Job Approval Upon Leaving Office

SOURCE: ABC News/Washington Post and Gallup polls

A predictable cycle develops. Presidents usually lose political capital when their approval ratings sink. A president in this predicament may be tempted to avoid divisive issues in favor of not making waves.

Because modern media coverage gives so much emphasis to the presidency, it serves to quicken and intensify these reactions. Because presidents can usually gain immediate publicity, they are expected to communicate their views and solve problems without delay. Precisely because they are supposed to be shapers of public opinion, they are expected to inspire the country to great causes and sensible, low-cost solutions.

Whatever they do, the more presidents strive to achieve favorable support in public opinion polls, the more they are tempted to engage in short-term transitory policies—policies that may not necessarily be good for the country in the long run.

WHY DISAPPROVAL RATINGS RISE

Presidents usually have the support of a majority of Americans just after their inauguration. A rallying around the newly elected president customarily takes place. Most people, including many who did not vote or who did not vote for the victor, give new presidents some benefit of the doubt. Plus, inauguration ceremonies usually promote patriotism, national pride, unity, and optimism in the new governing team.

Because the president serves as both head of government (the nation's chief politician) and head of state (the symbolic representative of the nation), the president is simultaneously—and paradoxically—the chief divider of the nation and its chief unifier. Ronald Reagan was a masterful head of state. In the aftermath of the Challenger space shuttle disaster, Reagan took on the role of the high priest and national healer for a nation devastated by tragedy. This role allowed Reagan, the nation's top politician, to rise above politics (at least for a while) and serve as a symbol for the nation.

Invested in the office of the presidency is respect, but also high expectations (typically exaggerated by presidential campaign promises). Yet the president's powers are seldom equal to the responsibilities or the public's expectations. This invariably leads to frustration, and also to a decline in popularity. Likewise, if the public continues to demand that the government deliver on contradictory expectations presidents are put in no-win situations. Given this paradox, what's a president to do?

To win the presidency, candidates make promises. Once in office, they find themselves battling with Congress and colliding with the Supreme Court on occasion, unable to exert as much influence over the federal bureaucracy as they had presumed, and constrained by public opinion, the press, interest groups, rogue nations, and other forces. A president's power today to make and implement policies is limited by the partisan and decentralized character of politics and government in America, which often results in gridlock. America's growing interdependence with the rest of the world, with all the negative fallout from globalization as well as the rise of worldwide terrorism, also can limit the flexibility of the office.

Thoughtful people realize that presidents are indeed constrained by a number of factors and should be constrained. That said, they still hold presidents responsible. Presidents are a convenient, highly visible scapegoat for the nation's problems. We oversimplify issues, we personalize them, and television is constantly featuring the president on the news. When things go wrong, people notice. When things go right, people are usually complacent. Reality may be far more complex, but it is easier for busy people to ascribe blame to a specific person—the president.

Americans evaluate presidents on the basis of social, economic, and international policy *outcomes*. Yet the public's perceptions of presidential performances are usually inexact. Their evaluation is based on a combination of their own situation and on their general judgment of how the nation is doing and how they think the nation will do. "When the economy falters, support for the president erodes, not so much because citizens blame the president for their private hardships, however vivid, immediate, and otherwise important they might be, but because citizens hold the president accountable for the deterioration of national economic conditions."[8]

People often acknowledge they hold unfair or unrealistic expectations. Thus when people are asked, "Why do you think presidents almost always lose popularity the longer they stay in office?" they give these reasons:

- Presidents can't please everybody.
- Presidents are scapegoats for our problems.
- Presidents can't spend money we and they don't have.
- They make too many promises they can't keep.
- Presidents often have to make unpopular decisions.
- Presidents are not as powerful as people often think.

In sum, people judge on whether or not they follow through on their pledges. Our support for presidents is influenced also by how long they have been in office, and questions of peace, prosperity, and integrity are key. Also, especially in recent years, partisanship looms large in how we judge incumbent presidents. Thus, while most Republicans favored Bill Clinton's impeachment, Democrats supported him in high numbers. Democrats far more than Republicans, on the other hand, lost confidence in George W. Bush and especially his handling of the war in Iraq. Democrats favored most of Obama's policy initiations, but Republicans quickly became critical of almost anything Obama proposed.

The public is not just tough on presidents but on Congress and the national government as well. We have a national government as well as a presidential expectations gap. As trust has declined in the government it has been increasingly a challenge for presidents of both parties to win support for initiatives that involve sacrifice or higher taxes. Presidents are expected to help make government work effectively, yet this is hard when the American public is skeptical and cynical about the prospects of good government.[9]

Donald Trump entered office as the least popular president in modern times (see Table 2.1). His confrontational style and divisive rhetoric, attributes that attracted many to Trump as a candidate, proved a problem as the new president tried to govern.

Table 2.1 Modern Presidents Popularity on Entering Office

YEAR	INCOMING PRESIDENT	POPULARITY (Gallup)
1993	Bill Clinton	68%
2001	George W. Bush	61%
2009	Barack Obama	83%
2017	Donald Trump	44%

Table 2.1 helps understand another unusual piece of information: President Obama left office with a very high approval rating of 60%. Obama started high (83%) and ended high. Part of the explanation of his final approval rating stems from "comparison shopping." Throughout most of his presidency, voters compared Obama to an image in their heads of what a great president is: FDR, JFK, or others. But in the last year of his presidency, voters began to see Obama relative to the two rival candidates Trump and Clinton. By comparison to the real, not the ideal, Obama does significantly better.

WHAT A PRESIDENT CAN DO

Can presidents appeal for public support and improve their standing with the public and use this to help enact their legislative initiatives? Leading the public is supposed to be a key responsibility as well as a key source of power for presidents. Yet the ability to *inspire* the nation and generate sustained public support takes enormous time and effort. Those who think this ability is somehow automatically conferred upon assuming office are mistaken.

Presidents with popular support can sometimes exert pressure on Congress to adopt their programs. Lyndon B. Johnson did this on landmark civil and voting rights legislation in the mid-1960s. Reagan did it on tax cuts and defense spending measures in his first term. Obama did it with his first economic stimulus initiative. Yet there are many more cases where presidents failed to win public support and consequently failed to secure congressional approval for their priorities. Thus, LBJ lost the public's support on Vietnam, Clinton lost it on health care, and George W. Bush failed to win public support for his social security and immigration policies.[10]

Is presidential popularity a predictable source of presidential power? Some scholars believe it can be a convertible source of political power—namely, that a president can convert popularity into congressional votes, better treatment by the media, greater party loyalty, and less criticism from political opponents.

Many legislative achievements have occurred during presidential honeymoons and when presidents were riding high in the polls. Also, if a president can convince Congress that he or she is popular and that to defy the White House is politically dangerous, that president has more political capital. *Perception* often counts as much as (and sometimes more than) *reality*. Under what conditions can a president sway public opinion?[11] While many political scientists believe that by "going public," a president can influence the public,[12] there is reason to doubt that presidents, using the so-called "bully pulpit," can move the public very much or very often.[13] Certainly, while presidents believe they can sway public opinion, and their efforts to often go public demonstrate that presidents are willing to invest time and resources into such efforts, evidence of significant presidential impact is spotty. In fact, so concerned are presidents about public opinion that since the Nixon years, the institutional efforts to communicate with and hopefully influence the public has mushroomed into a collection of pollsters, spokespersons, internal coordinators, message shapers, and media handlers.[14]

In any event, presidents are keenly aware of fluctuations in their popularity, and they routinely engage in efforts at dramatizing themselves and their initiatives in hope of currying increased public approval.[15]

Trying to understand the complications of when to lead, when to follow, and when to hold back or merely respond symbolically is the subject of a growing body of research. Complicating all this are the major changes taking place in the media. The golden age of radio and traditional network television has been replaced by twenty-four-hour cable television, YouTube, Twitter, Facebook, Internet bloggers, and a whole range of alternative news sources. It is harder now for a president to get media coverage and frame issues as they would like. And the public has become more skeptical if not cynical toward all of the media. Presidents keep "going public," yet the public either isn't listening or is increasingly skeptical. "Rather than being the voice of the nation, presidents in the new media age appear more spokespeople for special interests than they did in the golden age," writes Jeff Cohen. "When presidents are less able to lead the public, they seek other ways to get Congress to act favorably on their policies. With less opportunity or ability to lead the public in the era of the new media, presidents instead seek the support of interest groups, special publics, and their partisan base."[16]

Political scientist George Edwards concludes that while presidential popularity is obviously an asset for a president, presidential speeches to rally the general public to put pressure on Congress usually have little effect.[17] He recommends that a president may well want, in many circumstances, to engage in quiet negotiations, or deliberative discussions, with leaders in Congress. "Staying private," as opposed to using a bully pulpit to "go public" and thereby bypass Congress might "contribute to reducing gridlock, incivility, and thus public cynicism."[18]

Still, rightly or wrongly, many Americans want to believe presidents can lead public opinion and can provide vision and plans to at least set the policy agenda in Congress. Franklin Roosevelt said, "All our great presidents were leaders of thought at a time when certain historic ideas in the life of the nation had to be clarified." His cousin Theodore Roosevelt boasted, "People used to say of me that I . . . divined what the people were going to think. I did not 'divine.' . . . I simply made up my mind what they ought to think, and then did my best to get them to think it."[19]

Great presidents take risks. Those who merely want to be loved sometimes sacrifice conviction for wanting to be loved. Warren Harding was popular yet also a failure. JFK was popular yet often cautious until his third and last year. FDR once said, "Judge me by the enemies I've made." Historian Arthur M. Schlesinger, Jr., suggests that effective presidential leadership is provided by those who follow their convictions and, at least on important issues, ignore middle-of-the-road pragmatism.

"Middle-roading may be fine for campaigning, but it is a sure road to mediocrity in governing. The middle of the road is not the vital center: It is the dead center," writes Schlesinger. "The Greats and Near Greats all took risks in pursuit of their ideals. They all provoked intense controversy. They all, except Washington, divided the nation before reuniting it on a new level of national understanding."[20]

The unwritten presidential job description, the one we carry around in our heads, calls for a president to be a visionary problem solver, a unifying force for the nation, a healer and sage. Thus, every four years we search anew for a fresh superstar who is blessed with the judgment of Washington, the brilliance of Jefferson, the genius of Lincoln, the political savvy of FDR, the youthful grace of JFK, and the sunny optimism of Ronald Reagan. Expectations always rise as elections near. Yet an exaggerated sense of what one of us has called "the textbook president" inevitably blinds us to the limits of what a president can accomplish.

One difference in the evaluation between the public and experts is the perspective of time. Historians like to wait for twenty or thirty years and see how a president's policies played out. They also want to read the memoirs of the president and other top advisers and examine archival materials. The public, on the other hand, is plainly influenced by what historians call *presentism*. The people are more likely to remember presidents who were good ones in their own or their parents' lifetimes, rather than past presidents who were notable in the judgment of history. People who remember the youth and excitement of John Kennedy or the charm and patriotism of Ronald Reagan, especially in comparison to their successors who seem ineffective, dishonest, or boring, rank Kennedy and Reagan as greater than Thomas Jefferson.

All rankings of presidents, whether by the public or by experts, reinforce our inclination to attribute more power to presidents than they really had.

What Americans expect of a president depends on varying factors. Not the least of these is who is president, who has been recently in office, and what the times demand. If recent presidents appear to have been weak, the public will likely call for more decisiveness. If the recent presidents seem to have overreached, the public demands more humility, more honesty, or a more collaborative president.

The public does not always base its evaluation of presidents on policies, issues, or achievements. The public likes past and present presidents who elicit positive emotion—optimism, hope, strength, warmth, excitement—and made them proud to be Americans. Political psychologist Drew Westen argues that, whether we are looking at candidates or judging presidents, we should never underestimate the role that positive emotions play. "The most successful politicians know how to elicit a range of positive feelings—enthusiasm, excitement, hope, inspiration, compassion, satisfaction, pride. . . .[21]

HOW EXPERTS JUDGE PRESIDENTS

What constitutes presidential greatness? Experts judge presidents on the basis of: the scope of the problems they faced; their efforts (actions) and intentions (vision) in dealing with these problems; what they were able to accomplish; and long-term results. Experts admire presidents who are smart, skilled politically, and willing to tell people what they may not want to hear and who can lead these same people to where they may not, at least in the short term, want to go. Experts downgrade presidents whose administrations were rife with corruption, or who were lacking in character.

The process of rating presidents is fraught with potential biases, and the actions of presidents look different from different historical vantage points. There are dangers in trying to assess the effectiveness and achievements of a presidency too early, say within twenty years. Sometimes a spate of new biographies about a former president will cast a favorable light upon a presidency or, conversely, may downgrade a previously respected administration. Harding, for example, was popular at his death in office yet later was rated as ineffective by historians. Truman was unpopular when he left office in 1952 yet gained stature two generations later.

There are numerous expert rankings of presidents, but almost all have Lincoln, FDR, and Washington at the top, followed by Teddy Roosevelt, Wilson, Truman, Jefferson, and Eisenhower.

Do great crises encourage great presidential performance? Madison, Pierce, Buchanan, Andrew Johnson, Hoover, and George W. Bush all faced crises, yet their responses seemed lame or ineffective. On the other hand, Lincoln, Wilson, and FDR all rank as great or near great because they responded to crises effectively. Although severe crises do not necessarily bring forth great leadership, the so-called "greats" served in periods of military, social, and economic upheaval, and the way they met these tests justifiably enhanced their reputations. The old

The world's most exclusive club: the ex-presidents. AP Photo/J. Scott Applewhite.

Historians Survey Results Category

Total Scores/Overall Rankings

PRESIDENT'S NAME	2017 FINAL SCORES	OVERALL RANKINGS		
		2017	2009	2000
Abraham Lincoln	906	1	1	1
George Washington	867	2	2	3
Franklin D. Roosevelt	854	3	3	2
Theodore Roosevelt	807	4	4	4
Dwight D. Eisenhower	744	5	8	9
Harry S. Truman	737	6	5	5
Thomas Jefferson	727	7	7	7
John F. Kennedy	722	8	6	8
Ronald Reegan	691	9	10	11
Lyndon Baines Johnson	686	10	11	10
Woodrow Wilson	683	11	9	6
Barack Obama	668	12	NA	NA
James Monroe	645	13	14	14
James K. Polk	637	14	12	12
Bill Clinton	633	15	15	21
William McKinley Jr.	626	16	16	15
James Madison	610	17	20	18
Andrew Jackson	609	18	13	13
John Adams	603	19	17	16
George H. W. Bush	596	20	18	20
John Quincy Adams	589	21	19	19
Ulysses S. Grant	556	22	23	33
Grover Cleveland	540	23	21	17
William H. Taft	528	24	24	24
Gerald R. Ford Jr.	509	25	22	23
Jimmy Carter	506	26	25	22
Calvin Coolidge	505	27	26	27
Richard M. Nixon	486	28	27	25
James A. Garfield	481	29	28	29
Benjamin Harrison	461	30	30	31
Zachary Taylor	458	31	29	28
Rutherford B. Hayes	458	32	33	26
George W. Bush	455	33	36	NA
Martin Van Buren	450	34	31	30
Chester Arthur	446	35	32	32
Herbert Hoover	416	36	34	34
Millard Fillmore	393	37	37	35
William Henry Harrison	383	38	39	37
John Tyler	372	39	35	36
Warren G. Harding	360	40	38	38
Franklin Pierce	315	41	40	39
Andrew Johnson	275	42	41	40
James Buchanan	245	43	42	41

SOURCE: C-SPAN, 2017 Presidential Historians Survey

question of whether great times make for great leadership or great leaders make great times is never satisfactorily settled, in part because even admired presidents experienced failures too.

WHAT IS PRESIDENTIAL GREATNESS?

Attempts to define "presidential greatness" are necessarily subjective. It is a value judgment. We all have biases. We all live in a fixed historical era. We almost always approach the task with an eye on contemporary problems and with a partisan or ideological bias of some kind. Still, it is tempting, if not irresistible, to attempt such a definition.

Experts judge presidents as effective or outstanding when they have acted greatly in challenging times. Great presidents, they believe, had an appreciation of the dynamics of history as well as a deep sense of the needs, anxieties, and dreams of the American people. Did the president have the courage to fight for what was right? Did they bring out the best in the American people? Did they recruit a first-rate cabinet and advisory team? Did they display common sense, agility, decisiveness, and good judgment in picking priorities, and fights? Lesser presidents often shy away from, rather than join, a conflict.

Also, moral courage stands out. Were they willing and able to stand up and be counted, as Lincoln and FDR were, when the nation and the nation's allies were challenged by the forces of hate and oppression? Conservatives revere Reagan for his boldness in standing up to the Soviet Union, the bureaucracy, and unions.

George Washington faced intense hostility over the Jay Treaty, yet he saw it through. John Adams was prepared to break up his party to avoid war with France, and he did both. Lincoln defied public opinion by removing General McClellan of the Army of the Potomac, and Truman displayed similar courage nearly a century later in removing General Douglas MacArthur from his top military command in Korea. Though these actions were unpopular, history vindicated these presidents.

Most experts understandably evaluate past presidents on whether or not that president provided leadership to advance the nation's interests. But experts are seldom unified on what the nation's main interests are. Liberals admire those presidents who championed what they call the positive role of government to help all the people, not just the powerful stakeholders in society. Conservatives admire presidents who championed liberty, "free-market" economics, and a less regulated society.

Most everyone agrees that the best presidents put in place policies that encouraged long-term economic growth, expanded equality of opportunity, preserved and expanded civil liberties and human rights, and provided for long-term national security.

What did the great presidents do? George Washington, more than any other individual, converted the paper Constitution into an enduring document. With commanding prestige and character he set the precedents that balanced self-government and leadership, constitutionalism and statesmanship. Washington's success made possible the success of the Republic. That Washington owned at least 200 to 300 slaves and became wealthy as a result of their labor is hard for many modern Americans to accept. He held contradictory and varied ideas about the institution of slavery, and only at the end of his life did he begin to set his slaves free.

Jefferson was a skilled organizer and a resourceful chief executive and party leader. He made his share of mistakes, yet he adapted the office to countless new realities. His expansion of territory with the Louisiana Purchase, an achievement breathtaking in its consequences, assures him special status. Lincoln saved the Union and will be remembered as the foremost symbol of liberation, freedom, and tenacious leadership in our hour of ultimate crisis. FDR saw the nation through its worst economic crisis and rallied the nation and the world to defeat Nazism and Hitler. In a time of dictatorships he managed a democratic response to the Depression and war.

These accomplishments are admirable. Still, they raise many questions. If presidents alone were responsible for all those notable and enduring accomplishments, it is little wonder that our expectations of presidents are so high. Plainly, a variety of people and institutions (cabinet members, advisers, the military, diplomats, etc.) contributed to these achievements.

History seldom adequately honors the economic and social movement leaders, reform activists, and "disrupters" as opposed to "incrementalists" who often provide as much or more of an era's leadership than does the president of the time. Great leadership depends on its surroundings, on teams of leaders, and on people who demand leadership. Luck—sometimes "dumb luck"—also plays a part in greatness. Timing and knowing how to embrace and exploit paradoxes and context is also crucial.

Our fascination with presidential effectiveness and failure reveals much about ourselves, about qualities we admire and those we dislike. It tells us, too, about our dreams and national character. We yearn for heroism and courage in literature, film, sports, and in our own lives. And so we too look for certain heroic "Mount Rushmore" qualities in our presidents. We delight in presidents who have triumphed when they faced ultimate tests. We admire presidents who are smart and compassionate and who think and act constitutionally. We are diminished by those who reveal the darker side of human nature and public life.

A democratic republic puts its faith in the people—faith that they will not merely elect presidents who will be responsive to their desires but who will both educate them and do what is right. Americans want to be heard, yet they also want leaders who will independently exercise their own judgment. Although presidents, to be sure, must take care not to be so self-assured they become insensitive to advice, they also need a certain inner sense of what has to be done. In the end, the best presidents are likely to be those who can accurately interpret the sentiments of the nation and rally the people and other political leaders to do what must be done, and what the public will later respect. These presidents will commonly be strong political leaders with a vision, as well as policy proposals, of where they think the nation should go. We will ask of them: Did they preserve, protect, and enrich the liberty, the rights, and the economic opportunities of all the people? Did they so engage with the public as to educate and build support for what was right?

CONCLUSION

The United States has had some excellent presidents, yet Americans have reserved the label "great" to just one per century: Washington in the eighteenth century, Lincoln in the nineteenth century, and FDR in the twentieth century. Along the way, we have liked Teddy Roosevelt, JFK, Eisenhower, and Reagan, yet affection toward these presidents is a different matter from their place in history.

The presidency may have been designed to be more of an administrative than a political or leadership position. This has of necessity changed, and public views of what presidents should do are different now than they were in the 1790s or even a few generations ago.

Public support for presidents follows certain patterns, yet these patterns are somewhat unpredictable and the exceptions are sometimes as interesting as the patterns themselves. When ranking presidents we often learn more about the raters than the rated. As this chapter has also shown, even the most serious efforts at judging presidencies invariably involve some subjective or partisan biases.

The enduring challenge for presidents remains: Summon us to live up to our highest shared ideals of a generous, benevolent country that is a shining beacon for liberty and freedom; take prudent risks but anticipate and head off fiascoes; and pay close attention to our immediate shared aspirations such as national security, energy security, job creation, fair taxes, trade, prosperity, and equality of opportunity.

FURTHER READINGS

Bardes, Barbara A., and Robert W. Oldendick. *Public Opinion,* 4th ed. Lanham, Md.: Rowman & Littlefield, 2012.

Bose, Meena, and Mark Landis, eds. *The Uses and Abuses of Presidential Rankings.* Hauppauge, N.Y.: Nova, 2003.

Hetherington, Marc J. *Why Trust Matters.* Princeton, N.J.: Princeton University Press, 2012.

Leuchtenburg, William E. *The American President: From Teddy Roosevelt to Bill Clinton.* New York: Oxford University Press, 2015.

CHAPTER 3

Electing Presidents

Paradoxically, the candidate who won the popular vote in 2016 lost the election. Donald J. Trump won the Electoral College vote in 2016 by a comfortable 306-232 margin over Hillary Clinton. Yet, Clinton won the popular vote by over 2.9 million votes. In a democracy, Clinton should be president, but we do not live in a democracy, and there, once again, we see one of the paradoxes of the American Presidency. In the United States we have not one, but 51 presidential elections: the fifty states plus the District of Columbia. Winning electoral votes is the important thing, not winning a majority of votes. It is but one of the many paradoxes we will explore in this chapter.

THE WORLD'S MOST POWERFUL NATION
SELECTS A PRESIDENT

It was enough to make one blush from embarrassment: In the spring of 2015, one by one, a lineup of Governors, Senators, and other would-be presidents meekly stepped up pledging their allegiance, not to the United States of America, but to one rich 82-year-old Las Vegas casino owner, Sheldon Adelson, a Republican Party Sugar Daddy. New Jersey Governor Chris Christie profusely apologized to Adelson for referring to "occupied territories" (in reference to the West Bank and Eastern Jerusalem). Governor Jeb Bush broke from the normally rock-solid family loyalty to distance himself from Bush family consigliere and former Bush 41 Secretary of State James A. Baker III, who criticized Israeli Prime Minister Benjamin Netanyahu. For Adelson, absolute support for Israel was his one make-or-break issue, and his Republican courters knew it. One big check could make or crush a campaign.

Americans love their country, celebrate democratic ideals, and generally prize the American presidency, yet we are not especially proud of the way we elect presidents, or of the candidates who run. Many Americans were bewildered by the contentious presidential election of 2000, baffled by the Electoral College, embarrassed by the huge role money and the media play in presidential elections, and surprised by the way Donald Trump catapulted to the lead in the Republican 2016 race. People see the selection process as an often self-defeating system—a bit like a demolition derby, as much a process of eliminating good people as encouraging strong candidates to run for the White House. Many worry as well at a paradox noted in Chapter 1, that the qualities needed to win the White House are not necessarily the same as those needed to govern the country. The process by which we select presidents is complex and controversial: complex because there is not one law that covers presidential selection, but many. In some cases the federal government or national parties establish rules; in other cases, state laws governs presidential selection. For the most part it is the states that establish rules for elections. This means that there can be fifty different sets of laws governing a single election. And given the Electoral College, a presidential election is really fifty different, separate races.

The process is controversial because the campaign is *long, costly*, and rarely seems to produce *nominees* about whom we get excited. Too often cynics say we end up with the lesser of two evils, or the evil of two lessers.

Many of our presidential paradoxes apply to the way we elect presidents. The qualities we look for in a president are often at odds with one another. Yes, we want a "common man"—one of us—yet we insist that they also be extraordinary, above the rest. We want caring, compassionate, empathetic leaders who are also tough (even ruthless) when necessary. Americans want a leader to bring us together, yet to govern—even to get elected—is to be partisan, to be a divider at times. Finally, the skills and attributes that make one an effective candidate, are at times at odds with what it takes to govern effectively.

This chapter describes how we elect our presidents. We explore the following questions: Who becomes president? What do we look for in prospective presidents? What must a person do to be taken seriously as a presidential candidate? How important are the primaries and caucuses? What about the so-called advantages of incumbency? Why do people vote or not vote for president? What about the controversial Electoral College and its role in presidential elections? Finally, does the selection process do what we need in democratic and quality-of-outcome terms? After all, a presidential election is about more than merely determining who will assume office. It is also, or should be, the great conversation a democracy has concerning its future.

Elections matter, and the 2008 race was precedent shattering. Both of the final candidates vying for the Democratic Party nomination for president were from previously excluded groups: a woman, and a black male. Senators Hillary Clinton and Barack Obama broke barriers, opened up our democracy, and struck a blow for equality. Likewise, the choice of Sarah Palin as the Republican nominee for vice president added to the precedent-shattering nature of the election. It is hard not to look back at that race—regardless of your party affiliation—and not be impressed with how significant an event the 2008 race was for America (see Table 3.1). A black male with the middle name of Hussein won the presidency with

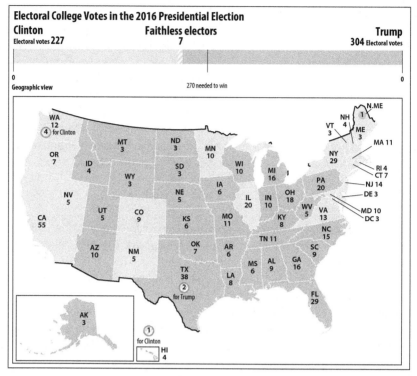

Map 3-1 2016 Electoral Map

53 percent of the popular vote and nearly 70 percent of the Electoral College vote (365 electoral votes). A corner was turned in America.

In 2016, the two finalists for the Democratic Party nomination were a woman and a Jew, and on the Republican side two of the final four candidates were of Cuban descent.

WHO BECOMES PRESIDENT?

Presidents *have usually been* middle-aged white male Protestant lawyers of European lineage from the larger states. Thirty-seven of our presidents trace ancestry to the British Isles, three were Dutch, and three were German. All but one, John Kennedy, were Protestants. About half have been lawyers and served in Congress. Most others held state or community elective office. Several were military heroes. Twelve were generals.

Long gone are the days when party leaders alone could select a candidate. Today, with the proliferation of state primaries and caucuses, the candidates who are well financed and can devote themselves to a year or two of full-time campaigning often have an advantage over public figures who occupy office or hold full-time jobs.

In a sense, there is an "on-deck" circle of at most thirty or so individuals in any given presidential election year: governors, prominent U.S. Senators, a few members of the House of Representatives, and a handful of recent governors or vice presidents who have successfully kept themselves in the news media. These men, and an occasional woman or outsider, form the core of electables whom "The Great Mentioner," that mythic conglomeration of prominent media figures and pundits, is willing to anoint as serious candidates.

No doubt there are talented business entrepreneurs, educators, military leaders, or other outstanding individuals who might make as capable a president as any of the activist politicians who inevitably become candidates. Seldom, however, are these nonprofessional politicians willing to enter the political thicket in their fifties or sixties. Dwight Eisenhower in the 1950s, and billionaire H. Ross Perot, who won 19 percent of the popular vote in 1992 and 8 percent in 1996, are the exceptions to the rule. And Donald Trump also defied the odds in 2016. Most potential presidential candidates do not want to spend several years on the campaign trail or raise the more than $100 million needed to run. Others may be reluctant to disclose their finances or subject their families to the brutal public scrutiny involved in a presidential race. Some potential candidates acknowledged that their spouses objected to their running for president. The demanding presidential campaign, especially with the more than thirty primary elections, is unappealing even to seasoned politicians.

The general public harbors a disdain for politicians. "If God had wanted us to vote," goes the saying, "He would have given us candidates." When asked about their career aspirations for their children, parents rate "politician" low on their list.

According to the Constitution, a presidential candidate must be at least thirty-five years old, must have lived within the United States for fourteen years, and must be a natural-born citizen. Whether a person born abroad of American parents is qualified to serve as president has never been fully decided. Such a person would probably be considered "natural born" even if not native born.

Beyond the constitutional requirements, American voters have a tough, unwritten set of demands for anyone driven enough to want to become president. We are often disappointed in the quality of our candidates because we invariably measure them against an idealized composite of what our greatest presidents and world leaders did, rather than against what our past presidents looked like prior to their becoming presidents. We remember past presidents primarily for their victories and on their best days.

Most of us yearn for so many talents and qualities in our presidents that it comes close to wanting "God—on a good day." We want vision, character, experience, organizational competence, intelligence, stamina, agility, inspiration, judgment, wisdom, emotional stability, and strength, and we especially want someone who shares our political beliefs, as well as our anxieties.

When looking for a new president, we often want a leader who can bring us together and bring out the best in us. Yet this is a tough assignment in a nation shaped by stalwart individualism and irreverence for government and centralized institutions, and today, hyperpartisanism.

We justifiably look at candidates with an unforgiving eye, but perhaps we are unfair with pop quizzes, "got you" questions, and denunciation of candidates for doing things we ourselves might have done. Then too, we simultaneously want a candidate to be like us and better than us.

Our ideal candidate, in addition to sharing our concerns and policy values, would have the following attributes, each of which is identified in the paradoxes that guide this book:

Courage. The willingness to take risks and try to serve all the people and not just those who bankrolled his or her candidacy; the intellectual courage to do what is right even when it is not popular or easy.

Experience and competence in bringing people together in teams to solve major political problems; great skill as a negotiator and builder of policy agreements.

Political savvy. An understanding of the necessity of politics and the ability to be an effective politician, someone who can work with people of all political views and who recognizes that coalition building is central.

An **understanding** of history and constitutionalism. A solid grasp of how governments and markets work and how trade and diplomacy operate, and a respect for the U.S. Constitution and the constraints it puts on leadership and government. Wanted too is a cosmopolitan respect for the diverse political culture in the United States.

The **ability** to recruit wise advisers and effective administrators, and the wisdom to delegate to teams of colleagues, is also important.

Listening, learning, and teaching skills. Paradoxically, a leader has to both listen to us and lead us. We want leaders who give us a sense not only of who they are, but more importantly, who we are, and who we might become.

Programmatic ideas and wisdom, and the ability to define plans, clarify options, and help set the nation's policy agenda. A president has to be preoccupied with the large, compelling issues of our day (economic opportunities for everyone, freedom, trade, nuclear proliferation, racism, equality, etc.)—a forest person, not overwhelmed by the trees or leaves.

Communication skills. Ideas and wisdom are of little use if a president cannot rally the public and empower teams and constituencies to enact new plans.

Tenacity and discipline balanced with emotional strength and humility. A thick skin helps in this generally thankless job, as do the ability to laugh at oneself and to admit flaws and mistakes. Not wanted are persons who are defensive, rigid, torn by self-doubt or self-pity, or individuals who blame their problems on "enemies."

Intellectual honesty. We want presidents we can trust, who have a basic respect for others and a commitment to serve the public interest.

Morale-building and community-building skills. The presidency is far more than just a political or constitutional job; it is also an institution that has to help us through crises and transitions, and help unify us when we experience national setbacks. Presidents at their best help remind us of our mutual obligations, shared beliefs, and the trust and caring that can hold us together.

Do we ask too much of our presidential candidates? Sure. History conditions different cultures to expect different things of their leaders. In the United States we exaggerate the capacity of what even heroic presidents can do to change the course of events.

But we won't lower our expectations.

WHY VOTERS VOTE THE WAY THEY DO

Most scholars believe the chief factors influencing how people vote in presidential elections are their *party orientation*, their *public-policy preferences*, the way they perceive the *integrity, character, and judgment* of the candidates, and *retrospective judgments* as well as *prospective judgments* on the performance of the incumbent or their political party.[1]

Parties are important factors when votes are counted. Roughly two-thirds of Americans identify themselves as Democrats or Republicans. Most of the time, most Republicans vote Republican, Democrats vote Democratic. For example, 90% of Republicans voted for Trump in 2016 even though several prominent Republicans refused to support him.

Issues or public policy preferences play an even more complicated role in how people cast their presidential votes. In certain years, like 1800, 1860, 1936, and 1964, issues played a larger, more clear-cut role. In other years, such as 1984 and 2000, issues weren't as important. Sometimes both major candidates take the

As crisis managers, presidents must both respond and be seen as responding to any disaster or crisis, lest they be criticized for inaction or lack of concern. AP Photo/Pablo Martinez Monsivais.

same position on a major issue, as in 1968 when both Richard Nixon and Hubert Humphrey said they favored ending the war, honorably, in Vietnam. In 2008, with the economic meltdown looming over the heads of voters, the issue of who might better handle the economy proved significant in voters' decisions. In 2016, a fear and change election, and a "whitelash," contributed to the outcome.

Effective candidates provide meaning and purpose in a confusing world. They help make sense of the times. A candidate, or president, who can give comfort, assurance, and hope amid this confusion, can generate loyal and wide support.

Often, honesty and integrity top the list of desired characteristics. We are keenly aware, more so because of Watergate, the Iran-Contra scandal, and Bill Clinton's and George W. Bush's various failings, of the need for a president to set a tone, and to serve as an example of credibility. Dishonesty and duplicity are qualities Americans dislike.

Most voters prefer a moderate candidate. They generally vote against extremists of any kind. This has led to an aphorism that "the only extreme in American politics that wins is the extreme middle." Ronald Reagan is somewhat of an exception to this rule, yet he was generally able to portray himself as a reasonable person and in his two terms as Governor of California he governed like a moderate; his rhetoric was often comforting and nurturing to the point that he appeared to be mainstream. In 2008 and 2012, Republicans tried to paint Barack Obama as too radical and dangerous, but Obama's reassuring style overcame such charges.

Personality and character also count. In local elections people often just rely on party labels. But with governors, U.S. senators, and especially presidents, and with the availability of extensive television and Internet coverage, people plainly exercise their own personal judgment about who is most fit to serve in office.

Some people deplore the fact that a candidate's personality and style are evaluated as equal to or more important than issues and substance. But a candidate's personality and temperament are perfectly legitimate and, indeed, proper subjects for voters to weigh. There is little doubt that a candidate's sense of self-confidence and personal style of conduct can and usually do affect how he or she would behave in office. Presidents have significant discretionary power, and their personalities can affect the way they decide public policy questions and handle crises.

The basic insecurities of certain presidents have also led to failure in the White House. We have reason to be alert to whether a candidate can accept criticism and whether he or she demands absolute loyalty from subordinates. We have suffered from presidents who have encouraged "group think" and developed "enemy lists."

In 2012 and 2016, the proliferation of big money into the race raised questions of whether one or both candidates had become captured by an elite oligarchy, as Bernie Sanders warned (the 1 percent). The 2012 race cost roughly $3 billion, leaving average voters to wonder if anyone was representing their interests. Hence the appeal of the self-financing billionaire Donald Trump in 2016.

Elections are also judgments about the past and hopes for the future. We base our vote in part on a retrospective assessment of how well or poorly we think the incumbent president or their party did in governing the nation. If we believe the state of the economy is going in the right direction, we are likely to reward the incumbent party.

We are usually drawn to candidates who are self-confident and self-aware, not given to defensive and compulsive behavior. The rise of Donald Trump in 2016 is the exception to this rule. He had plenty of self-confidence, yet was also combative and defensive.

To what extent are questions of private moral character relevant to presidential politics? While the president is, in many ways, a moral or symbolic spokesman for the nation, must the person who fills the office be personally "pure" to be a good president? It doesn't seem so. The public may want its presidents to be of the highest character, yet a look at the private lives of our great presidents reveals plenty of personal foibles.[2] The release of the "Access Hollywood" tape of Donald Trump bragging about sexual assault ("I just grab them by the . . .") suggests that voters pay little attention to the characters of candidates or perhaps, voted for Trump despite such comments.

One of the few modern presidents who might have passed today's "character test" is Richard Nixon. In his private life, Nixon was seemingly very upright. In his public life, however, Nixon left much to be desired. In a test of character "which Nixon passes and FDR fails, something is evidently amiss with our current prejudices about the kind of character we desire in political leaders."[3]

Precisely what do we mean by character? Some people with roguish private lives exhibit great public integrity. Others of spotless private life exhibit public qualities of duplicity. Today, journalists and rival candidates search the backgrounds of candidates, looking for any indiscretion. If found, that candidate is likely drummed out of the race. Is it fair to base our judgments of character on isolated events which may have occurred years ago, and from which the candidate may have drawn useful lessons?

Presidents, like the rest of us, are human; they make mistakes. Some learn from their mistakes, others don't. The perfect person does not exist. Our presidents come with a wide array of strengths and weaknesses. To disqualify a candidate because it was revealed they made mistakes years ago seems shortsighted.

Can a president be too nice, too honorable? Both Ford and Carter were decent people. Would they have been more effective if they had been more Machiavellian?

One clue into character may be how a person deals with adversity or defeat. FDR's polio would have overwhelmed most people, but Roosevelt overcame adversity, and in doing so, was even more convincing when he told us we had nothing to fear but fear itself. In Roosevelt's case, adversity made him stronger.

While no single definition of character adequately covers all our needs, the following qualities are certainly admirable in the person who becomes president: courage of conviction; internal moral compass; respect for others; commitment to the public good; respect for democratic standards; generosity of spirit, compassion and empathy, optimism, and emotional strength; sense of decency and fair play; and inner strength and confidence.

Voters often complain about the tone of presidential campaigns, seeing them as too negative. It is true that campaigns often go negative, and this is because generally, *negative works*.

In the end, questions of presidential character serve as yet another example of the paradoxical nature of presidential politics. What we applaud in one president we condemn in another. In the end, the real test of presidential character may well be, "Did this president bring out the best in all of us?"

However much we seek the well-rounded leader, we usually get ambitious, vain, and calculating candidates who often do not know what is to be done (though they are willing to try). The people who run and win view presidential campaigns less as dialogues or programs for adult education than as a fight to win office, a fight to get there. Once they get there, they will experiment and see what works. The voters may like a person who knows all the answers—but few candidates will make commitments that are not reversible once in office.

THE INVISIBLE PRIMARY

Today, candidates work for three, and even four years before the first primary to prepare for their race. Jimmy Carter announced his candidacy for the White House on December 12, 1974, almost two full years before the 1976 election, and he admits he made his decision in 1972, four years before the election. Many of the Republicans who ran for the 2016 nomination got started in 2013. Since 1936 active candidates who were ranked as most popular within their own party in the Gallup poll taken one month before New Hampshire's primary have won their party's nomination almost every time. Pre-primary activity is indeed significant. A candidate needs to be convincing on several "tracks" before he or she gets contender status. All of the following are needed:

- To become as well-known as possible
- To raise substantial sums of money
- To attract and organize a staff
- To pay numerous visits to key caucus and primary states, especially Iowa and New Hampshire
- To identify core issues and build a supportive constituency
- To devise a "winning" strategy
- To speak at scores of party functions (the rubber-chicken circuit)
- To court publicity and the media
- To develop a psychological preparedness and a self-confidence that radiates strength and energy.

These do not necessarily occur in this order, and this short list does not exhaust the self- and organizational testing of this period. However, without these a candidate isn't taken seriously.

The first need of a would-be president is to become known. No other effort commands as much time as the battle to gain name recognition. Candidates like Roosevelt, Eisenhower, Kennedy, Reagan, George W. Bush, and Trump had a leg up on most others because they had become celebrities or had inherited a well-known name even before they ran for the presidency. Candidates like Carter, Dukakis, Obama, and Kasich on the other hand, had to go out and become known the hard way—by crisscrossing the nation, visiting city after city, and giving unremitting, bone-numbing speeches, town hall meet and greets, and interviews.

The second major need for a presidential candidate is *money*. To realistically have a shot at the nomination, candidates have to raise millions and millions of dollars. Referred to as the "Green Primary," only those candidates who can raise big money are taken seriously. This, of course, gives the Donor Class significant power. It also undermines democracy by creating what is called a "weighted vote." Person A gives her vote plus $100 to her preferred candidate. Person B gives her vote plus $100,000 to a candidate, super PAC, and party. Whose vote carries more weight? Given the current interpretation of what is legal in fundraising, we can draw six conclusions regarding the importance of money in politics.

1. *Money does not guarantee victory.* Just ask Jeb Bush, the 2016 favorite who spent over $150 million and went nowhere.
2. *Not having big money guarantees defeat.* Just stating the obvious here.
3. *Wealthy individuals can buy their way in the race.* Steve Forbes and Donald Trump are prime examples.
4. *Dialing for Dollars.* As money serves as a gatekeeper, candidates must spend a great deal of time raising money, money that *may* come with strings attached.
5. *Working the Internet Magic.* An outsider—Obama in 2007, Sanders in 2015–2016—can now sometimes raise enough money to become a credible candidate using the Internet.
6. *Independent/outside money is not technically controlled and allows for "dark money" to corrupt or influence the selection process.*[4] The Koch brothers spent $400 million in 2015 trying to influence elections. And they are merely the tip of the iceberg.

How "independent" are these Super PACs? Most are led by and staffed by friends and former employees of the candidate, making them an "outside group of insiders," familiar with the candidate and aligned with the themes and goals of the campaign.

Large sums are needed to pay for staff, travel, and later in the campaign for crucial television and radio advertising. In 2008, Barack Obama raised more money than had ever been raised to run for president. In 2012, all candidates combined yet again set a record for fundraising.

In 1972, in *Bullock v. Carter*, the Supreme Court ruled that economic status should not be a significant impediment in seeking elected office. This case struck down a Texas law that established "filing fees" of up to $8,900 to get placed on the ballot. Today, after a series of "money-liberating" decisions, the Supreme Court has landed at the opposite end of the *Bullock* decision.

The "entry cost" for merely getting into the race today is roughly $1 billion. This discourages many considering a run in the first place. With money serving as a gatekeeper, only wealthy individuals (e.g., Steve Forbes in 199, and Donald Trump in 2016) or those willing to invest time—and perhaps their principles—in extensive fundraising need apply for the job of president. How many potential candidates, eyeing the race in 2016, decided not to even try given the staggering cost of presidential elections?

Candidates can now form super PACs that can accept unlimited donations. While candidates once went out of their way to avoid even the appearance of financial wrongdoing, today it is open season in the money race. That is because what once were blurred lines have now been erased. There is almost an "anything goes" attitude about fundraising today.

If the 1 percent dominate the American economy, they also dominate the presidential campaign financing system. Competition for billionaire backers is fierce, and this donor primary precedes the actual primary and caucus season by several months if not a year. Catch a billionaire sugar daddy and you can stay in the race (even if you capture few primary votes); fail to snare a big financial friend and your campaign is dead on arrival. Sheldon Adelson, the Koch Brothers, Norman Braman, Larry Ellison—these are the new American king makers.

It was in the 2012 Republican primaries that this new "billionaire boys' club" of the mega-donors became a key force in presidential selection when Adelson bankrolled former House Speaker Newt Gingrich in his failed nomination bid. Adelson's money kept Gingrich in the race for months and months, this despite the fact that Gingrich attracted few voters. But that set the stage for 2015–2016.

In the past electoral seasons, money tended to follow results: Do well in the early caucuses and primaries and the money would follow. Today, money precedes the race and several billionaires serve as the gatekeepers to the nomination.[5]

In the 2012 election, Barack Obama spent roughly $1.1 billion; Mitt Romney spent $1.2 billion. In 2016, Hillary Clinton was also a big spender, especially in contrast to the relatively small sums of money spent by Trump. She spend roughly $380 million, according to Open Secrets. With the rise of billionaire donors and "dark money" (where donors' names are undisclosed), average citizens are being both spent out of the system and kept in the dark about who is donating to whom.

The process of raising money in large sums is a compromising and sometimes corrupting one. The burden of having to raise millions for a presidential race is at the heart of why many able persons do not consider running for the office. It is also at the heart of why some people are turned off by our political process. All this raises serious questions about the selection process. When does a political contribution become a bribe? When does systematic campaign soliciting become equivalent to a conspiracy to extort funds? At what point does our democracy become a kleptocracy? The late Hubert Humphrey, who twice ran for president, put it bluntly:

> Campaign financing is a curse. It's the most disgusting, demeaning, disenchanting, debilitating experience of a politician's life. It's stinky. It's lousy. I just can't tell you how much I hate it. I've had to break off in the middle of trying to make a

decent, honorable campaign and go up to somebody's parlor or to a room and say, "Gentlemen, and ladies, I'm desperate. You've got to help me. . . .

. . . And you see people—a lot of them you don't want to see. And they look at you, and you sit there and you talk to them and tell them what you're for and you need help and, out of the twenty-five who have gathered, four will contribute. And most likely one of them is in trouble and is somebody you shouldn't have had a contribution from.[6]

Reliance on big money made the presidential selection process vulnerable to charges of corruption. In the aftermath of the Watergate scandal, Congress passed legislation for public financing of presidential elections. Enacted in 1974, the campaign finance reform effort called for public disclosure of all contributions exceeding $100, established ceilings on contributions, created a system of federal subsidies, and established spending limits. This law was challenged in court, and in *Buckley v. Valeo* (424 U.S. 1, 1976) the Supreme Court determined that while the Congress could regulate contributions and expenditures of campaign organizations, it could not prevent or limit independent individuals or groups from exercising free speech (and spending) rights.

Congress then passed the Federal Election Campaign Act (FECA), to revise existing laws to keep them in line with constitutional standards. These new guidelines have been in effect since the 1976 presidential election. But since that election, campaign organizations have discovered loopholes in the law that allow campaigns to get around it.

First the "independent" money exemption allows individuals and organizations to spend money for or against candidates as long as the effort is not conducted with the advice or assistance of a candidate's campaign organization. This has opened the door for "independent" spending on behalf of a candidate, or, as is more likely, negative campaign ads against a candidate. Second, the spending of what is called "soft money" allowed party organizations to raise and spend money for a variety of purposes in support of the campaign.[7]

In 2010 the Supreme Court, in a 5–4 decision in the case *Citizens United v. Federal Election Commission*, overruled important campaign spending precedents by allowing corporations (and labor unions) to contribute money to political campaigns. Asserting that corporations have the same rights as persons, the Court determined that the First Amendment rights of free speech—which included money—apply to corporations and that the government may not ban political spending (speech) by corporations in elections.

The Court's majority asserted that their decision was a vindication of the First Amendment's basic free speech right. The Court's dissenters warned that unleashing corporate money in campaigns would corrupt democracy. And the Court failed to account for the fact that many corporations are partially owned by foreign companies and individuals—a clear violation of U.S. law.

The 2010 decision marked a sharp shift in the Court's approach, overruling two precedents. Up to that point the Court decided in *Austin v. Michigan Chamber of Commerce* (1990)[8] *and McConnell v. Federal Election Commission* (2003)[9] that corporate and labor campaign contributions could be restricted. The recent decisions overturning these cases were major victories for Republicans and big businesses. The 2012 presidential election was the first where *Citizens United's* new rules applied.

This led to the development of what are called the "super PACs" (Political Action Committees). These super PACs are supposed to be "independent" of individual candidates, yet the line is often blurred. *Restore Our Future* promoted Governor Mitt Romney. This super PAC spent millions of dollars—mostly in negative television ads—attacking Romney's opponents. In this way an attack ad cannot be linked directly to the candidate who benefits because Super PACs are independent of the campaign and the candidates. President Obama had his super PACs as well.

The Citizens United Oligarchy

Less than 1 percent of the top 1 percent donated one-half of the money raised in the 2016 presidential primary campaign. Most of that money went to super PACs pledged to particular candidates. As of June 2015, more than $13.5 million of the $20 million raised by supporters of Governor Walker in 2014–2015 came from four donors. Twelve and a half million of the $16 million raised by Senator Marco Rubio's PAC, *Conservative Solutions*, came from four donors. Senator Ted Cruz raised $37 million, almost all of it coming from just these families. The largest donation to Governor Chris Christie's PAC came from a Boston investor who wanted to a build a $4 billion resort in New Jersey. Over 80 percent of Governor Rick Perry's money came from just three donors. Most of Governor Mike Huckabee's money came from poultry magnate Ronald Cameron. More than half of Senator Rand Paul's money was provided by two donors.[10]

This green primary allows fringe candidates, or those with little popular support, to wage a long campaign, staying in the race long after any of hope of winning has been exhausted.

The Supreme Court further opened the door to big money in campaigns with its 2014 decision in *McCutcheon v. Federal Election Commission*. In a 5–4 vote, the Court equated money with speech (as opposed to property). By deciding that money was speech, the Court further gutted campaign finance restrictions, striking down the limits on how much a person could donate to a candidate per election cycle. Welcome to the Wild West of campaign financing.

Once the Supreme Court opened up the money spigot, it wasn't long before enterprising candidates found new and creative ways to exploit these new conditions. In 2015, Jeb Bush postponed his formal announcement that he was a candidate so he could personally raise over $100 million for his PAC, *Right to Rise*. Such PACs are supposed to be strictly independent of the campaign, but as Jeb Bush had not yet declared himself a candidate, he was able to claim that the money was for his PAC, not his campaign. Once he announced, he cut off formal ties to *Right to Rise*, but the PAC was headed by Bush friends and former associates.

Super PACs allow candidates to circumvent campaign finance laws. Current law limits the amount individuals can contribute to a candidate to $2,500. Normal

PACs (corporations, unions, etc.) are limited to giving $5,000 to any single candidate. *Citizens United* made a mockery of this. Now, individuals and organizations can spend unlimited amounts of money to support—or attack—a candidate. The only requirement—a cosmetic one at that—is that the organization not directly work with a candidate.

While both liberal (DreamWorks CEO Jeffery Katzenberg gave $3 million to *Priorities USA Action*) and conservative (the Koch brothers gave $200 million to their Super PAC, *Americans for Prosperity*) Super PACs have sprung up, and spending in 2012 and 2016 heavily favored Republicans.

To put U.S. campaign spending into perspective, the 2010 general election in Great Britain cost roughly $130 million for all its races. The U.S. 2012 presidential race alone cost roughly $3 billion.

While it would be misleading to say that money literally buys elections, money nonetheless plays a significant role in influencing who the eventual winner will be. The primary candidate who spends the most money almost always wins. In fact, 91 percent of the time in congressional races, the better financial candidate wins.[11]

Campaign contributions are often given to reward and influence candidate positions. Steel magnate Henry C. Frick complained of Teddy Roosevelt, "We bought the son of a bitch and then he did not stay bought."[12] Campaign contributions are seen as investments in the future, and contributors do expect, and often get, returns on their investments.

In 2008, Democratic nominee Barack Obama raised eyebrows when he bypassed public funding for the general election, believing, correctly, that he could raise and spend substantially more money outside the public financing parameters. Obama's rejection of the public funding regime will doubtless spell its doom for the public option. Increasingly, campaigns are utilizing the Internet in the race for the White House. YouTube did not exist in 2004. In 2008 and 2016, it had a significant impact in the presidential contest. And in 2016, Donald Trump used Twitter to reach out to his supporters, leading some to refer to the 2016 race as the Twitter campaign.

New campaign technologies dramatically impact both the way campaigns are conducted and how citizens connect to the campaign and candidate.[13] These technologies give us more quantity, but do they give us more quality? As new forms of social media rise, interest in "serious" news has declined.[14] New media—the Internet, YouTube, blogging, social networking, Twitter—has a generational bias as well.

The rise of online news sources (and "Fake news") has contributed to the decline of newspapers, network news, even local television. It has also led to the ability to cocoon oneself from hearing news or opinion different from one's own. A liberal can read like-minded blogs. A conservative can watch Fox News, or listen to Rush Limbaugh, and never be bothered by a different perspective. In this way, we have no common reference points. We speak past each other, isolated on our own comfortable islands, safe from the challenges a healthy public discourse requires.

The new media has shaped campaigns. In 2008, the musician will.i.am produced a "Yes We Can" music video which attracted over 15 million hits. CNN even partnered with YouTube to produce a presidential debate with questions coming from YouTube users. In 2016 Bernie Sanders was able to attract young people into his camp by spreading his message on Facebook and via the Internet.

From campaigning to governing, the Obama team experimented with new ways of governing and new ways of connecting the president to citizens, as well as citizen to like-minded citizens, creating a virtual community of political cohorts. The village green has morphed into the village screen, and Barack Obama's innovative use of emails, text messages, YouTube, Facebook, and other social-networking sites continues past the campaign to a bold experiment in governing. Obama's Internet strategy has "rewritten the rules on how to reach voters, raise money, organize supporters, manage the news media, track and mold public opinion, and wage—and withstand—political attacks."[15] It was, as Mark McKinnon, senior advisor to President George W. Bush, remarked, "The year we went into warp speed [on the use of the Internet]. The year the paradigm got turned upside down and truly became bottom up instead of top down."[16]

In the 1930s, Franklin D. Roosevelt utilized the "new" medium of radio to reach out directly to voters. In the 1980s, Ronald Reagan effectively used television to bypass the press and go directly to the public. Barack Obama used the "new" medium of the World Wide Web to make a "direct" connection to voters, closing the gap between candidate and citizen and creating a virtual community of supporters. In 2016, it was Donald Trump, tweeting.

The exacting invisible primary period is always an exhausting ordeal and a formidable test, as well, of whether an individual can hold up physically and can control himself or herself emotionally. Barack Obama gained voice and self-confidence as he endured and grew during the grueling primary season of 2008; by contrast, the Republican field in 2012 and 2016 seemed to push each other further to the right, perhaps weakening electability in November.

PRESIDENTIAL PRIMARIES

Presidential primaries began as an outgrowth of the Progressive movement's efforts in the early twentieth century to diminish "boss rule" and to encourage popular participation in government. Presidential primaries began to take shape after 1905 when the La Follette Republicans in Wisconsin provided a system for the direct election of members of the state's delegation to the national nominating convention. Now most of the big, electoral-rich states are using some type of presidential primary.

The concept of popular participation in the nomination of the presidential party nominees evolved slowly. First we relied upon the congressional caucus system, which did not allow for direct popular participation at all. Until 1828 members of Congress from each party met and selected the person they wanted as their nominee. With the growth of democratic sentiment and the coming of the Age of Andrew Jackson, the national nominating convention system began to emerge as the replacement. In 1828 state legislatures and state party conventions were relied upon to nominate party nominees. After that, national conventions took hold, although it was not until 1840 that national party conventions were accorded full recognition.

Not until 1912 did primaries begin to be used regularly (about twelve states used them that year) in enough places to begin to have a serious impact on the presidential nominations. Some party leaders, however, have never been enthusiastic about primaries, in large part because they believe they undermine the two-party structure by strengthening the hand of candidate loyalists and issue-oriented zealots at the expense of the party regulars. Primaries allow people to vote who may have little or no loyalty to the party and little stake in the party's future. Today, the primaries are now essential in winning the nomination, as most delegates are won in these primary contests.

The rules for primaries vary from state to state and from party to party. Usually, however, as in Ohio or Florida, voters elect delegates directly or by showing a preference for a presidential candidate. Some of the early primaries, such as those in New Hampshire and South Carolina, can be important in giving a psychological lift to a front-runner or a new challenger. Later primaries can be important in giving the final edge to one candidate over others as the front-runner heads into the national convention. The late primaries, as in the case of California, usually have less impact, since the front-runner often has a sufficient number of committed delegates.

In recent years the system of presidential primaries has become one of the most debated aspects of the presidential selection process. Critics say it is a case of "democracy gone mad" and a "questionable method of selecting presidential candidates."

Nearly always, the criticism of the primaries ends up focusing upon these alleged flaws: the system takes too long, costs too much, highlights entrepreneurial personalities at the expense of issues, makes pseudo-enemies out of true political allies, invites factionalism, undermines parties, often favors colorful ideological candidates over moderates, and frequently does not even affect the outcome of the nomination process. Critics point to the Goldwater (1964) and McGovern (1972) nominations as prime examples of flaws in the primary system.

Primary voters tend to be older, have higher incomes, are more educated, and are more politically active and extreme than those who do not vote in primaries. Turnout is usually low (yet much higher than in caucuses), though we witnessed greater turnout, especially in some of the Democratic primaries, in 2008 and in some of the Republican primaries in 2012 and 2016.

The frequent and sustained criticism of primaries leads some observers to suggest that we should abolish or at least reform them. Many people support a national primary, a one-shot, winner-take-all event in August or September of election year. Others favor regional (multi-state) primaries or a return to state conventions as a better means by which to select competent presidential nominees. Still others favor letting smaller states go first, then mid-size states, followed by the big states.

The primary system has its blemishes, yet it has also served us reasonably well. Although "the people" do not fully control the nominating process, it is clear that primaries have increased the public's potential to influence who will be convention delegates and has opened the process to some candidates and ideas which might otherwise have been excluded.

Even with the party appointed "super delegates," primaries have decreased the party leaders' control over the nomination process. Students of our party system are worried about this. They would prefer a system that sends responsible party regulars of the state and local parties to the national convention, not bound by rigid instructions from a primary verdict but as representatives, free to seek out the national interest according to their best judgment. They believe these party regulars would be delegates concerned with the majority of the party's rank and file and also with the acceptability and electability of a candidate as well as that candidate's ability to serve effectively as president. This view celebrates party regulars as those who are most informed and best qualified to select the nominee. Donald Trump's "hostile takeover" of the Republican Party would not, these critics assert, have been possible if party regulars had more control over the nomination.

Another criticism of the primary system stems from the undue weight placed upon the first primary in New Hampshire and the first caucus in Iowa. These two states are atypical and largely rural and Caucasian.

It is true that primaries do allow, on occasion, for a weak candidate to be nominated. But primaries also allow for fresh faces and young new blood to emerge, as happened in 1960, 2008, and 2016. By giving candidates several opportunities to present themselves to the public, our present procedures make it possible for a candidate to win substantial support during a relatively short period of time.

While 2008 for the Democrats and 2016 for the Republicans were exceptions, the generally modest participation in the primaries prompts reform suggestions. Universal voter registration, or the motor-voter bill (allowing people to register to vote at the time they register for a driving license), slightly increases participation. A Sunday voting day or a national holiday on voting day may also encourage voting.

To win their party's nomination, candidates in primary races—unless there is a clear and undisputed front-runner—must compete for the votes of party activists who vote in primaries at a higher rate than do mainstream party members. As activists tend to be more ideologically extreme, Democrats—in order to attract partisan activists—must usually move farther to the left, and Republicans farther to the right. Once the nomination has been secured, they usually scurry to the center to appeal to the more numerous moderate and independent voters of the general election.

When an incumbent president faces a tough challenge from his own party, as Jimmy Carter did in 1980 with Senator Ted Kennedy, or Gerald Ford in 1976 with Ronald Reagan, they emerge severely weakened and usually end up losing in the general election. An inside challenger forces the incumbent to take stands that will appeal to the base yet not always play well in the general election. They also face challenges and criticism that may weaken them in the eyes of the public and give the opposing party a good sense of which criticisms work and which do not. Also, the unchallenged incumbent does not have to spend much money, keeping his campaign treasury full for the general election. And the incumbent will not have to actively campaign, saving precious time and energy for the battle ahead.

Our paradoxical approach to electing presidents can further be seen in our hunger to elect an "outsider" to the White House. Where at one time experience, demonstrated ability, and policy knowledge mattered a lot, today those candidates who run as outsiders, against the "Washington establishment," (e.g., Donald Trump) have the advantage.

It began after Vietnam and Watergate. Four of the five presidents elected before these tragic events had served as U.S. senators. The fifth, Dwight D. Eisenhower, had a great deal of insider experience as Allied Commander in Europe. After Vietnam and Watergate, four of the next six presidents had no Washington experience, and all ran "against the system." Governors replaced Senators in the White House. Outsiders replaced insiders. The inexperienced in the workings of Washington replaced D.C. veterans.

One of the virtues of the primary system is that candidates are required to present themselves to the people. Candidates have got to organize their thoughts, to clarify and define key issues. They are required to communicate with all kinds of people and to react under pressure. Often, it is an excellent learning experience for both candidates and the public. It also allows room for the people to sharpen and alter their initial views of candidates.

Return to state conventions or the ancient congressional caucus procedure would serve only to increase the influence of political bosses and special interests, who find it easier to bring pressure to bear on a few individuals in those old "smoke-filled rooms" than on entire electorates. Moving to a national or even a regional primary would lessen contact between candidate and voter, virtually preventing the less well-known candidate from running, and increase reliance on television advertising.

CAUCUSES

While most of the delegates to presidential nominating conventions are selected in primaries, caucuses also have a significant impact on the electoral process. A caucus is a meeting of citizens who select delegates to represent them—and their chosen candidate—in state conventions where the actual delegates are selected.

The Iowa caucus, which occurs before the first primary (in New Hampshire), is especially important in that as the first test of the candidates' organization, appeal, and electability, it tends to elevate some and eliminate other candidates from the race. While a relatively small and electorally less significant state, Iowa nonetheless has clout as the first electoral contest of the campaign season.[17]

By January or early February of an election year, Iowans meet in over 2,000 precincts to elect delegates to the county convention. Then, another meeting is held in each of the ninety-nine counties of the state. These county conventions select delegates to the state's congressional district convention and the state convention. These conventions select state delegates to the national party convention.

In contrast to primaries, where an individual casts a vote in secret in a voting booth, caucuses are community exercises in political participation. They allow for interaction, party-building, and community-building. They are, however, time-consuming, and critics argue that some—the sick and elderly, military stationed out of state, people working two jobs, and parents of small children—are effectively prevented from participating. Unlike primary elections, there is no absentee or mail ballot voting in a caucus.

A candidate who has a strong state organization, has a bit of money, and is willing to spend several weeks in the dead of winter sloshing around in the snows of Iowa can emerge out of "nowhere" to become a legitimate contender. Several lesser-known candidates were able to emerge from the pack in Iowa. Jimmy Carter surprised pundits by winning the 1976 Iowa caucuses and emerged as the party front-runner. Similarly, Ted Cruz gained traction from his relentless personal campaigning across Iowa in 2016.

Several other states, such as Nevada, Washington, Maine, and Idaho, use caucuses to select their delegates.

NATIONAL CONVENTIONS

Over time, national conventions have performed (or tried to perform) several functions. They have nominated presidential candidates acceptable to most factions within the party. By winning plurality victories in the primaries a candidate can secure the nomination without being acceptable to virtually all elements within a party. It is only the acquiescence of these other interests at the convention that signals to the party's rank and file that the nominee is the legitimate party standard-bearer. Carter and Ford won that legitimization at the 1976 conventions; Mitt Romney and Barack Obama did so in 2012. Goldwater and McGovern failed at their conventions in 1964 and 1972, respectively.

It has always been the purpose of a convention to select or ratify nominees who possess a strong likelihood of winning voter support in November. The goal is to produce a winning ticket. A more general function of conventions is the task of trying to unify a party that is not inherently unified. Conventions are not a time to debate differences but to promote unity in the face of disagreements and diversity. It is naturally in the party's interest to build enthusiasm and rally the party faithful to work for the national ticket.

Conventions also hammer out party platforms. Platforms are generally less meaningful than the campaign statements of the presidential candidates, but they are a useful guide to the major concerns of a party. They are often "something-for-everyone" reports. A platform is invariably a compromise of sectional views, diverse caucuses (women, blacks, etc.), and the policy preferences of dominant party elites. The winning candidate is often willing to concede a plank or two in the platform to the wishes of one of the runners-up in the primaries. This can be a quid pro quo offer to a faction or a candidate-based organization within the convention that must be won over to unite the party.

If the party has an incumbent president, the platform is often drafted in the White House or pre-approved by the president and his top policy advisers. Seldom does the party adopt a platform at variance with its incumbent president.

Criticism of the national party nominating conventions has been frequent. President Eisenhower called them a national disgrace, and social critic H. L. Mencken once wrote that "there is something about a national convention that makes it as fascinating as a revival or a hanging."[18] Critics contend conventions are too long, unwieldy, unrepresentative, irresponsible, boring, and a waste of time. Others say they function with too much concern for selecting a winner rather than the best qualified person. Similarly, critics say vice presidential choices are often made too hastily, with too much regard for balancing the ticket and not enough regard for selecting a person who may eventually become president. The selections of Agnew (1968), Eagleton (1972), Quayle (1988), and Palin (2008) are cited as examples.

Television and the proliferation of presidential primaries have altered the role of modern conventions. Today, conventions are less about selecting candidates and more about political theater; less about where the party wishes to lead the nation and more about entertainment and marketing the party's heroes, principles, and tickets.

Yet another complaint about national conventions came about in the wake of the Democratic Party's reforms of the early 1970s. A commission was established to try to improve the delegate selection processes and to "open up" the Democratic Party. The basic goal of these reforms was to end the traditional dominance of regular party leaders and make the Democratic convention more representative of the party rank and file.

A key criticism, however, is that according to the new rules many delegates to the convention are not acting as dedicated members of a party, with all the memories, past participation in, and commitment to its future. Instead, they are acting as members of a candidate-centered organization whose loyalties are almost exclusively to specific candidates and their issues. This may lead, critics charge, to allowing the "zealots" to rule.

This is a serious charge, yet it does not stand up to critical analysis. Greater openness does not mean the end of influence by party leaders, only that they would have more competition for influence. Nor are issue activists inclined to be party wreckers.

While party activists and convention delegates are more ideologically to the left or right than the general public, it is not true that this leads them to nominate extremists for the presidency. Of those nominated after 1972, only Ronald Reagan somewhat leaned to the political extreme, yet he rarely seemed extreme to the voters who elected him twice.

One wag commented that "Democrats have to control their left-wing extremists and Republicans have to worry about their right-wing extremists." And we should not be surprised when committed true believers get active in politics in pursuit of their cherished agenda items.

On balance, the national conventions have served us rather well, if imperfectly. New rule changes, the far greater role of television, and the reality that nominees are more and more "selected" and "nominated" in the state primaries require us to reexamine the traditional functions of the convention. Although substantial change has taken place, the conventions still serve many intended goals.

Conventions remain a uniquely American pageant. Where most Western democracies select their leaders from a closed party caucus, away from the hustle and bustle of mass politics, in the United States selecting a president is the people's job, as messy and chaotic as this may be.

Many of the criticisms of the convention process are really criticisms of elections in general. Elections may not be our finest hour, they may not always address our better selves, they may not be the ideal way to select leaders, yet they remain the most reliable of the known available devices.

INCUMBENCY: ADVANTAGE OR DISADVANTAGE?

It is often thought that we have a two-term presidential tradition and therefore incumbent presidents enjoy a reelection advantage. But, in fact, only fourteen of our presidents served out fully eight consecutive years in office. Most U.S. presidents have served one term or less or one term plus a year or two.

Still, for a sitting president, the benefits of incumbency are easily distinguishable: instant recognition, full access to government research resources, the ability to dominate events and make news and attract constant media exposure, party organizational structure at one's disposal, ability to dispense government contracts, and some ability to manipulate the economy.

Regardless of a president's record of accomplishment, an incumbent president is supposed to benefit from a public relations machine that shows the president as a person of action, a commander in chief, a traveling statesman, and a strategic crisis manager. Not the least of a president's assets is a loyal White House staff that, in the unavoidable blurring of presidential and political functions, performs a myriad of services. A president and the national party can also raise money more easily than the opposition, and the resources of the office provide millions of dollars' worth of free publicity.

A rival for the presidency is generally a political candidate and little more. He or she is a seeker whose motives are unclear, a pursuer with a feverish gleam in his or her eye. Such candidates covet what their rival already possesses. The most they can give are promises.

Perhaps the most important asset for the incumbent is the selective or manipulative use of government contracts, patronage, and other political controls over the economy. President Nixon's manipulation of milk prices is alleged to have aided his campaign treasury in the 1972 election. In what was called "the incumbency-responsiveness program," Nixon aides sought to maximize their control over the federal government's enormous resources to their best advantage. Federal grants were evaluated according to political benefits. Political appointments and ambassadorships were sometimes promised in exchange for large campaign contributions. And corporations were "encouraged" to contribute to the upcoming Nixon campaign in a near-extortionist manner.

One of the paradoxes of recent years can be seen in the incumbency advantage sometimes being transformed into the incumbency disadvantage. In 1968, incumbent Lyndon Johnson was compelled not to seek renomination when faced with mass protests over his Vietnam policy. His successor, Richard Nixon, was forced to resign from office one step ahead of impeachment. Nixon's successor, Gerald Ford, nearly lost his nomination bid and ended up losing the election in 1976, and the man who defeated him, Jimmy Carter, also faced a serious nomination challenge and lost in his 1980 bid for reelection. Reagan's successor, George H. W. Bush, lost in his 1992 reelection bid to Bill Clinton. Plainly, being the incumbent can sometimes be dangerous to the president's political health.

Incumbency, then, is a double-edged sword. It can help a president who presides over a period of prosperity and peace and projects an image of being in charge of events. But it can just as readily act against a president associated with troubled, perplexing times, who does not seem to be in full possession of the office. If prosperity favors the incumbents, recession favors the challengers. Distrust of politicians and low morale in the nation favors the challengers; strong confidence in the national government favors the incumbent.

An incumbent is necessarily on the defensive: His record is under detailed scrutiny, his administration's every flaw and unfulfilled promise is exposed to microscopic examination. The American people can conveniently, if often unfairly, blame a whole range of problems on a president, whereas the astute challenger presents a smaller target.

The incumbent is often judged against the idealized model of the perfect president, and, naturally, is found wanting. Paradoxically, the incumbent may at times be the symbol of the nation's pride but may just as readily be the nation's most convenient scapegoat.

GENERAL ELECTIONS: WHAT MATTERS?

People with higher family incomes are more likely to vote than those with lower incomes. Older people, with the exception of the infirm, vote more often than younger people. Women vote in higher percentages than men. White turnout is slightly higher than African-American turnout, but Hispanic voting is lower. The more formal education one has, the more likely one is to vote.

Yet, why do so many people not vote in presidential elections? Forty-two percent of eligible voters did not vote in the 2016 presidential election. The easiest explanation is that people are lazy and apathetic about national issues. Paradoxically, however, American citizens are more aware of and interested in political issues than are citizens in most other democracies, yet American participation is far lower.

There are a variety of reasons for not voting. Most states require advance voter registration. Some people say they are too busy, too ill, or don't feel the outcome of the election will make that much difference. In a number of states voter suppression efforts have been implemented in order to depress the vote among groups such as the young, minorities, or recent immigrants who are likely to vote Democratic.

One analysis of voter turnout suggests it is also partly due to the fact that political parties may have declined in importance, that the media dwells so much on the negative aspects of candidates and campaigning, and that presidential campaigns go on for so long that elections become a mind-numbing experience. One proposed remedy might be to shorten the nominating process, yet this is unlikely to make a significant difference. Others suggest a system of early voting, as practiced in thirty-four states, to encourage higher turnout. Still others favor same-day voter registration and online voting.

In general, those who vote participate out a sense of duty, believing that it is a part of their civic responsibility. Most also believe that their vote sometimes matters, that their political and economic interests are at stake. They want their party nominee to win because they either strongly or mildly adhere to the policies championed by their party.

So *political parties* do matter. In addition, *candidate appeal* and *special issues* being debated in a particular election can matter. But for issues to really matter requires that the issues in question matter to a large number of voters and that the main candidates take clearly opposing stances on the issues. Rarely do candidates focus on only one issue, and candidates often blur their issue positions in order to broaden their appeal.

Candidates such as Dwight Eisenhower in 1952, John F. Kennedy in 1960, Ronald Reagan in 1980, and Barack Obama in 2008 plainly benefited from candidate appeal.

Presidential candidates are not free agents who can choose among strategies at will. Strategy is seldom based on mere choice; it is usually forced by circumstance. For example, about every eight or twelve years there is a strong underlying desire to throw out the party in office (1980, 1992, and 2016 voters seemed in part to be punishing those in office who seemed unable to improve things). Slogans such as "It's time for a change" or "Throw the rascals out" are familiar refrains as voters turn incumbents out of office with an almost predictable alternation. Since the 1950s, only George H. W. Bush was able to defy the "eight years is enough" rotational phenomenon.

Most voters have made up their minds as to how they will vote by the end of the national conventions, a good eight or ten weeks before election day. The basic organizational effort of a candidate must be aimed at stirring up the support of voters at the grass roots and maximizing the vote of your base. The strategy that makes the most sense is to get out all possible supporters and potential supporters and independents and largely ignore resources aimed at converting the opposition. Supporters need general reassurance on both substantive and stylistic matters, but opponents want to know specific policy plans and program ideas.

A lot depends on how candidates conduct themselves. We carefully watch how they answer tricky questions and whether they keep their cool with hecklers as well as in heated presidential debates. Acting "presidential" is usually an important part of the voter's equation when deciding on a preferred candidate. High-profile endorsements can sometimes help as well.

More than anything, presidential electoral politics is coalitional politics. Interest groups help to get others involved in a campaign. They can help mobilize voters on Election Day. Groups are seldom neutral. They lean to one party or one kind of candidate over others. Groups want access to the political system and they want someone favorable to their interests in the White House.

Candidates find the general election fraught with dynamic tensions. Issue-oriented enthusiasts urge them to "speak out on the vital issues." Party regulars urge them to work closely with the party bosses. Television consultants urge them to devote most of their time to brief television spots and talk-show appearances. Public relations aides urge them to invoke patriotic symbols and quote from prestigious heroic sources. Campaign managers generally urge that debating all the issues and trying to educate the public is not the best way to win a campaign. Issues which attract some groups drive others away.

The study of voting patterns in presidential elections reveals several notable findings. Sometimes referred to as "gapology," voting studies reveal several gaps between Democratic and Republican voters.[19]

There is a "race gap" that is especially apparent in white versus black voters. In 2004, George W. Bush won 58.7 percent of white votes (which comprised 77.1 percent of all votes) yet only 27.6 percent of non-white votes. Nine out of ten African-American voters supported John Kerry in 2004, and roughly 95 percent of black votes went with Barack Obama in 2008 and 2012, and in 2016, Clinton won the black vote by an 88 to 89 percent margin. Fifty-eight percent of whites voted for Romney, 93 percent of black for Obama, and 69 percent of Hispanic went with Obama.

There is also a "marriage gap." In 2004 Bush received 58 percent of the married vote, and John Kerry received 59 percent of votes from the unmarried. In 2008, John McCain received only 52 percent of the married vote.

One can also see a "church attendance" gap, with three-fifths of those who regularly attend church services voting Republican in 2004. In 2008 there was roughly a 10 percent gap favoring John McCain. In the 2008 race, 54 percent of Protestants voted for McCain, 54 percent of Catholics for Obama, 78 percent of Jewish voters supported Obama, and 74 percent of white evangelical voters supported McCain.

One often hears of the "gender" gap, and while not as determinative as the previously cited gaps, women do tend to vote more Democratic and men more Republican. In 2008, men voted at a 49 percent rate for Obama and women voted for him at a 56 percent rate.

A "generation" gap is sometimes evident. Voters age fifty and older tend to vote Republican; the under-forty group tends to vote Democratic. The generation gap in voting was especially evident in 2008 with the eighteen- to twenty-nine—year-old votes going almost 2–1 for Obama. Older voters, sixty-five and older, voted 53 percent for John McCain. Yet it is instructive to remember that in 1984, Ronald Reagan won every voter age group, including a majority of younger voters.

There is also a "rural–urban" gap, with rural voters more likely to vote Republican and urban voters, Democratic. Again, in 2008, this gap closed a bit as the vote for Barack Obama in rural areas rose by 5 percent, but dropped by 3 percent in small towns.

Do elections matter? They do, although elections seldom give a president or a country a specific mandate. A national election in the United States is rarely a plebiscite or referendum on specific issues. Because of candidate's policy ambiguity, we often vote without a clear idea of what the candidates will do if elected.

Presidents invariably try to convince the Washington community they have some sort of mandate, believing that if the public and Congress believe that there is a mandate they will have an easier time governing. A mandate is based on three features: the *size* of a president's electoral victory; the *type* of election (issue-oriented or personal); and the *number* of candidates from the president's party elected to Congress (the president's coattails and the aggregate numbers.) Often these factors are negligible enough to prevent any legitimate claim that the victor earned a "mandate to govern."

The debate over whom to vote for usually centers around which candidate is best equipped to handle the job and the problems at hand rather than around the detailed specifics of how to solve the big issues of the day. Thus, our elections may represent mandates to get the job done, yet we leave the means up to the judgment of the president. Elections sometimes set limits on what can be done, but they usually only moderately determine the precise future course of public policies.[20]

Unlike their parliamentary counterparts, elections in the United States do not confer *power*. They merely grant office, which grants the opportunity to seize power. Presidents must work at translating an electoral victory into political power.

The 2016 election was yet another *angry voter*, change election. On the right, nativist, anti-politician anger was the catalyst for the Donald Trump insurgent campaign; on the left, Senator Bernie Sanders captured the attention of the young and the Occupy Wall Street voters. Most analysts underestimated the force of the anti-incumbent, anti-status quo vote in 2016. This is most clearly seen in the fact that several traditionally Democratic rust-belt states went for Trump, swinging the election in his favor. Trump was able to build on the anger of white middle class voters who felt that the government was not looking out for their interests, that income stagnation worked against them, and fear of loss left them insecure and vulnerable, to forge a winning coalition among disaffected, angry, and alienated largely white voters.

Millions of Americans—left and right—had lost faith in the political system and gravitated to insurgent candidates. With trust in government at an all-time low, insiders were blamed for the country's problems, and many voters believed the government was not working for them. Political outsiders—beginning in 1976 and repeatedly recurring from that election on—became attractive as they were seen as untainted by the sins of the Washington, D.C., beltway. In 2016, the way was paved for an anti-establishment candidate like Donald Trump to come along and appeal to voters with an anti-government message. In this change election, the American voters went with the candidate of change.

The Debates Reflect Voter Disapproval of Government Insiders

The first Republican primary debate—widely anticipated due to the interest generated by the Trump candidacy—was the most-watched primary debate in history, pulling in more viewers than Game 7 of the 2014 Baseball World Series. Those waiting for Trump to implode or explode may have been disappointed. Perhaps as much as 20 percent of campaigning deals with theater and stagecraft. Trump, the experienced television star, was able to shine, especially compared to the dull performance of his rivals.

In the early stages of the race, the two heavy favorites, Hillary Clinton and Jeb Bush, were soon challenged by two insurgent candidates: Donald Trump for the Republicans and Bernie Sanders for the Democrats. Clinton and Bush looked flat and tired next to the high-energy Trump and Sanders. Both Bush and Clinton hoped to be the tortoise to the Trump and Sanders hare.

The 2015–2016 Republican primaries got off to an unusually crowded start. While the Republican field of seventeen serious candidates overflowed with presidential hopefuls, one candidate trumped the field: Donald Trump. He was different, brash, confrontational, and a non-traditional candidate in a year of change. Week by week he railed against Bush, then Rubio, then Cruz, and week by week his rivals dropped from the race, until in the end, the last candidate standing was Donald Trump. He was a magnet for television coverage, and he quickly eclipsed all his more conventional rivals. One by one they fell until, in the end, Trump was the only Republican left.

On the Democratic side, Hillary Clinton simply outlasted rival Bernie Sanders. While Sanders had the enthusiastic crowds, Clinton had the Democratic Party establishment, the money, and the organization to top her challenger.

THE ELECTORAL COLLEGE DEBATE

The controversial and virtually tied presidential election of 2000 was troubling. Some of our worst fears about the anachronistic Electoral College came true. Popular vote winner Al Gore lost to electoral vote winner George W. Bush. Bush carried thirty states and won 271 electoral votes. Gore won twenty states and the District of Columbia and won 267 electoral votes.

The Florida vote ended up in nearly a statistical tie, yet all twenty-five electoral votes went to Bush, rather than a proportional allocation of twelve and a half electoral votes to each of the leading contenders.

There were at least some puzzling aspects of the election in 2000. Bush and Gore all but ignored California, New York, and Texas, the three largest states in terms of population and electoral votes. These states were conceded well in advance—California and New York to Gore and Texas to Bush.

Both before and after the 2000 election, the American public told pollsters they favored abolishing the Electoral College and moving to the more simple and presumably much more democratic "one person, one vote" direct election procedure for selecting a president. Between 60 percent and 70 percent of Americans regularly support this. Yet weeks after the Bush–Gore election was settled, there was little public clamor and even less political maneuvering for amending the U.S. Constitution to bring about this change.

As we were reminded in 2000, and again in 2016, presidents are elected by the Electoral College, not directly by the voters. Many people and many political observers grumble about the Electoral College system. Yet most people are resigned to the fact that we seem stuck with the Electoral College. Leading scholars who have examined the Electoral College and its consequences generally conclude we need to devise a better way to pick our presidents.

The Electoral College system was adopted for a variety of complicated reasons at the Constitutional Convention in 1787 and was more an afterthought than a carefully constructed method of selection.

HOW THE ELECTORAL COLLEGE WORKS

In making their presidential choice in November, voters technically do not vote for a candidate but choose between slates of "presidential electors" selected by state political parties. In almost all of the states, the slate that wins a plurality of popular votes in the state wins all the electoral votes for that state. In Maine and Nebraska, the plurality of the votes in congressional districts determines how to distribute electoral votes, respectively. This is called the district plan.

Each state has one electoral vote for each senator and each representative. The District of Columbia has three votes, which were granted it by the Twenty-Third Amendment to the U.S. Constitution. There are 538 votes in today's Electoral College, and one must earn 270 or more to win. George W. Bush's much-debated 271-electoral-vote victory was plainly a close call.

According to this system, a president is not officially elected on Election Day. Victorious slates of electors travel to their respective state capitols on the first Monday after the second Wednesday in December—no wonder most people don't remember how this system works!—where they cast ballots for their party's presidential ticket. Ballots are then sent from the state capitals to Congress, where early in January they are formally counted by House and Senate leaders and the next president is officially announced.

There is yet another unusual and rather undemocratic aspect to the Electoral College. In the event that no candidate secures a majority of electoral votes, the decision would then go to the House of Representatives. This has happened twice, once in 1800 and again in 1824. It was a possibility in 1968, 1992, and again in 2000.[21] In the House, the delegation from each state casts a single vote. If a delegation is evenly divided, this state forfeits its vote. Thus, the influence of a third-party "spoiler" candidate can on occasion pose a significant threat to the two main parties, because the House of Representatives chooses a president from among the top three candidates. Consecutive ballots are taken until a candidate wins a majority (twenty-six) of the state delegations.

Defenders of the Electoral College contend we should not lightly dismiss a system that has served us reasonably well for so long. The Electoral College continues to attract devoted supporters. Political scientist Norman Ornstein argues that as imperfect as the Electoral College may from time to time seem, overall it has served the republic quite well for more than 200 years.[22] And conservative columnist George Will argues that the Electoral College supports "America's federalist republic," with an emphasis on federalism.[23]

Attorney Tara Ross argues that the framers saw democracy as dangerous, and instead invented a "federalist republic," of which the Electoral College is a key component. For Ross and others, the framers "deliberately created a federalist republic, rather than a pure democracy."[24] Why risk the intended or unintended consequences of change?

Defenders are fond of the old saying that "the evil best known is the most tolerable" and "when it is not necessary to change, it is necessary not to change." They also cite John F. Kennedy, who once defended the Electoral College by arguing that the question does not merely involve certain technical details of the election process, but a whole solar system of subtle, interrelated institutions, principles, and customs.

Supporters of the Electoral College process claim that eliminating this system might:

- weaken the existing two-party system and encourage splinter parties, possibly triggering contingency elections
- weaken the federal character of America's constitutional system
- encourage presidential candidates to pay less attention to smaller states as they concentrate on major metropolitan areas
- encourage even more simplistic media-oriented campaigns.

Perhaps the greatest fear of moving from the Electoral College system to a direct vote system is that relatively small third parties or single-cause candidates might be able to magnify their strength. "In direct elections," writes historian Arthur Schlesinger, Jr., "they could drain enough votes, cumulative from state to state, to prevent the formation of a national majority—and to give themselves strong bargaining positions in case of a run-off."[25]

Critics of the Electoral College call it an antidemocratic relic and the most embarrassing part of the current Constitution. They cite several problems, among them that the vote of the people (popular) might be undermined, that faithless electors could violate the will of voters, that there is a small-state advantage, and that contingency elections in the House could lead to chaos and questions of legitimacy on the part of the winner. A 1967 report by the American Bar Association called the Electoral College "archaic, undemocratic, complex, ambiguous, indirect, and dangerous."[26]

Further, given that many states are solidly red (Republican) or solidly blue (Democratic), presidential elections are conducted primarily in "purple" states (those eight or ten that are "in play"), ignoring most of the nation. The purple states are battleground states, the rest mere spectator states.[27]

One of the most compelling critiques of the Electoral College system is offered by political scientist George Edwards. He argues against the Electoral College, favoring direct popular election of the president. After systematically debunking the main claims of Electoral College advocates—that the current system protects the interests of smaller states, and some minority voters, supports federalism, strengthens the two-party system, protects against voter fraud, and gives the newly elected president a clearer mandate—Edwards explores several other options for selecting presidents: the *Automatic Plan* (bypass an Electoral College and directly award delegates to each state's winning candidate), the *District Plan* (awarding votes to the winner in each Congressional district, plus giving two additional electoral votes to the overall winner of the state), the *Proportional Plan* (awarding votes in each state based on the proportion of votes received within each state), and the *National Bonus Plan* (giving 102 additional electoral votes to the popular vote winner). In the end, Edwards argues that "political equality" is the key feature of a viable electoral democracy, and as such, since "every voter's ballot does not carry equal weight,"[28] in the current system only the direct election of a president meets standards of democratic fairness.

The direct election method means quite simply that the person who gets the most votes wins. There is no Electoral College. Advocates of the direct popular system contend everyone's vote should count equally, people should vote directly for the candidate, and the candidate who gets the majority or plurality of votes should be elected.

With the Electoral College method, a president can be elected who has fewer popular votes than his opponent, as was the case in 1824 when John Quincy Adams, with 30.92 percent of the vote, defeated Andrew Jackson who had 41.34 percent of the vote. This happened again in 1876 when Rutherford B. Hayes, with 47.95 percent of the popular vote, won over Samuel J. Tilden, with 50.97 percent of the vote; and in 1888, when Benjamin Harrison, with 47.82 percent, won over Grover Cleveland, with 48.62 percent. And, of course, it happened most recently in 2000 when George W. Bush won 47.9 percent of the popular vote while Al Gore won, and in 2016 when Hillary Clinton beat Donald Trump by over 2.9 million votes, yet lost the presidency. This can happen because all of a state's electoral votes are awarded to the winner of the state's popular vote regardless of whether the winning candidate's margin is one vote or three million votes.

The direct-vote method is appealing in its simplicity. Since it is based on a "one person, one vote" principle, it more clearly makes a president the agent of the people and not of the states. Governors and senators are elected by statewide direct popular voting, and they are supposed to be agents of the state. The president, however, should be president of the people, not president of the states—or at least this is what reformers say.

In the aftermath of the confusing 2000 presidential election, a wide array of ideas surfaced, many dusted off from earlier efforts at reform. Most efforts were, as noted, some type of direct vote or proportional allocation. One intriguing, if unlikely, proposal called for a new format for voting that asks voters to choose not only their first choice, but also their second and third choices. If no candidate receives 50 percent, the candidate with the fewest votes among the top three would be eliminated. Those who voted for the eliminated candidate would then have their second choice receive their vote. This is repeated with lesser candidates until only two candidates remain or there is a clear winner. It is, in essence, a built-in "instant runoff" procedure, a runoff without having to hold a new election.[29] While this and similar ideas attracted interest, it was instructive how quickly demands for reform faded and the United States went on as usual, as if the bizarre events of the presidential election of 2000 had never happened.[30]

FROM ELECTION TO GOVERNING

Campaigns, while interesting in and of themselves, are designed to determine who shall govern. Ironically, elections tell us *who* shall govern, yet they do not automatically confer the power to govern to the newly elected presidents. In a separation-of-powers system, elected officials are given the *opportunity* to govern, but not necessarily the *power* to govern.

Some scholars believe that getting elected requires one set of skills, governing another. This paradox has led some recent presidents to engage in what is called "the permanent campaign" where a president is constantly in campaign mode as a means to drum up support in order to govern. This "going public" strategy is sometimes done at the expense of "going Washington" (bargaining, cajoling, and deliberating at length with congressional insiders) and may actually make governing more difficult. Understandably, however, presidents engage in both strategies.

Power in the American system is akin to a greased pig contest at the county fair. There, you grease up a pig, put it in a pen, and have a dozen or so children run after the pig, trying to catch it and bring it to the judge's table to get their hard-earned prize. The problem is, the pig doesn't want to be grabbed, and even if you can grab the pig, it squirms and is slippery, and difficult to hold on to. And there are a bunch of other kids who are grabbing at your arms, and pulling the pig out of your hands, trying themselves to gain control of the pig. In the greased pig contest, the game is funny and entertaining. If you are the president, grabbing for power rarely seems funny.

To answer the power question, we must begin with the incoming president-elect's "level of political opportunity" or political capital, the fuel that drives the American system. Not all presidents are created equally. Some enter office with a full tank of high-octane gas, while others assume office depleted and running on fumes. Franklin D. Roosevelt came into office with a wealth of political capital;

Gerald Ford did not. Thus, the stage was set for FDR to succeed, while the cards were stacked against Ford.

How does one convert electoral victory into political clout? The level of political opportunity is largely derived from factors extrinsic to the president himself. In trying to calibrate political capital, first look at conditions or circumstances. Are these routine or crisis times? If routine, expect the president to be constrained by the separation of powers and checks and balances. If a crisis, the president's powers expand. Witness George W. Bush prior to, then after, 9/11.

Next, what is the size of the election victory? If a double-digit victory, power expands. Were there clear issues discussed and promoted in the election or was it largely an election about personality? If several key issues were promoted by the victor, he may claim that he was elected to accomplish his policy agenda and thereby gain some clout.

How long were the president's coattails? Did they bring other members of their party into the House and Senate as a function of their attractiveness at the top of the ticket? We measure coattails by how much of a difference there was between the vote in a district or state for the president and for the candidate running for Congress. If the president outpolled the local candidate, he had coattails and can claim that one of the reasons the local candidate won was because of the pull the presidential candidate had in that district. All this may give the president an opportunity to claim a *mandate* for governing. If others in the political universe think the president has a mandate, they may be less likely to oppose a president's policies. Also, the key is: does the president's party have majority status? If so, the president may well be able to govern.

Does the public demand change? If so, the president has another power leg on which to stand. Is the political opposition in Congress united and determined or divided and uncertain? A distracted and self-absorbed opposition is a weak opposition.

Finally, is the incoming administration ready to "hit the ground running" with a few clear policies they will focus on, or do they hit the ground stumbling, and have a vast and undisciplined list of "must haves" on the legislative agenda? The general rule is that a short, disciplined, focused agenda is best. During the honeymoon period, early victories on key agenda items will pave the way for future success as the impression is cemented that this is a president to be reckoned with.

Not everything is extrinsic to the president. An array of personal and skill factors also help shape power. Experience counts, as do management skills and the ability to persuade. Judgment is essential. Charisma helps. One's power or strategic sense is valuable. Empathy is a key. So too is the team one puts together.

CONCLUSION

Our presidential selection process is neither tidy nor easy to understand. It is and will continue to face criticism because of its expense and length, because of the biases of the Electoral College, and because many people believe it tests candidates more for their fund-raising and media skills than for the ability to govern and make tough economic and foreign policy choices.

The election process has evolved in varying and often unpredictable ways since the framers met in Philadelphia. It seeks to achieve a variety of often contending and conflicting purposes. Yet it is one of the compromises so often found in the structure of the American political system that seek to paper over regional, political, and even ideological differences. Old tensions of how strong a central government we really want and of how strong and powerful a central leader we are willing to tolerate are never far behind the scenes. Questions of just how much democracy we really want and how much we actually trust the judgment of the average citizen are often involved in our attitudes about the presidential election system. The politics produced by this complicated process is not always pretty, not always democratic, and, as we have tried to suggest, has its share of paradoxes. Yet, this selection process is part of the continuing American quest to preserve a politics of compromise, coalitions, moderation, and pragmatism.

FURTHER READINGS

Brown, Lara M. *Jockeying for the American Presidency: The Political Opportunism of Aspirants*. Amherst, N.Y.: Cambria Press, 2010.

Edwards, George C. *Why the Electoral College is Bad for America*. New Haven, CT: Yale University Press, 2004.

Wayne, Stephen J. *Is This Any Way to Run a Democratic Election?* 3rd ed. Washington, D.C.: CQ Press, 2007.

CHAPTER 4

Presidential Power and Leadership

"Power" is a much used yet little understood concept. The problem is particularly vexing when we wrestle with the concept of presidential power. What do we mean by power? How much does a president have? How much should the president wield in a constitutional democracy?

Several of our presidential paradoxes apply directly to the dilemmas of power and leadership. One says Americans want powerful leadership, yet we distrust authority and fear the abuse of power. Another explains that we want our presidents to solve problems, yet are hesitant to grant the discretionary power equal to our demands and expectations.

One of the most striking paradoxes is that we expect presidents to govern successfully, yet we trust or support them only reluctantly. Since the 1950s, trust in government has generally declined. While there was a rally effect after 9/11, trust quickly dropped to its lowest point since we began measuring.[1] How can a president govern in such an atmosphere?

Part of the challenge is that the very term "democratic leadership" is paradoxical. How can a democracy—government of, by, and for the people—look to one person, or even a small team of people, for leadership? It sounds so antidemocratic. The words "leader" and "leadership" imply that someone provides direction. The word "democracy" implies consent of the governed, widespread participation, and representative government. Are these concepts irreconcilable?

While there is certainly a tension between democracy and leadership, it can be a creative tension that enhances both aspects of executive governance. Yet all too often, this potentially creative tension degenerates into forms of behavior that can undermine both democracy and leadership.

In this chapter, we begin by discussing how Americans view presidential power and leadership, and cycles of leadership over time. We then examine the president's constitutional and political power, as well as critiques of executive power. Finally, we discuss components of presidential leadership, and implications for American democracy. While democratic leadership may be our goal, the road to achieving it can be difficult, especially in a political system that encourages high expectations of the president but contains significant structural constraints in policy making.

HOW DO AMERICANS VIEW PRESIDENTIAL POWER AND LEADERSHIP?

Several hurdles stand in the way of strong presidential leadership. A system organized around a separation of powers as opposed to a fusion of power (Great Britain and Canada fuse legislative and executive power, for example) structurally inhibits strong leadership. America's political culture also undermines strong leadership.

Ours is in many ways an anti-authority and therefore an anti-leadership culture. Political scientist Samuel Huntington describes us as having an "American Creed," characterized by a commitment to individualism, egalitarianism, democracy, and freedom.[2] Admirable goals all, yet these qualities are not especially supportive of strong leadership or strong deferential followership. Political scientist Clinton Rossiter captures this paradox well: "We have always been a nation obsessed with liberty. Liberty over authority, freedom over responsibility, rights over duties—these are our historic preferences. . . . Not the good man, but the free man had been the measure of all things in this 'sweet land of liberty'; not national glory but individual liberty has been the object of political authority and the test of its worth."[3]

How does this American creed shape our views on leadership? While it creates a fundamentally anti-leadership disposition, the American propensity for individualism generates a type of hero worship that encourages a heroic model of the presidency. Thus we honor Washington the patriot, Jefferson and Jackson the great democrats, Lincoln and FDR the saviors. But such hero worship masks, in some ways, our notable fear of power and resistance to authority. In general, we still distrust leaders. Libertarian presidential candidates Ron and Rand Paul, and Green Party presidential nominee Ralph Nader have reflected deep strains of individualism, if not irreverence toward the political establishments of their day. The unexpected election in 2016 of Republican presidential candidate Donald Trump, a businessman who held no political office before seeking the White House, illustrates the appeal of "outsider" politicians whose professional success is not grounded in the traditional political process.

Given their underlying skepticism and distrust of political leadership, the American public typically does not expect elected officials to make demands of them. It is difficult, except in a crisis, for presidents to ask the people to make major sacrifices for the common good or move beyond self-interest. When Jimmy Carter back in the 1970s asked citizens to turn their thermostats down to 68 degrees Fahrenheit in an oil crisis, he was rebuked. When President Bill Clinton called on the American people to provide military peace forces in Haiti and Bosnia, Americans were hesitant if not hostile to his requests.

President George W. Bush, perhaps realizing that the American public responded harshly to calls for sacrifice, told voters in the immediate aftermath of the 9/11 attacks on the United States, not to tighten our belts, pay higher taxes to fund a new war against terrorists, or otherwise settle for less, but to "Get on board. Do your business around the country. Fly and enjoy America's great destination spots. Go down to Disney World in Florida. Take your families and enjoy life, the way we want it to be enjoyed."[4] In his memoirs, Bush noted, "I was surprised by critics who suggested I should have asked for more sacrifice after 9/11. I suppose it's easy for some to forget, but people were making sacrifices. Record numbers of volunteers had stepped forward to help their neighbors."[5]

While Americans occasionally demonstrate patriotic fervor, they seldom demonstrate a deep-seated sense of community. When the public lacks a strong sense of community, leaders have a difficult time pulling the nation together (except in a crisis) to respond collectively, politically, as one nation. In his inaugural address, President Trump emphasized the importance of patriotism to overcome political divisions, stating that "At the bedrock of our politics will be a total allegiance to the United States of America, and through our loyalty to our country, we will rediscover our loyalty to each other."[6] The Women's March on Washington the day after the inauguration, as well as other marches that day in the United States and around the world, demonstrated the challenge of moving beyond the divisive 2016 presidential election; whether the Trump administration's leadership and policies will achieve that objective remains to be seen.

THE MOODS AND CYCLES OF AMERICAN POLITICS

Leadership seldom occurs in a vacuum. There are different "seasons" of leadership, times when presidents are afforded more or less room to exercise power.[7] These cycles take many forms: a business cycle of economic growth followed by recession; a political pendulum of liberalism followed by a conservative period; strong presidents followed by weak ones; a mood swing of public confidence in government followed by a retreat into private, more self-centered interests; a foreign policy shift from isolationism to international involvement. Such cycles are, for the most part, beyond the control of presidents, yet they do have an impact on presidential power.

In crises, presidents are afforded considerable leverage. Then there are times when presidents are kept on a short leash. In the aftermath of the war in Vietnam and of Watergate, the public turned against the government and presidential power and questioned much of what presidents did. Thus Presidents Ford and Carter were restricted in their opportunities to exercise power. The public was more suspicious, the press was more skeptical, the Congress tried to reassert its authority, and if that weren't enough, the economy was sluggish. Even if Ford and Carter had been skilled, gifted politicians, their level of political opportunity was so low, there was little way they could have been successful.

FDR, by contrast, a skilled politician, benefited from a level of opportunity that was unusually high. He came to office when the public yearned for strong leadership, and when Congress was willing to accede power to the president. Hence the mixture of high skill and high opportunity encouraged FDR to pursue power.

"Political time" is also important. During periods of social upheaval, certain types of leadership will be more necessary, while during periods of normalcy a different type of leadership may be required. Moreover, a different sort of leadership is required during periods of crisis. There is not one leadership style for all seasons. Effective leaders improvise accordingly.

Several cycles are especially relevant to presidential leadership. One is the succession cycle. Major policy shifts are most likely when new leaders come to power. Thus, leadership change is connected to policy change. Another cycle is the cycle of decreasing popularity. Over time, presidents tend to lose popular support (as discussed in Chapter 2), which makes it more difficult for them to put together political coalitions as their terms progress. Another presidential cycle is the cycle of growing effectiveness. A president's learning curve is at its lowest at the beginning of the term and rises as time goes by. Yet a president's power is usually at its zenith early in the term, when knowledge is lowest.

The cycle that seems most relevant to presidential leadership deals with the long-term ebb and flow of American politics. Historians suggest that this cycle is like a pendulum swinging back and forth. The United States alternates between periods of "conservatism versus innovation" and "diffusion versus centralization"; such mood swings reflect "a continuing shift in national involvement, between public purpose and private interest."[8]

America has long encouraged freewheeling entrepreneurial capitalism. But America has learned, too, that government and governmental leadership are necessary for the country to flourish. We of course depend on the government to provide for the common defense, but the government also provides many other opportunities for the public, such as scientific, technological, and medical innovation.

The U.S. federal government has made mistakes in many areas, such as the Vietnam War, the costly and ineffective War on Drugs, and misdirected corporate or agricultural subsidies. On the other hand, the famed Manhattan Project in World War II that produced the atomic bomb, the interstate highway system launched during the Eisenhower years, the National Aeronautics and Space Administration, the National Science Foundation, and the Centers for Disease Control are just a few examples of the programs through which creative governmental leadership can promote both the economy and society.

"The combination of energetic markets and effective governance," write Jacob Hacker and Paul Pierson, "has delivered truly miraculous breakthroughs." The United States has prospered when government plays its proper role in promoting basic research, investing in education and infrastructure, and performing a benevolent regulatory role in encouraging markets to serve broader public purposes.[9]

Different political climates require different types of political leadership and different sets of political skills. A president's level of political opportunity is based upon factors such as crisis versus normal conditions (as the post-9/11 political environment demonstrated, a crisis president has expanded powers), the results of the previous election (landslide versus a close election), the number of a president's political party in Congress (a large majority versus divided government), issue ripeness, and a public demand for action. Opportunity, combined with resources and skill, determines how much power a president is likely to have.

PRESIDENTIAL POWER: CONSTITUTIONAL AND POLITICAL

One of the more persisting of presidential paradoxes from the standpoint of presidents is the realization that the office carries much less power, however power is defined, than the candidates had thought when they ran for office. Yet presidential power is neither fixed nor static. It fluctuates depending on the demands of the times, skills of the president, types of issue areas, and needs of the public.

Constitutional Powers

All presidents on assuming office have formal constitutional powers. The founding fathers arranged for an office broadly defined as well as vaguely outlined. Power was available, yet it would be subject to various checks. A president is open to challenges or possible vetoes from a number of political institutions.

There is a plasticity in our fundamental conception of presidential powers. The exact dimensions of executive power at any given moment are largely the consequence of the incumbent's character and energy combined with the overarching demands of the day and the challenges to the system. Some presidents have been maximizers—Jackson, Lincoln, and the Roosevelts, for example. Certain of them became shrewd party leaders. Some saw themselves as direct agents of the American people, as the people's choice with mandates to carry out in exchange for the conferring of power. Still others employed the "take care that the laws be faithfully executed" clause of the Constitution to broaden the notion of executive power well beyond the boundaries envisioned by most of the framers of the Constitution. Plainly, an office under-defined on paper has become enlarged with the accumulation of traditions and the legacy of some often brilliant achievements.

If the United States had remained a small nation, isolated from the other nations of the world, the role of the executive would doubtless have remained weak, certainly much weaker than the presidency we have come to know. Had the presidential office not been capable of expanding, the nation may well not have survived. Presidential power and leadership have been essential for progress.

In normal or routine times when dealing with domestic matters, presidential power is limited. In such circumstances the separation-of-powers system distributes and shares powers between the three branches. However, in crisis or war, presidents often seize or are delegated significant, even imperial, powers. In a crisis, the checks and balances of the separation of powers recede, and the president has at least the chance to wield greater power.

And therein lies the irony. In domestic policy during normal times, presidents may have too little power. In foreign policy during a crisis, they may wield too much power. Thus we have the "Goldilocks problem" of presidential power. In normal times presidential power is "too cold," in a crisis "too hot." It is hard to get it "just right."

Political Power

Political scientist Richard Neustadt appreciated how hard it was for presidents to be effective. His classic text *Presidential Power*, first published in 1960, is a manual of personal power: how to get it, how to keep it, and how to use it. [10] Neustadt broke away from the traditional emphasis on leadership traits, the compartmentalized listings of functional tasks, and the then-dominant tendency to study the presidency in legal or constitutional terms. Instead, he used organizational and administrative behavior as frames of reference for the study of what presidents must do if they want to influence events and why and how presidents often lose the ability to influence. His stress was on the shared powers of the office rather than the separation of powers. He emphasized the reciprocal character of influence, the constant personal calculations that motivate people to cooperate or not to cooperate with presidential initiatives.

Presidential Power was rightfully hailed as a pioneering contribution to our understanding of the operational realities of presidential leadership. It succinctly explains how the presidency is not as powerful as many people think, nor should its strengthening automatically be feared, as many have argued. Neustadt called on future presidents to acquire as much power as they could, for formal institutional powers were fragile, even puny, compared with the president's responsibilities.

Neustadt said presidential power is the power to persuade, and the power to persuade comes through bargaining. Bargaining, in turn, comes primarily through getting others to believe it is in their own self-interest to cooperate. Presidents are depicted as being constantly challenged by threat to their power and constantly needing to enhance their reputation as shrewd bargainer. Tenacity and proper timing are also essential.

Neustadt put great emphasis on "professional reputation" as a source of presidential influence. A president who was, in Machiavelli's classic formulation, both loved and feared, could be a powerful leader.[11] But the effective president needs to be respected and trusted. To succeed in policy making, a president must maintain a strong professional reputation with other political elites, whom Neustadt identifies (probably too narrowly) as "Washingtonians." These elites include politicians in Washington, D.C., such as members of Congress and lobbyists, as well as political leaders outside the capital, such as governors. In addition, a key variable for building coalitions with Washingtonians is a president's approval ratings, or what Neustadt terms "public prestige."

Presidential Power held out hope that a shrewd and artful leader could and would be a powerful Hamiltonian engine of change. Aggressive, ambitious, strategic politicians, determined to get their way and ever distrustful of the motives of others, seemed to be the remedy for the post-Eisenhower years. A key problem of the presidency at the time was how the president could regain control over the drifting Washington policy apparatus. Forceful leadership was needed, and only the president, Neustadt suggested, could fill the leadership vacuum.

Neustadt's contribution to the understanding of the presidency is his notion that the power of presidents rests on their ability to persuade others. Because presidents share authority with other institutions, they cannot merely command. Thus, they must constantly bargain and negotiate in an effort to achieve results, as Figure 4.1 illustrates on page 90.

Unresolved Questions

The most frequent criticism of Neustadt's analysis is that it seemed too preoccupied with the acquisition of power and stockpiling the power, divorced from any discussion of purposes to which power should be put. Such an emphasis on means without a clear discussion of ends left the impression that the art of leadership is mainly the art of manipulation. Neustadt was faulted too for a failure to emphasize the role that a "sense of direction" plays in presidential leadership, and how presidents would call on or consider ideological values in their power exchanges.

One critic went so far as to suggest that Neustadt "baptizes" political ambition just as Dale Carnegie or Wall Street manuals baptize greed.[12] Many readers would have liked a more thoughtful discussion of the ends of presidential power, of the ethical boundaries. What are the higher claims on a president, and how does the creative president balance the ethic of responsibility and the ethic of ultimate ends?

A second criticism of Neustadt's book was that it is too approving of the personalization of presidential power. It seems to say: Find the right president, teach them what power is all about, and progress will be realized. It portrays presidents as potential saviors. It comes close to suggesting we need a heroic, charismatic, larger-than-life figure on whom to lean to make the system work.

Two problems arise from this emphasis on presidents as the answer to our needs. First, Neustadt failed to take into account the degree to which presidents are, more often than not, stabilizers or protectors of the status quo rather than agents of redistribution or progressive change. Neustadt gave little attention to the way prevailing American elite values, and market capitalism, often limit a president's freedom. One gets the impression from reading Neustadt that he thought presidents can and should roam at will, providing they are shrewd enough to be able to persuade others that their share the same interests. In fact, however, all of our presidents have had to prove their political orthodoxy and their acceptability to a wide array of established powers, especially corporate leaders, entrenched interest-group leaders, and so on. Thus, Neustadt raised perhaps myopic hopes that the presidency might regularly be an instrument for the progressive transformation of American politics. In short, Neustadt's *Presidential Power* and similar writings too often seduce us to place too much faith in and unrealistically high expectations of individual leaders to achieve what in reality has to be the collaborative work of large cohorts, movements, and teams of citizen-leaders.

Second, just how much and how often can we turn to the White House and hope that a benevolent, bright, and energetic president will provide truly inspired leadership? Surely this is what Obama supporters in 2008 were hoping for from their candidate, but the Obama presidency did not achieve the campaign promise of moving beyond partisan divisions. Whether this was due to shortcomings in presidential leadership or recalcitrant political opposition continues to be debated. Donald Trump's successful presidential campaign was based on a comparable outsider approach to changing Washington, though with a very different professional background and policy platform. Apart from the president, history suggests that breakthroughs and leadership often come from the bottom (or at least the middle) up. Civil rights workers, consumer organizers, women's rights activists, environmentalists, tax-reform champions, and anti-war protestors are illustrative of the catalysts that more often than not bring about policy change in the United States.

Did Neustadt's call for strong presidential leadership betray a liberal bias? For most of the post–World War II era, the heroic/strong presidency that Neustadt promoted was considered the model for political progressives of his day. Neustadt and others advocated a powerful activist presidency in the pursuit of more government intervention in problem solving. Conservatives had generally advocated more limited government, less presidential power, and a smaller role for the federal government, except in defense spending and national security preparedness.

But the heroic presidency could, conservatives found, be used to pursue the conservative agenda. Emboldened by Ronald Reagan's rhetorical skills and the promise of the "Reagan Revolution," conservatives saw the presidency as a vehicle for political power. From that point on, and through most of the George W. Bush presidency, conservative presidentialists emerged as a powerful force in the Republican Party, and Neustadt's strong presidency view became a philosophy for multiple political leanings.[13]

From Persuasion to Other Forms of Power

Who can doubt that prestige and persuasion comprise key elements of presidential leadership? And yet, persuasion does not exhaust the opportunities of presidents to lead. Presidents also have power, the ability to act, to command, to assert, to initiate. Presidential leadership is about persuasion and power, leadership and command.

The American political system positions presidents in an advantageous spot. While they share power with Congress, and many of the key elements of power are blended, split, and shared by the president and Congress, the president is often well positioned to develop comprehensive national plans to initiate action, and thus to lead or even preempt Congress.

By using executive orders and national security directives, initiating action, acting unilaterally, or by invoking administrative methods (discussed in Chapter 7), presidents can increase their governing powers and, if Congress does not fight back, often win. While the Madisonian system requires the president to govern with Congress, certainly there are formal powers as well as political opportunities that sometimes allow presidents to govern alone.

James Madison anticipated that individuals would seek to aggrandize power. This led to the establishment of a separation of powers designed to give competing institutions power and leverage to counterbalance aggrandizing efforts. In the modern era however, Congress has sometimes been remiss in standing up for its institutional powers, and presidents have been able to acquire power, sometimes unchallenged. This is especially the case in foreign policy, where presidents waged the Korean and Vietnam Wars without a declaration of war from Congress. Even after passage of the 1973 War Powers Resolution (over a presidential veto), Congress is typically supportive of the president in military intervention. The 2002 joint congressional resolution authorizing the use of military force in Iraq, for example, was a White House initiative, with relatively limited debate and strong support in Congress, despite reservations that many legislators stated after the invasion, when expected stockpiles of weapons of mass destruction were not found, and costs escalated far more than anticipated.

If, constitutionally, presidents are dealt a relatively weak or limited power hand, there are still ways for them to engage in direct, unilateral actions and exercise power. A president with skill, persuasive ability, prestige, popularity, and strong personal attributes can add to this arsenal of power by taking direct or unilateral action. The modern American chief executive is not either the personal presidency *or* the direct action presidency. Smart, effective presidents employ the lessons of Neustadt and unilateralism. They survey the political landscape and utilize the strategy most likely to prove effective.

The direct actions a president can employ that might lead to successful leveraging of unilateral power include: taking the initiative; executive orders; signing statements; and prerogative authority. Presidents may be constitutionally as well as politically vulnerable, but they are not helpless. They may employ an array of unilateral actions that might—under the right conditions (e.g., crisis, war, or when they have unified government)—give them independent power to act above and beyond the constitutional limits of the office.

In addition to persuasion and command, presidents must do much more. For presidents to be effective, and govern within the bounds of democratic leadership, they must also develop a "strategic sense." They must know what to accomplish and how to accomplish it. And, their means and goals must aim to further the will of the people, empower citizens, and strengthen democratic accountability. Success is not measured merely by getting one's way but also by the ends to which policies are directed.

By "strategic sense" we mean the ability to devise an overall plan that is designed to integrate means and ends, that shows what to do and how to do it, that links smaller tactical steps to a broad guiding vision. To overcome the roadblocks built into the system a president must develop a strategic sense of governing. Some elements of presidential leadership remain fairly constant over time—the Constitution, the separation of powers. Others are variable—the skill level of the president, the context or situation at hand, the nature of the president's mandate, the president's party strength in Congress. The president must develop a strategy designed to maximize political capital.

Presidential leadership refers to a complex phenomenon involving influence— the ability to move others in desired directions. Successful leaders are those who can take full advantage of their opportunities, resources, and skills. Institutional structures, the immediate situation, the season of power, the political culture, the regime type, and the dynamics of followership define the opportunities for the exercise of leadership. The resources at a leader's disposal include constitutional and statutory powers, advisers, media, level of popularity, nature of the congressional majority, and political environment. We often mistake resources for power. A successful leader converts resources to power. This does not happen automatically. To convert resources to power requires skill.

The founders wanted a government of energy, yet a specific type of energy, energy that resulted from deliberation and collaboration. What model or type of leadership is required to move such a system? A model based on consensus-building, bargaining, influence, and cooperation. Such a model of power requires presidents to think strategically.[14]

PRESIDENTIAL LEADERSHIP

The words "leadership" and "power" are often used interchangeably. This is misguided. Leadership suggests influence; power is command. Leaders inspire and persuade; power wielders order compliance. Leaders induce followership; power holders force compliance. Officeholders have some power by virtue of occupying an office. Leaders, on the other hand, must earn followership. The officeholder uses the powers granted by the virtue of position. Leaders try to reshape their political environments, aligning their initiatives together with their allies toward achieving the common good.

As discussed earlier, while presidents derive some of their power from constitutional sources, they derive other parts from political and personal sources. Effective presidents use all the resources available to them. True leadership occurs when presidents are able to exploit the multifaceted nature of opportunities to both command and influence.

It is primarily presidential leadership, then, that can overcome the natural lethargy built into the American system and give focus and direction to government. Congress can, on occasion, take the lead in policy making, as was the case when the Congress overcame presidential opposition from Ronald Reagan and imposed economic sanctions on the white minority government of South Africa. More recently, after the 2011 budget showdown between the White House and Congress, the failure to reach a budget agreement two years later that cut spending by required amounts spurred members of Congress to endorse a sequester on federal spending in early 2013, followed by a government shutdown that fall. Both budget conflicts constrained the executive policy agenda. But such cases are

infrequent. Congress simply is not institutionally well designed to provide consistent national leadership over extended periods of time. Not surprisingly, citizens
have most often looked to the White House for leadership and direction. If the
president does not lead, gridlock inevitably prevails. In sum, presidential leadership usually remains the key for moving the machinery of government.

The Building Blocks of Presidential Leadership

Vision

The most important "power" a president can have is to rally the public around a
clear and compelling goal. A meaningful, positive vision that is rooted in building
blocks of the past, addresses needs and hopes of the president, and portrays an
image of a possible future opens more doors to presidential leadership than all the
skills and resources combined. A powerful vision can transform a political system,
recreate the regime of power, and chart a course for change. Aspirational vision
energizes and empowers, inspires and moves people and organizations.

Presidents have long relied on public appeals to win support for their initiatives. Theodore Roosevelt called this "the bully pulpit" power—the effort to sway
the public and the Congress. Many political scientists believe that a president is
forced to "go public" with such appeals, especially given the party polarization and
gridlock of today's political environment. [15]

But some political scientists contend that presidential speeches usually fall
"on deaf ears" and that presidents rarely move the needle of public opinion. [16] An

Ronald Reagan, an inspirational leader who challenged voters with a new vision and direction
for the nation, exercised significant influence on the politics of his era.
© SHEPARD SHERBELL/CORBIS SABA.

example would be Obama's appeals for more gun regulation. More likely, such appeals work only occasionally, on specific issues at certain times. White House advisers also say the so-called "bully pulpit" by and large no longer exists, if it ever did, in large part because of the fragmented media and the short public attention span.

Visions are empowering. They are derived from the shared values of a community, flow from the past, and are about the future. Visions inspire, give meaning and direction to a community, and are about achieving excellence. A visionary leader gives direction to an organization and gives purpose to action.

Visionary leaders are remembered and have an impact after they have left office. Thus, long after FDR, Martin Luther King Jr., and Ronald Reagan were gone, the power of their ideas and the impact of their words remain symbolic and emotional forces in the political arena. Ronald Reagan was able to inspire followers because he was skilled at presenting his vision. In contrast, the Bushes often had trouble providing a compelling vision that rallied the nation.

Few people are better positioned to present a vision to the public than a president. Already the focus of much media and public attention, presidents can become "highlighters" of important issues to be addressed as a part of the president's agenda.

Skill

Even the most skilled of presidents face formidable roadblocks. Skill can help determine the extent to which a president takes advantage of or is buried by circumstances, but circumstances set the parameters of what is possible regarding leadership. Presidents recognize they have "windows of opportunity," referring to how open or closed circumstances are for exercising presidential leadership. Skilled presidents who face a closed window (e.g., the opposition party controlling Congress during a period of economic troubles where the president's popularity is low) will be limited in what they can accomplish. Presidents of limited skill, when the window of opportunity is open, will have much greater political leverage, even though their skill base is smaller.

It is thus entirely possible for a president with limited skill to be more successful than a president with great skill. If one is dealt a weak hand, there is only so much skill can do. This is not to say that skill is unimportant. But in the constellation of factors that contribute to success or failure, skill is but one, and probably not the most important, element.

Before an election one often hears political cynics complain, "It really doesn't matter who gets elected, they all end up doing the same thing anyway." Social science lends some support to this view. After all, social scientists widely believe that the institution, role, expectations, fortune, and other factors play a significant role in determining behavior. The cynic has a point, yet it should not be taken too far. Individuals are constrained, but individuals do matter; leaders matter.

One way of looking at the skill/opportunity dilemma is to focus on what is referred to as a president's "political capital." Is a president's political capital like a bank account where a one-time deposit is made at the beginning of the term, invested carefully, and drawn upon prudently, in case the president runs out of resources? Or may a president add to the bank account from time to time, renewing political resources?

Despite initial conflicts, Democratic President Bill Clinton worked successfully with a
Republican-led Congress for much of his administration. AP Photo/Greg Gibson.

President George H. W. Bush believed that his capital was a fixed sum, and
in spending it, he dissipated it. Bill Clinton, on the other hand, viewed political
capital more flexibly. He sometimes spent it, then tried to replenish his assets as
best he could. In the end Clinton had to listen and work more closely with the
Republicans who had won control of Congress. But he benefited from a booming
economy in his second term.

Do individual leaders make a difference? Sometimes. The effect of individual
presidents in specific policy areas is unmistakable: Lyndon Johnson and civil rights,
Richard Nixon and China, Ronald Reagan and negotiations with the Soviet Union,
Bill Clinton and the Brady Bill (gun control), George W. Bush and the War on Terror,
and Barack Obama and health care. These presidents made choices, moved in new
directions, and were often consequential. Yes, they were limited, yet they were able
to overcome the natural lethargy of the system and succeed in selected policy arenas.

Determining the precise role skill played in these events is a challenge.
Could another president have opened the doors to China? Perhaps, yet maybe
not. Could any president emphasize human rights in foreign policy? Certainly.
So where are we left? When does skill matter, and how can we recognize or
measure political skill? Regrettably, it is too elusive a concept to measure precisely. High levels of skill, task congruence, and high opportunity sometimes
lead to presidential success, and low levels of these often lead to failure.

If skill is of some importance, it is useful to ask, what skills are most useful to a president? Political expertise often is cited as a requirement for effective leadership, and while this sounds like common sense, the correlation between expertise and achievement is not clear. Some of our most experienced national leaders were, in many respects, failures (Hoover, LBJ, Nixon, and George H. W. Bush come to mind). Overall, more experience is better than less experience, although by no means a guarantee of successful performance. Thus, other factors determine to a great degree the success or failure of a president.

Ronald Reagan, Bill Clinton, George W. Bush, and Barack Obama serve as excellent examples of amateurs, in Washington D.C. terms, who sometimes behaved amateurishly in the White House. Reagan in Beirut, Clinton in Somalia, Bush in Iraq, and Obama in Libya all made fundamental errors. In all cases, leaders with little or no foreign policy experience made blunders that might have been avoided. More experienced hands might have known better. The start of the Trump presidency in 2017 raised several questions about how the 45th president's career in business, not politics, would affect his leadership and policy decisions.

Presidents also need people skills. They must know how to persuade, bargain, cajole, and co-opt. They must be masters of self-preservation. They must be able to motivate and inspire, to gain trust and influence. And occupants of the White House must master the art of "presidential schmoozing."

Personality skills are also a significant part of the arsenal of presidential requirements. All presidents have a strong drive for power. To be effective, presidents should be self-confident, secure, and flexible. Presidents consumed by self-doubt, insecurity, and rigidity are often dangerous and more apt to abuse power.

Presidents also need self-knowledge. We all have weaknesses, but we need not let our weaknesses consume us. Good presidents recognize their strengths and weaknesses, and attempt to deal constructively with weakness. Thus, presidents who are inexperienced in foreign policy may need to compensate by surrounding themselves with experienced foreign policy insiders.

Managerial skills are also important if a president is to succeed. Upon taking office presidents tend to see only the personal as important; the historical and institutional are often downplayed. Effective presidents must be disciplined. By this we mean they must be intelligent, have stamina, show sound judgment, and carefully focus their efforts.

Good presidents are also creative, empathetic, and expressive. They need to be optimistic. They must also have senses of humor and learn to control their tempers. President Reagan's self-effacing sense of humor served him well; it disarmed opponents and won supporters.

Political Timing

The "when" of politics also matters greatly: when the legislation is introduced, when the public is ready to accept change, when Congress can be pressured to act, when to lead and when to follow, when to push and when to pause. A sense of political timing, part of the "power sense" all great leaders have, helps a president know when to move, when to retreat, when to hold firm, and when to compromise. The transition and honeymoon are especially important periods.

Getting a good start, or "hitting the ground running," is a key element of political success, and during the transition, the eleven-week period between the November election and the January inauguration, some of the most important work of an administration is done. Here the groundwork is laid for much that will follow, and a tone is set that shapes the way others see the new administration. During the transition, the president makes key decisions on who the top advisors will be, who will fill important cabinet positions, how the staff will be instructed, what decision style will be employed, whether to pursue a partisan strategy or try to woo the opposition, how to mobilize the public, and what issues the administration will push during the first year.

As political scientist James Pfiffner writes, "Power is not automatically transferred, but must be seized. Only the authority of the presidency is transferred on January 20; the power of the presidency—in terms of effective control of the policy agenda—must be consciously developed."[17] To seize power, presidents must adopt a strategic approach to the transition, one that leaves little to chance and that deals self-consciously with the use of power.

A president's first 100 days and first six to ten months are a crucial period for setting the agenda. It is important to win at least a few key legislative victories as soon as possible.

Strong presidents such as Woodrow Wilson, Franklin Roosevelt, Lyndon Johnson, and Ronald Reagan began with explicit goals and pushed Congress to enact bold new programs. Indeed, each new president is in effect invited in the first year to share a vision and a national agenda with attentive Washington, national, and international audiences.

When Reagan took office, for example, his administration self-consciously chose to focus on a select few big-ticket items: tax cuts and increased defense spending. Nearly all else, including important foreign policy matters, were put on the back burner. This allowed his administration to concentrate its energies.

In contrast, George H. W. Bush virtually relinquished the advantages offered by the honeymoon period. He got off to a slow start and appeared more concerned with managing a response to events as they happened than with shaping events by his actions. His early weeks were marked by caution.

A president's strategic sense must also take into account other key elements of presidential power maximization: party majority in Congress, public approval ratings, relations with the leaders of the other party in Congress, media relations, management skills, agenda control, and coalition and consensus building.

ARE WE TOO PRESIDENCY-CENTRIC?

When things are going well, we praise presidents and celebrate presidential power. Yet we have little patience when things go badly and usually point the finger of blame—whether merited or not—directly at the president.

Part of the problem is what political scientist Brendan Nyhan terms the "Green Lantern Theory of Presidential Power." Nyhan suggests that we hold a mistaken view of presidential power and capability. We view the president as having all the power needed to succeed, much like the comic-book superhero. If only presidents worked harder or applied the correct political strategy, then they could move Congress as they wish. The executive institution is fine—recent officeholders are the problem.

There typically are two variants to the Green Lantern view: the LBJ model and the Reagan model. The LBJ model posits that if only the president tried harder to work with Congress, then they would enact legislation. The Reagan model suggests that if only presidents did a better job of selling programs to the public, then they would rally people to their side, thereby compelling Congress to follow. Both models are informative, but they do not apply directly to current political conditions and challenges.

While hard work and a sound strategy would help, the Green Lantern view neglects the very real checks built into the American political system, checks that often prevent even the smartest and hardest-working presidents from achieving the most modest of goals. Presidents are not the government; they are a part of the government and must share powers with others, most notably with Congress and the states. The public sees the president as a national problem solver but fails to take into consideration the many obstacles, roadblocks, checks, and balances that confront all presidents. Consequently, we often end up savaging our presidents when they fail to meet our inflated expectations; only in a crisis do we give the president sufficient power to do anything substantial. Political scientists William Howell and Terry Moe contend that the constitutional system of separation of powers, and especially the parochialism and polarization in the U.S. Congress, hinders the federal government's ability to address pressing national needs today. Consequently, presidents require more "fast-track" legislative power to provide coherent national policy making.[18]

Libertarian Gene Healy presents a different perspective on presidential power, arguing that the presidency has become far more powerful than the framers anticipated or wished. The swelling of presidential power, Healy says, has led to "romanticization of the presidency," with the president as our "national guardian." He asks, "Is that vision of the presidency appropriate for a self-governing republic? Is it compatible with limited constitutional government?" and concludes, not surprisingly, that "it is not."[19]

In the end, libertarians like Healy typically call for a "constitutional presidency," one more in line with the model invented by the framers. They are aware of the many forces that have contributed to the growth of presidential power, and may also be aware that the president is tilting at windmills. Yet this view offers a correction to those conservatives who promote the "unitary executive" or presidentialist model of presidential power. Some progressives similarly warn of the dangers in idealizing the presidency. Presidential scholar Louis Fisher, for example, reminds us that the presidency is a constitutional office, defined and redefined over time, yet still embedded within a constitutional framework.[20]

Richard E. Neustadt's Model of Presidential Power

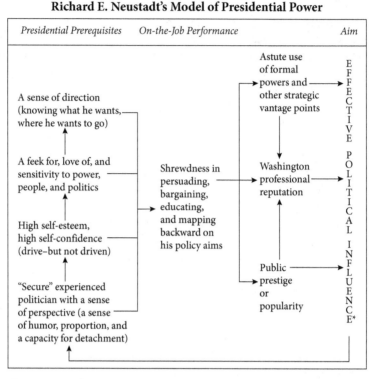

Figure 4.1 *Defined as the capacity to acquire power and use it to frame and implement policy.

CONCLUSION

Bold, effective, sustained presidential leadership is uncommon. In those rare periods of leadership (which usually are in a president's honeymoon period, or in a major crisis, or when a president enjoys strong party majorities in Congress), presidents are able to animate citizens and mobilize government, develop a vision and establish an agenda, move Congress and lead the bureaucracy. Such presidents recast the arena of the politically possible. It has not happened often. The forces arrayed against a president usually have the upper hand. Both our Constitution and the array of forces in our complex political and economic system almost conspire to leave us with a limited leadership system—or at least guarantee only gradual shifts in public policy.

The preconditions for effective presidential leadership are rarely in synchronization: skill, the right timing, a consensus, a governing coalition, popularity, vision, and a mandate. Presidents, to be effective leaders in a democratic system, must bring Hamiltonian energy to our Madisonian system of checks and balances in order to achieve Jeffersonian and Rooseveltian ends of liberty, justice, and equality of opportunity. Few presidents can achieve this, save on occasion.

To succeed, presidents must be masters of the light (education, vision, mobilization) and the heat (power, bargaining). Given the incredible array of skills and circumstances necessary for presidents to succeed, it is no wonder that many of them fail to live up to our expectations.

Some of the difficulty rests with individual presidents who lack programmatic ideas as well as sufficient political skill. Part of the challenge rests with the structural design of the American constitutional system, which separates and fragments power. Part, too, is because the American people resist sweeping or bold changes—especially if those changes may raise taxes.

In a democracy, leaders have a responsibility to educate, enlighten, inform, and listen to the people. They must identify problems and mobilize public support. By informing and educating the citizenry, as well as themselves, leaders also engage in a dialogue that ultimately seeks to develop a vision, grounded in the values of the nation, that will spur needed action.

FURTHER READINGS

Greenstein, Fred I. *The Presidential Difference: Leadership Style from FDR to Barack Obama*, 3rd ed. Princeton, N.J.: Princeton University Press, 2009.

Howell, William G., and Terry M. Moe. *Relic: How Our Constitution Undermines Effective Government—And Why We Need a More Powerful Presidency*. New York: Basic Books, 2016.

Howell, William G. *Power Without Persuasion: The Politics of Direct Presidential Action*. Princeton, N.J.: Princeton University Press, 2003.

Neustadt, Richard E. *Presidential Power and the Modern Presidents*. New York: Free Press, 1990.

Rudalevige, Andrew. *The New Imperial Presidency*. Ann Arbor: University of Michigan Press, 2005.

Schlesinger, Arthur M. *The Imperial Presidency*. Boston: Houghton Mifflin, 1973.

Skowronek, Stephen. *Presidential Leadership in Political Time: Reprise and Reappraisal*, 2nd ed. rev. and exp. Lawrence: University Press of Kansas, 2011.

CHAPTER 5

The Presidential Job Description in a System of Shared Powers

Anyone searching for the paradoxes of the American presidency need look no further than the president's informal as well as formal job description: high expectations, yet limited power; many demands, constrained resources. We expect presidents to accomplish great things, yet often we tie their hands. Of course, as discussed earlier, the job of the president has changed and enlarged dramatically since 1789. While the constitutional provisions relating to presidential power remain virtually unchanged, the responsibilities and expectations of the office have increased significantly.

Further, the president is embedded in the separation-of-powers system. In this three-branch system of government some powers are separated, some shared and blended, but little is given exclusively to the president. As such, on most issues, the president must elicit the cooperation of other branches to act legitimately. In the midst of the war against terrorism, this system has come under particularly acute strain.

Historians still debate the motives of the framers of the U.S. Constitution. They believed in the consent of the governed, yet they also were worried about democracy. The framers harbored grave concerns about both mass-based democracy and executive tyranny. These concerns are evident when one examines the inventing of the American presidency.

To understand what is expected of presidents today, we need to examine the invention of the presidency as well as its evolution over time. Only then can we fully appreciate the many roles and demands placed upon the presidency.

Several of our paradoxes apply here. We want a powerful president, yet the separation of power enchains the office. We like presidents who are above politics, yet dealing with Congress demands great political as well as partisan savvy. We want visionary policies, but we also want presidents to follow the public will—however difficult it is to define.

In establishing a separation of powers system with checks and balances, the framers of the Constitution sought to both empower a presidency with energy *and* limit the reach of the office. They wanted "republican energy" in the new executive, an energy animated by shared and separated powers that *both* the president and Congress exercised, often together.

EVOLUTION OF PRESIDENTIAL JOB DESCRIPTION

The Presidency as Defined and Debated in 1787

The presidential job description as outlined in the Constitution was a medley of compromises. The framers wanted a presidency strong enough to do what was asked of it and yet not one that would use governmental authority for selfish ends or contrary to the general welfare. In almost every instance presidential powers were shared powers. Perhaps only the pardon power was a truly imperial grant of power.

Despite the administrative, diplomatic, commander-in-chief, and veto powers granted to them, presidents found they had to act within a set of strong constitutional, political, and social restraints. They had to be sensitive to the dominant elites, the cultural "rules of the game," and, of course, the threat of being impeached or turned out of office at the next election.

The writers of the United States Constitution created, by design, what some call an "anti-leadership" system of government. Their goal was less to provide a system of government than one that would not jeopardize liberty. Freedom was their goal; governmental power their concern. The men who toiled in that hot summer of 1787 in Philadelphia thus created an executive institution, a presidency, with limited powers.

The framers primarily wanted to counteract two fears: the fear of the mob (democracy, or mobocracy) and the fear of the monarchy (centralized, tyrannical executive power). The menacing image of England's King George III, against whom the colonists rebelled and whom Thomas Paine called "the Royal Brute of Britain," served as a powerful reminder of the dangers of a strong executive. To contain power, they set up an executive office which was constitutionally rather weak (Congress had, on paper at least, most of the power), based on the rule of law, with a separation of powers, ensuring a system of checks and balances.

To James Madison, a chief architect of the Constitution, a government with too much power could be a dangerous government. A student of history, Madison believed human nature drove people to pursue self-interest, and therefore a system of government designed to have "ambition checked by ambition" set within rather strict limits was the only hope to establish a stable government which did not endanger liberty. Realizing that "enlightened statesmen" would not always guide the nation, Madison embraced a checks-and-balance system of separate but overlapping and shared powers. Madison's concern for a government that controlled and limited powers is seen throughout his writings, yet nowhere is it more vivid than where he wrote in *Federalist Paper* No. 51, "You must first enable the government to control the governed; and in the next place, oblige it to control itself."[1]

Yes, government was to have enough power to govern, but no, it could not have enough power to overwhelm freedom. If one branch were empowered to check another, tyranny might be thwarted. There is scant concern in Madison's writings for the needs of a strong government. Thus, the Constitution was both an enabling and a constraining document.

Alexander Hamilton was the convention's chief defender of a powerful executive. An advocate of strong central government, Hamilton promoted a version of executive power quite different from Madison's dispersed and separate powers. Where Madison wanted to check authority, Hamilton wished to enhance authority; where Madison believed that the new government's powers should be "few and defined," Hamilton wanted to infuse the executive with "energy."[2] A feeble executive implies a feeble execution of the government. A feeble execution, in Hamilton's words, is but another phrase for a bad execution, and a government ill executed, whatever it may be in theory, must be, in practice, a bad government.

Hamilton wanted a strong president within a more centralized federal government. Yet such a system would undermine Madison's determination to check government power—the presidency, a unitary office headed by one man, would have no internal check. Thus Madison insisted on the need for strong external checks, that is, a strong Congress. While Madison won the day at the Convention, creating a presidency with fairly limited powers, history and presidential precedent often have been on Hamilton's side.

Looming in the background was the influential presence of Thomas Jefferson. Supportive of small government and democracy, Jefferson was suspicious of centralized power. But Jefferson's vision of small government, an agrarian economy, and a robust democracy was given little attention at the Convention. A Madisonian model emerged.

Like most of the founders, Madison feared government in the hands of the people, yet he likewise feared too much power in the hands of any one person. Thus, the Madisonian model called for both protections against mass democracy and limits on governmental power. This is not to say the founders wanted a weak and ineffective government. Had that been their goal, they could have kept the Articles of Confederation. But they did not want a government which could act too easily. The theory of government which the Madisonian design necessitates is one of consensus, coalition, and cooperation on the one hand, and checks, vetoes, and balances on the other.

As a result, the presidency is a rather limited institution with few independent powers. The paradox thus created, especially in the modern period, is this: How can a president bring Hamiltonian energy to this Madisonian system for Jeffersonian ends? The founders did not make it easy for the government to act or for presidents to lead. That was not their intent. They left the powers and contours of the office somewhat vague—expecting Washington to fill in the gaps. This created "an invitation to struggle" for control of government. A modern efficiency expert, looking at the framers' design for government, would likely conclude that the system could not work well: too many limits, too many checks, not enough power, and not enough leeway for leadership. Yet this is the way most of the framers wanted it.

What did the framers create? The chief characteristics, or mechanisms to control and empower the executive, are:

- Limited Government: A reaction against the arbitrary, expansive powers of the king or state, and a protection of personal liberty.
- Rule of Law: Only on the basis of legal or constitutional grounds could the government act.
- Separation of Powers: The three branches of government divided but sharing in power.
- Checks and Balances: By separating power, each branch could limit or control the powers of the other branches of government.

The Constitution both empowers and restrains government. Article I is devoted to the Congress, the first and constitutionally the most powerful branch of government. Article II, the executive article, deals with the presidency. The president's power cupboard is, compared to the Congress, nearly bare or at least vague. Section 1 gives the "executive power" to the president but does not reveal whether this is a grant of tangible power or merely a title. Section 2 makes the president commander-in-chief but reserves the power to declare war for the Congress. Section 2 also gives the president power to grant reprieves and pardons, power to make treaties (with the advice and consent of the Senate), and the power to nominate Ambassadors, Judges, and other public ministers (with the advice and consent of the Senate). Section 3 calls for the president to inform the Congress on the State of the Union and to recommend measures to Congress, grants the power to receive Ambassadors, and imposes upon the president the duty to take care that the laws are faithfully executed. These powers are significant, yet in and of themselves they do not suggest a strong or independent leadership institution.

Thus, the president has two types of power: formal (the ability to command) and informal (the ability to persuade). The president's formal powers are limited and (often) shared. The president's informal powers are a function of skill, situation, and political time. While the formal power of the president remains fairly constant over time, the president's informal powers are variable, dependent on the skill of each individual president. This is not to say a president's formal powers are static—over time presidential power has increased significantly—but the pace of change has been such that it was over 100 years before the presidency assumed primacy in the U.S. political system.

The structure of government dispersed or fragmented power; there is no recognized, authoritative vital center; power is fluid and floating; no one branch could easily or freely act without the consent of another branch; power was designed to counteract power; ambition to check ambition. It was a structure designed to force a consensus before the government could act. The structure of government created by the framers did not create a leadership institution, but three separate semiautonomous institutions that shared power.

The Presidency as Redefined by Washington and His Successors

The Constitution was the result of bargains and compromises. One area of dispute was the power the new president would be granted. Unable to come to terms with this question, the framers were forced to leave the powers of the president somewhat ambiguous. This was not especially troublesome because they knew who the first president would be: George Washington. The founders held Washington in such high regard that they were confident he would set the proper tone for the office.

George Washington loomed large in the early republic. Washington sailed in uncharted waters and is credited with establishing sound precedents. He lent dignity to this newly invented presidency, developed a version of consensus leadership where possible and executive independence where necessary, was guided by the rule of law and recognized the limits of his power, and generally remained true to the requirements of constitutional government. Above all, he established the legitimacy of the office of president.[3]

Keenly aware that as the first occupant of the presidential office every act of commission and omission would be noticed, scrutinized, and perhaps established as precedent, Washington was careful to establish the independence of the office yet still respect the integrity of the Congress. He was well aware that nearly everything he did, however trivial, was setting precedent for those who would follow. Washington also imposed his semi-regal persona and his republican sentiments on the new office, and in effect, brought to life what the framers had merely invented.

Following Washington, the power of the presidency rose and fell depending on circumstances, the will of the president, and the demands of the time. Thomas Jefferson (1801–1809) stretched the powers of the presidency, using the nascent political party to aid in achieving his goals. Andrew Jackson (1829–1837) asserted the independence of the presidency and linked his power to the people. Jacksonian democracy represented a broadening of democracy and a connection between the president and the people of which the Framers were suspicious. Jackson portrayed himself as the "tribune of the people" and asserted a brand of leadership linked to popularity.

Abraham Lincoln (1861–1865) demonstrated that during a crisis, the powers of the presidency could be expanded. Using a combination of claimed emergency and war powers, Lincoln took bold action during the Civil War. He blockaded Southern ports, called up the militia, arrested persons suspected of disloyalty, and suspended the writ of *habeas corpus*, all without congressional authorization. Lincoln knew he had intruded into areas of congressional authority, yet claimed the doctrine of necessity as his justification.[4]

During the presidency of Theodore Roosevelt (1901–1909), the United States emerged as a world power, intent on making its mark on the international stage. TR aggressively asserted presidential power both at home and abroad, and reestablished presidential primacy. Roosevelt viewed the presidency as a "bully pulpit" and contributed to the rise of what is called the "rhetorical presidency,"[5] seeing the president as the "steward of the people." Viewing power expansively, TR asserted that "it was not only his right but his duty to do anything that the needs of the nation demanded unless such action was forbidden by the Constitution or by the laws. . . . Under this interpretation of executive power I did and caused to be done many things not previously done by the president and the heads of the departments. I did not usurp power, but I did greatly broaden the use of executive power."[6]

The presidency of Woodrow Wilson (1913–1921) further established the United States as a world power and the presidency as a pivotal center or lever of American government. Wilson used his powerful rhetorical skills in conjunction with a reliance on party and programmatic leadership to establish the presidency as the guiding force for the nation's mixed economy. When combined with his leadership during World War I, Wilson's governance elevated the office of presidency to one of national and international leadership.

Mixed in between these active presidents were a series of lesser or even lackluster presidents who often diminished the office. For every Jackson, there was a Tyler, for every Lincoln, a Grant, for every Wilson, a Harding. Yet if there were presidential underachievers along with those who stretched the boundaries of presidential power, clearly the institutional trend was in the direction of growing influence.

The Presidency as Redefined by FDR and the Modern Presidents

The institution of the presidency as we know it today was born in the 1930s. The stepchild of the Depression and war, it was during the Franklin D. Roosevelt era (1933–1945) that the presidency became a modern institution.

The start of the Great Depression in 1929 and World War II a decade later contributed to the presidency-centered nature of our national government, and the leadership style and skill of FDR established the United States (for better or worse) as a presidential nation.

FDR, considered by presidential scholars to be one of the nation's greatest presidents, was a powerful and effective chief executive. Under his leadership, and with a supportive Congress, the presidency became the prime mover of the American system, and people began to look to the federal government and to the presidency as the nation's problem solver. The federal government had grown, and with it presidential responsibilities, ending the era in which presidents such as Calvin Coolidge could claim that his greatest accomplishment was "minding my own business."

Roosevelt's success transformed both the presidency and public attitudes about it. He created expectations of presidential leadership which would be imposed on his successors. The "heroic" model of the presidency was established as a result of FDR's leadership, and for the next forty years, presidential scholars would often promote the model as good and necessary. FDR's successors would labor in his dominant shadow.[7]

If Roosevelt was an important president, the myth of FDR took on even greater stature. An inflated view of Roosevelt passed for fact in popular and scholarly mythology of the presidency. He was, of course, not as powerful as many remembered him.

Truman assumed the presidency in the final days of World War II. To the surprise of most of his contemporaries, Truman became an effective president, though his popularity could never match FDR's, and many of his enduring policy achievements would be appreciated only much later. The last president to not have a college education, Truman's common-sense approach to governance and general humility illustrated an ability to rise to the call for leadership that has received much scholarly and public acclaim in recent years.

After Dwight D. Eisenhower successfully won the Republican nomination and then the presidency in 1952, he enjoyed strong bipartisan public support through two terms in office. While not an openly activist president, Eisenhower sometimes exerted a hidden-hand style of leadership in an era where the public seemed supportive of a less activist government at home and abroad.[8] He set a clear direction in national security policy, developing a strategy that relied on nuclear deterrence instead of high defense spending to wage the Cold War, and he confidently maintained that position even amid growing concerns (which later proved to be incorrect) in his second term that the United States was falling behind the Soviet Union in military strength.

If FDR's legacy of public leadership seemed to be missing in the Eisenhower years, Eisenhower's successor was determined to revive it. John F. Kennedy campaigned on a platform of energetic executive leadership as much as Democratic policy change. After some early missteps, Kennedy achieved some notable successes in his tragically short presidency, from peacefully resolving the Cuban missile crisis to calling for major civil rights legislation in 1963.

From FDR's presidency through the 1960s, a presidency-centered model came to dominate scholarly thinking and enjoyed broad public support. Scholars endorsed a philosophy of government with strong executive leadership that directed public opinion. In so doing, they placed less emphasis on public democratic responsibilities and failed to recognize the potential dangers of a heroic model of presidential leadership.

Lyndon B. Johnson's remarkable legislative achievements in the aftermath of John Kennedy's assassination confirmed for many the wisdom of the strong presidency model. In response to the civil rights movement, which spurred long-overdue social reform in the United States, Johnson enacted landmark civil rights soon after taking office. He achieved this success through the force of persuasion and bargaining with members of Congress, as well as with both support and pressure from African-American political leaders. After winning election overwhelmingly in 1964, Johnson further expanded his domestic-policy agenda, leading the passage of legislation in voting rights, housing, transportation, education, and many other areas.

The Vietnam War forced scholars and the public to rethink assumptions about heroic presidential leadership. U.S. involvement in Vietnam began quietly, escalated incrementally, and led to tragedy. By 1968, the U.S. was engaged in a war that it could not win, and from which it could not honorably withdraw. It was a "presidential war," and it brought the Johnson administration to its knees.[9]

After important legislative successes, the problem of Vietnam would overwhelm Johnson and the nation. Most Americans supported U.S. intervention in

Vietnam initially, but this support gradually eroded. Divisiveness overtook the nation as LBJ persisted in escalating the war. The strong presidency, so long seen as critically important for the American system, now seemed too powerful, too unchecked, and alas, even a threat to democracy. After years of hearing calls for "more power to the president," by the late 1960s the plea was to rein in the overly powerful White House.

If Vietnam led to questions about the power of the presidency, the actions of Johnson's successor, Richard Nixon, raised new concerns about that power. With the constitutional crisis known as Watergate, Richard Nixon, named an "unindicted co-conspirator" by the grand jury, became the nation's first president forced to resign from office.

In reaction to the abuses of power by Johnson and Nixon, Congress attempted to reassert its power. The Ford and Carter presidencies, rather than being imperial, seemed imperiled. Presidential constraints largely defined the post-Nixon era in the 1970s.

Then, in the 1980s, Ronald Reagan began to reassert presidential power. Claiming a bold mandate and focusing on several key economic initiatives, Reagan succeeded in enacting much of his early policy agenda, including tax cuts and increased defense spending. After winning re-election in 1984 with a forty-nine-state landslide victory in the electoral college, Reagan also achieved landmark tax and immigration reform. He additionally redefined American foreign policy, shifting from maintaining a firm Cold War policy in his first term to having four summit meetings with the Soviet Union in his second term, and signing the first U.S.-Soviet treaty to decrease nuclear weapons. But overreach of executive power took place in the Reagan presidency as well with the Iran-contra scandal, which also illustrated the risks of presidential delegation and limited engagement in policy details.

After serving eight years as Reagan's vice president, President George H. W. Bush led as a manager at a time when the nation needed a visionary leader. Bush was at his best when he had a clear goal to achieve—for example, the Persian Gulf War, for which Bush successfully built a global coalition, drawing upon his extensive international network from a career in diplomacy. But he had difficulty setting an overarching mission for his presidency, and after breaking a campaign pledge not to raise taxes and facing an economic recession later in his term, he lost re-election.

The Clinton presidency demonstrated both strengths and limits of presidential leadership. Clinton was a gifted and masterful politician who also revealed significant character challenges in office. His serial affairs and dishonesty about them prompted the most extensive investigations ever launched into the private life and conduct of a president.

After failing to achieve his major campaign promise of health care reform and witnessing the Republican midterm electoral landslide, which returned Congress to Republican control after four decades in the House (and just a six-year period of Democratic control of the Senate in that time), Clinton seemed on track to having a single-term presidency. But when Republican House Speaker Newt Gingrich initiated budget battles that resulted in two government shutdowns in 1995–1996,

Clinton prevailed with the public, decrying Gingrich's proposed budget cuts as draconian.

Clinton's "Third Way," between the liberal left of the Democratic Party and the hard right of the Republicans, allowed him to "triangulate" between extremes and offer voters moderate alternatives. After negotiating a budget agreement and enacting legislation to increase the minimum wage, allow workers to keep health insurance when changing jobs (albeit with potentially high premiums), and create major welfare reform, Clinton handily won reelection in 1996. But a special investigation by Independent Counsel Kenneth Starr into Clinton's pre-presidency business ventures revealed a sexual affair during his presidency that Clinton initially denied. After impeachment (the second president in U.S. history to face this charge) and acquittal, Clinton continued to enjoy public support, but his political capital, despite his claims to the contrary, was greatly diminished.

The hotly disputed 2000 presidential election suggested that the George W. Bush presidency might face challenges to strong executive leadership. Nevertheless, Bush fulfilled his signature campaign promise of tax cuts soon after taking office, and made progress on promised education reform as well. But the Bush 43 presidency changed dramatically after the terrorist attack against the United States on September 11, 2001.

The attack changed the political circumstances in which Bush governed and created a "crisis presidency." Power shifted to the White House, as the public, Congress, and much of the world community rallied behind the president. With a veteran national security team, whom President Bush had selected in consultation

President Bush comforted and rallied the nation in the immediate aftermath of the 9/11 terrorist attacks against the United States. AP Photo/Doug Mills.

with Vice President and former Defense Secretary Dick Cheney, the Bush White House had a clear goal: Stop terrorism and defeat the enemy. To do so, the United States initially attacked the al-Qaeda terror network and overthrew the Taliban government in Afghanistan. With an international coalition, the United States achieved key early victories in the war against terrorism.

Domestic and international support for the president became more divided with the 2003 Iraq invasion. The Bush administration decided to wage war against Iraq to overthrow the dictatorial regime of Saddam Hussein, who had flouted international requirements for weapons inspections for several years. President Bush did secure a unanimous United Nations Security Council resolution that declared Iraq would face "serious consequences" if it continued to violate inspections obligations, but the Council would not agree to a second resolution explicitly authorizing military action. The Bush White House then built its own international coalition and launched a war against Iraq that quickly toppled Hussein, but then continued throughout the rest of the Bush 43 presidency, as the United States attempted to establish stable democratic governance in Iraq.

Toward the end of Bush's second term, a financial crisis hit the United States, then the global economy. A few large corporate institutions crumbled, the stock market plummeted, several banks failed, home foreclosures skyrocketed, and the administration scrambled for a rescue plan. With a plan for massive government intervention, the administration tried to stop the economic bleeding. But the snowball effect was too much to stop and the president left office with approval ratings in the low twenties, comparable to Truman leaving office during the stalemated Korean War.

Given the financial crisis, the ongoing Iraq war, the Bush administration's controversial surveillance and interrogation policies to combat terrorism, and Republican governance of the White House for two terms, a Democratic presidential victory in 2008 seemed likely. But the election of Barack Obama, the country's first African-American president and a first-term U.S. Senator from Illinois in 2008 (with just four years of national political experience), was completely unexpected. Obama waged a relentless battle for the Democratic nomination against then-U.S. Senator Hillary Clinton, ultimately prevailing with a narrow margin of victory in both delegates and votes. In the general election, Obama won decisively over Republican candidate John McCain, promising to bring "change we can believe in" in both politics and policy choices to Washington.

Once in office, Obama found bipartisanship difficult to achieve. His economic stimulus package received just three Republican votes, and his signature campaign issue of health care reform passed on a party-line vote with no Republican support in the spring of 2010. That fall, Democrats lost control of the U.S. House of Representatives, and Obama faced a budget showdown with Congress in the summer of 2011, as well as legal challenges to the Affordable Care Act, which the U.S. Supreme Court upheld in the summer of 2012. Nevertheless, Obama won re-election in 2012 over business executive and former Massachusetts governor Mitt Romney, and Democrats kept control of the U.S. Senate, though that would change in the 2014 elections.

In his second term, Obama's budget conflicts with Congress continued, leading to sequestration of federal funds (automatic budget cuts) in 2013 as well as a government shutdown for the first time in nearly two decades. In foreign affairs, Obama had kept his original campaign promise to withdraw U.S. troops from Iraq in his first term, but the rise of Islamist militants in the Middle East known as ISIS, or the Islamic State of Iraq and Syria, prompted criticism that the Obama administration lacked sustained assertive leadership abroad. Obama's reluctance to send troops to the Middle East to combat terrorists without congressional support further bolstered this view. But in other areas where the administration acted unilaterally, such as expanding the use of drone strikes to attack terrorists in Pakistan, Somalia, and Yemen, or in enacting immigration reform, Obama faced criticism for not working with Congress. In many respects, expectations for executive leadership in the twenty-first century contain so many paradoxes that presidential performance is almost certain to disappoint in some area.

THE JOB OF THE MODERN PRESIDENT

Nowadays presidents are asked to be countless things that are not spelled out with any clarity in the Constitution. We want the president to be a national cheerleader of morale as well as international peacemaker, a moral leader as well as the nation's chief economic manager, a politician in chief, and a unifying representative of all the people. We want every new president to be everything, at least of virtue, that all our great presidents have been. No matter that the great presidents were not as great as we think they were. Rightly or wrongly, we believe our greatest presidents were people of talent, tenacity, and optimism, individuals who could clarify the vital issues of the day and mobilize the nation for action. Our great presidents were transforming leaders who could not only move the enterprise forward but could summon the highest kinds of moral commitment from the American people.

Yet, rarely is a president a free agent. The president nearly always mirrors the fundamental forces of society: the values, the myths, the quest for order and stability, and the vast, inert, and usually conservative forces that maintain the existing balance of interests. Ours is a system decidedly weighted against unilateral leadership, a system that encourages most presidents, most of the time, to respond to the powerful, organized, and already represented interests at the expense of the unrepresented. Moreover, a president today must preside over a highly specialized and sprawling bureaucracy in the executive branch.

Reality, as well as expectations, has expanded and recast the presidency and organized it around three major interrelated policy areas that we may call sub-presidencies:

1. Foreign affairs and national security.
2. Macro-economics.
3. Domestic policy, or "quality of life," issues.

The president's time is absorbed by one or another of these competing policy spheres, and the executive staff and cabinet have come to be organized around these three substantive areas.

The Foreign Affairs Presidency

Modern presidents concentrate on foreign and national security policy, often at the expense of the other policy areas. This is understandable. Since World War II, the United States has been the hegemonic, or dominant, power of the Western alliance. Since the devolution of the Soviet empire in 1989, the United States has been recognized as the major super-power in the world. U.S. global leadership typically is linked to presidential power: A strong America necessitates, many believe, a strong presidency. Thus, presidents focus increased attention on this policy domain, over which they can sometimes exercise significant influence.

To be sure, an exclusively foreign, economic, or domestic problem is a rarity, and many issues intersect all three areas. Critical issues such as trade, inflation, energy development, drug abuse, or environmental problems, not to mention war, require planning and policy leadership that cut across the three policy areas. Still, a close examination of how presidents since FDR have spent their time suggests that foreign policy issues, often crises, can overshadow domestic and economic policy concerns.

The founders did not intend that presidents would become the dominant agent in national policymaking, yet they did expect the president to direct foreign affairs. In the eighteenth century, foreign affairs generally were viewed as an executive matter. After all, the top priority for a national leader is the nation's survival and national defense. Today, especially in the nuclear age, foreign-policy responsibilities cannot be delegated: They are executive in character and presidential by tradition.

After the disastrous Bay of Pigs invasion in 1961, President Kennedy vividly emphasized the central importance of foreign policy: "It really is true," he told a visiting Richard Nixon, "that foreign affairs is the only important issue for a President to handle. . . . I mean, who gives as—if the minimum wage is $1.15 or $1.25, in comparison to something like this [the Bay of Pigs]?"[10] Kennedy frequently said the difference between domestic and foreign policy was the difference between a bill being defeated and the country being wiped out.

White House advisers from recent administrations agree that presidents spend at least half of their time on foreign-policy or national security deliberations. In some instances, this emphasis on foreign policy and national security has occurred by choice, most notably for President Nixon, who said, "I've always thought this country could run itself domestically—without a President; all you need is a competent Cabinet to run the country at home. You need a President for foreign policy; no Secretary of State is really important; the President makes foreign policy."[11] But presidents cannot focus on foreign affairs at the exclusion of the nation's domestic needs.

Political scientist Edward S. Corwin famously described the Constitution's provisions for foreign policy making as "an invitation to struggle" between Congress and the presidency. Presidents claim their use of foreign policy power is grounded in the Constitution, but such claims of independent authority are debatable. Congress has the broadest and clearest constitutional mandate, but its power has atrophied due to lack of use. Even the power to declare war, which is expressly granted to the Congress, has slipped through the hands of the legislature. The 1973 War Powers Resolution, enacted over President Nixon's veto, established clear provisions for how the president must inform Congress when sending U.S. troops abroad, and how Congress must approve military interventions that last more than two months. If Congress orders the president to bring troops home, then the president must comply. Every president since Nixon has declared that the War Powers Resolution is unconstitutional; no president has openly defied the law, but neither has Congress provoked a confrontation with the president, most likely because that could be dangerous for U.S. troops in action, and because Congress's authority would be diminished if the president refused to comply.[12]

Perhaps a president's most significant political power in foreign policy is speaking for and representing the nation to the world. This allows a president the opportunity to act, make decisions, and announce policies, thereby preempting much criticism. To defy the president on a matter of national security often risks appearing unpatriotic, especially in moments of international crisis. Thus, presidents can muffle potential critics and pressure Congress to submit to their will. For example, Theodore Roosevelt sent part of the U.S. Navy, the Great White Fleet, halfway around the world in defiance of congressional budget restrictions, and then said, "I sent the fleet . . . will they leave them there?" George H. W. Bush sent U.S. troops to the Middle East following the 1991 Iraqi invasion of Kuwait, prepared for war, built international and domestic public support, and *then* challenged Congress to pass a resolution authorizing the war. These examples show how presidents, by taking action that makes congressional resistance difficult, usually can get their way—though this has been more difficult recently, as Obama's second-term conflict with Congress over taking military action in the Middle East to combat terrorism illustrated.

Over the course of a term, presidents spend more time on foreign affairs, perhaps in part because they so often get frustrated being rebuffed in domestic and economic policy. Since presidents need to demonstrate accomplishments to maintain their reputation for leadership, they almost naturally gravitate to the area in which their power is greatest. The irony, of course, is that presidents have greatest political power in the area where they probably are most potentially dangerous and in need of checks and balances.

When Obama took office, he faced two wars, a crushing economic recession, and a budget crisis of massive proportions. In foreign policy, Obama sought to lower bellicose rhetoric, reengage with allies, pursue multilateral policies around the world, disengage from the Iraq War, devote more attention and resources to the war in Afghanistan, close the detention camp in Guantanamo, end torture, and, in general, develop a more nuanced liberal internationalist approach to foreign affairs.

While Obama came to the presidency with little foreign policy experience, he quickly assembled an experienced and respected team of advisers and cabinet officials. His major foreign-policy achievements included withdrawing U.S. troops from Iraq (though critics said this created a leadership vacuum that allowed terrorists to gain a foothold in the region); increasing U.S. involvement in Afghanistan to strengthen anti-terrorist efforts before downsizing the American presence there; reaching a nuclear arms deal with Russia; authorizing the killing of terrorist Osama bin Laden by U.S. Navy Seals; toppling the dictatorial regime of Muammar Qaddafi in Libya; reopening diplomatic and commercial ties with Cuba; and negotiating an agreement for Iran to halt its program to build a nuclear weapon in exchange for having the United States lift some sanctions.[13]

But Obama was no miracle worker. Some critics complained he was indecisive about confronting ISIS's attacks in Syria.[14] Others faulted him for expanding the use of drones to kill terrorists and for failing to close the detention center at Guantanamo Bay. Just as Obama's foreign policies were sometimes viewed as similar to his predecessor's, so, too, did Obama receive a wide range of criticism and praise for his foreign-policy choices, much like George W. Bush. Without a doubt, both were consequential foreign-policy presidents, with their legacy still a work in progress.

The Macro-Economic Presidency

As the economic crisis of 2007–2009 demonstrated, the president is also held responsible for promoting a prosperous economy. In fact, the second-largest portion of presidential policy time is spent on macroeconomics—that is, issues of monetary and fiscal policy such as trade and tariff policy, inflation, unemployment, the stability of the dollar, and the health of the stock market. Toward the end of the George W. Bush administration, with the sub-prime collapse of the U.S. housing market and the subsequent stock market crisis, the president was compelled to spring into action in an effort to bring stability to the falling economy. But just how much control does a president have over the economy?

In the early days of the Republic, presidents had less involvement in the development of economic policies. The nation was young, not yet a world power, and Congress was in primary control of determining the budget and setting economic policy. Presidents began to get more involved in setting economic policy with passage of the Budget and Accounting Act of 1921. This law directed the president to formulate a national budget and created a Bureau of the Budget. Then, beginning with Franklin D. Roosevelt, presidents began to expand their involvement in economic and budgetary matters.

While the expectations of presidential responsibility and control of the economy have grown enormously in the past sixty-five years, the president's power to manage the economy has not risen accordingly, creating yet another presidential paradox. We expect presidents to bring about economic breakthroughs but rarely give them the power necessary to work miracles.

Historical circumstance, presidential initiative, legislative acquiescence, and public expectations all have contributed to the emergence of a powerful, but limited, presidency in economic affairs. While congressional efforts to recapture their constitutional duty over the "power of the purse" are evident (e.g., The Congressional Budget and Impoundment Control Act of 1974), the president remains a central figure in setting national economic policy.

A president can scarcely hide from visible quantitative economic indicators, such as unemployment rates, consumer-price indexes, the gross domestic product, interest and mortgage rates, commodity prices, oil import price levels, and stock-market and bond-market averages. In the era of instant cable and electronic news, these figures are available to everyone, at any time, and the American people increasingly judge and measure their presidents on whether they can cope aggressively with recession and inflation, offer effective economic game plans (preferably without tax increases), and use the nation's budget as an instrument for ensuring a healthy and growing economy. The complex issues of tax reform and income redistribution are always on the national political agenda.

But a president's statutory responsibilities for pursuing stable and prudent fiscal policies are not matched by political resources or available expertise. In most areas of our economy, consumers are relatively weak or unorganized, but uneven economic performance will bring immediate pressure on the president from wealthy business executives, unions, and farmers, and from their large delegations of congressional allies.

A further paradox of the president's role as economist-in-chief of the nation pertains to the contradictory demands we place upon the national government. We want to cut spending, cut taxes, and cut the deficit, but we don't want any of "our" favorite programs cut (and every line in the budget is somebody's favorite).[15] Most people want the government to do more but spend less. In a robust economy, the hard choices become much easier, but in a staggering economy, or one burdened with debt, all the choices become painful—as George W. Bush and Barack Obama found out in recent years.

When the economy crashed in 2008, President Bush, a free market devotee, found himself confronted with a frightening choice: stick to principle and watch as the world sank into an international depression, or intervene and try to stop the financial bleeding. "America's financial system is at stake," Treasury Secretary Hank Paulson told the president. "Did I," Bush asked himself, "want to be the president overseeing an economic calamity that could be worse than the Great Depression?" Bush decided "to be Roosevelt, not Hoover."[16] He acted, pouring money into the financial system via the Troubled Asset Relief Program (TARP). Bush got the federal government actively involved in bailing out Wall Street and American business. It was only a beginning. President Obama would inherit the financial mess.

Perhaps the most critical problem President Obama faced on taking office was what to do about the economy. He inherited an economy still in a free-fall after the 2008 recession. The housing bubble had burst, the stock market plummeted, unemployment was near 10 percent, and the economic meltdown threatened to get even worse.

Obama acted swiftly and relatively boldly. He engineered a stimulus package, the American Recovery and Reinvestment Act, putting nearly $800 billion into the economy. He coordinated mortgage relief, a bailout of the auto industry, achieved greater protection for credit card holders, and initiated Wall Street regulations. These policies helped stabilize the economy, yet the recovery proved slow and uneven. [17]

President Obama deserves some credit, along with his predecessor, President Bush, for responding to the economic meltdown. Some credit their actions for pulling the United States out of what otherwise would have been a massive international depression. Stabilizing the economy was one thing, but guiding the economy to expand prosperity was much harder to achieve. Indeed, many people believe, along with U.S. Senator and presidential candidate Bernie Sanders (who voiced these concerns in the 2016 campaign), that the American economy was influenced only by Wall Street bankers and the very rich. Supporters of President Donald Trump voiced similar concerns about a small group of Americans gaining much of the benefits of national economic prosperity, but they largely viewed the Washington political establishment as responsible for the problem.

A late 2015 national survey of public attitudes about inequality shows that many Americans are disappointed with the lack of economic opportunity in the United States and the elusiveness of the "American Dream." (See Table 5.1.) Presidents are expected to promote the economy, and their approval ratings and re-election prospects are greatly affected by economic progress and setbacks.

Table 5.1 NBC News/Esquire National Survey November, 2015 (N = 3257)

1. Do you think elected officials generally enact pollices that favor the interests of:
   - all Americans 20%
   - the wealthy 78%
2. The gap between the wealthy and everyone else in the U.S. is:
   - getting larger 74%
   - staying the same 22%
   - getting smaller 4%
3. Do you think the American Dream—if you work hard, you'll get ahead—is alive and well?
   - still holds true 36%
   - once held true, but not any more 52%
   - never held true 11%
4. Which best describes your family's financial situation?
   - make enough to save and buy some extras 35%
   - make just enough to pay bills and obligations 46%
   - don't make enough to pay all the bills 18%

Selected questions from NBC News/Survey Monkey/Esquire Online Poll, November 21-24, 2015. See Esquire Editors, "American Rage: The *Esquire*/NBC News Survey," January 3, 2016. Available at http://www.esquire.com/news-politics/a40693/american-rage-nbc-survey/

The Domestic Presidency

Presidents concentrate on those policy areas in which they think they can have most influence, typically areas in which interest groups and public opinion can be readily rallied. Leadership in domestic policy is costly, both financially and politically. Moreover, newly elected presidents find that budgets are virtually fixed for the next year and a half if not longer, and that in domestic matters they are dependent on Congress, specialized bureaucracies, professions, and state and local officialdom. Is it surprising, then, that enacting and implementing domestic policy can lose presidential attention? Presidents may rationalize that they must concern themselves with foreign and macroeconomic policy as they lose heart with complicated and often highly divisive domestic problems.

From Roosevelt through Obama, recent presidents have learned that progress on the domestic front was more difficult than they had imagined it would be. They complain that they face greater limits on their ability to produce favorable results in the domestic sphere than they had realized before entering the White House. Clinton's efforts to restructure national health care programs and policy are a notable example. George W. Bush's efforts to enact social security reform are another.

Domestic failures, while not generally as dramatic as failures abroad, can nonetheless undo a president. President George W. Bush's tepid response to Hurricane Katrina's devastation of the Gulf region in September of 2005 significantly tarnished his image as an effective leader. The political consequences of not moving forcefully can be severe; as Bush writes:

> In a national catastrophe, the easiest person to blame is the president. Katrina presented a political opportunity that some critics exploited for years. The aftermath of Katrina—combined with the collapse of Social Security reform and the drumbeat of violence in Iraq—made the fall of 2005 a damaging period in my presidency. Just a year earlier, I had won reelection with more votes than any candidate in history. By the end of 2005, much of my political capital was gone.[18]

Presidents usually are more successful at influencing foreign affairs than domestic policy. In fact, presidents often face major defeats in the domestic arena: Clinton with health care reform, George W. Bush with social security and immigration reform, and Obama with gun control and immigration reform all illustrate the challenges with enacting domestic policy. Counting on domestic legislation to cement your political legacy is rarely a winning formula; FDR's New Deal and LBJ's Great Society were the exceptions, not the rule.

President Obama entered office with an ambitious domestic agenda. This made him a polarizing figure, and Republicans in Congress wasted no time going on the attack. Obama's campaign call for changing Washington politics would not be achieved; indeed, Obama faced hyper-partisan politics through most of his presidency. Further, his domestic agenda was severely restricted by the ongoing deficit crisis: There simply was not enough money—even if the United States went further into debt—to do all Obama wanted. Thus, Obama had to set priorities, and economic recovery and affordable health care insurance became his priorities.[19]

The Obama White House made efforts to build a bipartisan coalition in support of health-care reform, but to no avail. While the medical profession, pharmaceutical companies, and groups such as Catholic hospitals supported the legislation, Republican opposition remained firm. And Obama, perhaps wishing to avoid some of the criticism leveled against President Clinton who handed Congress "his" bill in 1993, neglecting to get sufficient congressional advice or buy-in prior to submitting the legislation, gave Congress an exceptionally high amount of authority to devise its own bill, within some agreed-upon parameters. After a long, difficult, and costly struggle, Obama signed the Affordable Care Act into law in the spring of 2010. Not a single Republican voted for the final legislation.

Even after passage, opponents refused to accept the law, attempting to get the courts to override "Obamacare," stoking political opposition that contributed to the rise of the Tea Party movement, and using radio talk shows and cable television to attack health care as budget busting. While health care was a policy win for Obama, it also came with hefty political costs.

In his second term, Obama had even greater difficulty passing domestic initiatives. As discussed earlier, just getting annual budgets approved became a major battle. The Tea Party and libertarian elements of the Republican Party successfully pressured the national government to cut domestic spending in many areas, thereby fostering general opposition to federal-government initiatives. Unprecedented levels of party polarization and public distrust of the national government further complicated policy making. Mutual antipathy undermined the political trust that is necessary for governance as well as the deal-making that underlies the Madisonian political system.[20]

Sustained presidential lobbying for major domestic initiatives in the face of strong political opposition is challenging. But the success and prosperity of the nation depends on public investment in such programs, from research and development to education to highways, airports, and other infrastructure projects.

Social Security, the GI Bill, Medicare and the Affordable Care Act, the National Science Foundation, and the National Institutes of Health are just a few programs that have advanced U.S. prosperity. Women's suffrage, the Civil Rights Act of 1964, and repealing the "Don't Ask, Don't Tell" policy that had prohibited openly gay and lesbian individuals from serving in the military, are examples of government acting to achieve fairness and inclusiveness. A graduated income tax and Pell grants for deserving students are examples of government seeking to further equality of opportunity. A strong case can be made that more of these national government decisions are needed to supplement the traditional market-based economic system that has served the United States so well. American cities, highways, and infrastructure all have deteriorated to an alarming degree because of gridlock and hyper-partisanship in, and weakened legitimacy of, the national government.[21]

Presidents alone cannot reverse this trend. But presidents, political parties, and other national leaders need to be fully aware of the dysfunctional character of the contemporary U.S. political culture. Americans have become markedly less trusting of the national government in the twenty-first century, and this is the key challenge shaping the presidential job description today.

CONCLUSION

Several incentives help shape the performance of the presidential job. As they have operated in the recent past, these incentives ensure that certain responsibilities get special attention, whereas others become neglected. Preoccupation with problems of national security and macroeconomics often leaves too little time for leadership in the area of domestic policy. Crisis management, symbolic leadership, and priority setting also crowd out the tasks of lobbying and program implementation and supervision. Creative follow-through is seldom adequate; the routines of government often go neglected. Program evaluation and the imaginative recruitment of program managers for appropriate tasks never receive the sustained attention they merit. On balance, White House officials often do what is easy to do or what they perceive as urgent, sometimes to the neglect of doing what is important.

Presidents tend to concentrate on several areas of the presidential job. In part this may be because we have created a nearly impossible presidential job description—we give our presidents too much to do and too little time in which to do it. In part, however, recent presidents have also been, or so it would appear, lulled into responding to those parts of their job that are more glamorous, and more prominent. Presidential activity in symbolic, priority-setting, and crisis contexts can convey an image of strength, vigor, and rigor.

The true measure of presidential effectiveness is the capacity to integrate multiple responsibilities in order to avoid having initiatives in one area compound problems in another, or having problems go unattended merely because they defy the usual organizational boundaries. Another challenge of presidential leadership is the intricate balancing of each aspect of the presidential job with the others. A close examination of presidential performance in recent years relative to the whole matrix of the job suggests that presidents are strong in some areas and weak in others, and that the overarching job of synthesis and integration is seldom performed adequately.

FURTHER READINGS

Fisher, Louis. *Presidential War Power.* 3rd ed., rev. Lawrence: University Press of Kansas, 2013.

Hacker, Jacob S., and Paul Pierson. *American Amnesia: How the War on Government Led Us to Forget What Made America Prosper* (New York: Simon & Schuster, 2016).

Hudak, John. *Presidential Pork: White House Influence over the Distribution of Federal Grants.* Washington, D.C.: Brookings Institution Press, 2014.

Jones, Charles A. *The Presidency in a Separated System.* 2nd ed. Washington, D.C.: Brookings Institution Press, 2005.

Pfiffner, James P. *The Strategic Presidency: Hitting the Ground Running.* 2nd ed., rev. Lawrence: University Press of Kansas, 1996.

Raphael, Ray. *Mr. President: How and Why the Founders Created a Chief Executive.* New York: Vintage, 2013.

CHAPTER 6

Presidents and Congress

In September of 2008, the United States—indeed the entire international financial system—seemed on the verge of a meltdown. The sub-prime lending crisis in the United States led to the collapse of some of the largest banks and financial companies in the nation, and there was the very real threat that this would lead to an international depression.

The Bush administration called for a $700 billion bailout. But the president did not—on his own—have the authority to disburse such sums. He had to get congressional approval. In a matter of days, the intense, often contentious back-and-forth exchange between the administration and members of Congress led to a revised proposal that authorized the $700 billion bailout, but with added protection for the taxpayers and added regulations on the financial sector.

On September 29, 2008, the House voted against the bailout 227–206. House leaders twisted arms, and Bush administration officials feverishly called members in an attempt to turn twelve votes and save their plan. After defeat in the House, the bill went to the Senate, where a series of "sweeteners" were added. On October 1, the revised bill passed the Senate 74–25 and the new proposal went back to the House where, on the second go-around, it passed on October 3 by a comfortable margin of 263–171.

After a whirlwind of activity, "the system worked." A Republican president and a Democratic Congress, facing a potential crisis, had hammered out an agreement intended to lend stability to the teetering markets. It wasn't easy, it wasn't pretty, yet it demonstrated how two separated institutions could come together to solve problems. Yes, it worked, but only for a time. And a crisis had forced everyone's hand. It wasn't long before cooperation degenerated into open conflict.

The relationship between the president and Congress is at the center of the separation-of-powers system. It can animate or debilitate the governing process, and it is central to understanding the paradoxes of the presidency. For example, one paradox posits that we admire the "above politics," bipartisan approach (that Obama hoped to bring to Washington politics), yet the presidency is perhaps the most political office in the American system (witness Obama and the contentious, party-line passage of health care reform in 2010). Likewise, another paradox reminds us that we want a president who can unify us (as Obama tried to do in the 2008 general election), yet the job requires taking firm stands and making controversial decisions that often divide us (again, Obama's health care reform).

In this chapter we look at our system of separate branches and the conflict between the branches. Later in the chapter, we examine some of the measures Congress has taken in recent decades to try to assert its authority in its continuing struggle with the White House, focusing on foreign policy and confirmation politics for executive and judicial appointments.

SEPARATE INSTITUTIONS SHARING POWERS

The principal designer of the nation's capital, Major Pierre L'Enfant, had more than mere space in mind when he located the president and Congress at opposite ends of Pennsylvania Avenue. Congress, he decided, would be housed atop Jenkins Hill, giving it the high ground. The president would be a little over a mile away, at the end of a long street which would serve as a threadlike link connecting these two separated institutions. Not only did the Constitution separate the executive and legislative branches, but geography would as well.[1]

Yet if the U.S. system is to work, both branches must find ways to bridge the gap and join what is separated. The founders saw the separation of powers not as a weakness but as a source of strength, as a way to ensure deliberation and prevent tyranny. Cooperation between the president and Congress was what the framers required if energetic government was to be achieved. But how was a president to develop the collaboration necessary to make the system of separate institutions sharing power work?

The relationship between president and Congress is the most important one in the American system of government. Only Congress can allocate resources, and presidents who consistently attempt to go around Congress cannot long succeed. A president may not like it, but sustained cooperation with Congress is a necessity. Presidents may act unilaterally in a few areas, but most of the president's goals require a partnership with Congress.

This is no easy matter. As one long-time presidential adviser noted, "I suspect that there may be nothing about the White House less generally understood than the ease with which a Congress can drive a president quite out of his mind and up the wall."[2]

It is common to see the president as the driving force behind new initiatives, relegating Congress to a supporting role. While this is sometimes true, it does a disservice to the rich and complex interactions in presidential-Congressional relations. The president sometimes leads, but often takes up ideas already percolating up in Congress. Lawmaking is a "two-way street,"[3] with the president sometimes influencing Congress and at times Congress influencing the president.

In matters requiring legislative authorization, Congress ultimately has the upper hand. While a president is sometimes seen as leader of the nation, agenda setter, vision builder, and legislator-in-chief, it is Congress that has the final say. And since there are multiple veto points in Congress, any of which may block a president's proposal, the forces wishing to prevent change usually have the advantage. The American system has many roadblocks, yet few avenues for easy change.

People nowadays expect presidents to lead Congress. But public expectations notwithstanding, a president's legislative powers are constitutionally (Article II, Section 3) thin. The Constitution grants Congress "all legislative power," but it also establishes a relationship of mutual dependence and power sharing. The more ambitious a president's agenda, the more dependent that president is on congressional cooperation. Presidents have the veto power, but Congress can override with a two-thirds vote. They can nominate and appoint many officials, but the most important positions require Senate confirmation. They report on the state of the union and, by precedent that has become accepted, they may propose legislation, lobby Congress, help frame the agenda, and build coalitions. Still, presidential powers over Congress generally are limited.

The peculiar paradox is that in a real sense, no one is completely in charge. Responsibility and power are fragmented. This often creates a fascinating blame game with presidents blaming Congress for the nation's ills and Congress blaming the president. In this respect, the United States stands in contrast to parliamentary systems such as that of Great Britain. Rather than having a separation of powers, parliamentary systems have a *fusion* of power. The prime minister is elected from and by the majority party in the Parliament. Prime ministers are responsible to, yet also have power over, the majority party, and are thereby granted more legislative power than a U.S. president possesses. Fusing the executive and legislative powers together creates more power and greater accountability. If things go well or ill, the voters know who is responsible.

The United States is notable among major world powers because it is neither a parliamentary democracy nor a wholly executive-dominated government. Our Constitution invites both Congress and the president to set policy and govern the nation. Leadership and policy change are encouraged only when two, and sometimes all three, branches of government concur on the desirability of new directions.

Often, presidents, and especially their budget directors and secretaries of the treasury, develop "parliament envy," in the sense that they surely wish their proposed budget and tax reform proposals could be sent to Congress and be assured, in most instances, of majority support. But this is clearly not how our separation-of-powers, bicameral system functions.

The Framers' Perspective and Historical Evolution

Constitutional democracy in the United States was designed to be one of both shared powers and division.[4] The framers wanted disagreement as well as cooperation because they assumed that the checks and balances within the government would prevent a president and Congress from "ganging up" against the people's liberties. The framers actually made such disagreements inevitable by providing a president, Senate, and House of Representatives elected by different constituencies and for different lengths of service.

The framers anticipated that the president and Congress would often disagree over policy, for they gave the president veto power over legislation, but gave Congress the power to override that veto. They gave the power to nominate top personnel to the president but gave the Senate power to confirm. They authorized presidents to negotiate treaties but required the Senate's approval by a two-thirds vote before the president could ratify a treaty. The framers also knew from their study of history that heads of government were more prone to going to war than were the people's representatives, so they vested the final authority for war in the legislature.

Congress was established as the dominant and constitutionally most powerful branch of government, and the first few presidents were minimally involved in the legislative process. But the founders' vision soon gave way to political reality, and slowly presidents began to pull power into the White House. Congress was often a willing participant in giving additional power to the presidency. The rise of the legislative presidency did not follow a clear, unobstructed path. Some of the more ambitious chief executives, such as Jefferson, used the newly forming political parties to exert influence in Congress. Others, such as Jackson, exploited popular opinion to gain influence. Still others, such as Lincoln and FDR, gained additional powers during crisis.

Sprinkled among these power-aggrandizing presidents were less assertive or weaker chief executives. Thus, an institutional ebb and flow characterizes power relations between the president and Congress. Over time, however, this tug of war has moved toward a stronger president in the legislative arena. Still, Congress has a way of frustrating even the most skilled of presidents, especially when there is divided government, with the control of the presidency and Congress in the hands of vying political parties.

While the popular expectation is that the president is a "chief legislator" who "guides Congress in much of its lawmaking activity,"[5] reality is often different. The decentralized nature of power in Congress, the multiple access and veto points within the congressional process, the loosely organized party system, the independent and entrepreneurial mode of legislators, and the weakness of legislative leadership all conspire against presidential direction and leadership. This means that presidents often influence Congress only "at the margins" and are more "facilitators" than leaders.[6] But the theory upon which the U.S. government is based assumes a reasonable amount of cooperation between the two branches. As Supreme Court Associate Justice Robert Jackson wrote in 1952, "while the Constitution diffuses power the better to secure liberty, it also contemplates that practice will integrate the dispersed powers into a workable government."[7]

Challenges of Shared Power with Divided Government

For recent presidents, the politics of shared power has often been stormy, as Bill Clinton's health care proposal, George W. Bush's social security reform attempts, and Obama's immigration reform efforts illustrate. (All failed; Obama tried to institute immigration reform unilaterally, but his actions were stalled in the courts.) The politics of shared powers is characterized by changing patterns of cooperation and conflict depending on the partisan and ideological makeup of Congress, the popularity and skills of a president, the strength of the political parties, and various events that shape the politics of the times. As we will discuss, the politics of shared powers in an era of divided government can be described aptly as the politics of Congress's varying success in asserting itself in response to presidential initiatives and leadership.[8]

Today, divided government has become the rule rather than the exception. Since 1952 there has been a split in partisan control of the presidency and Congress for about two-thirds of the time. And while even in eras of divided government, presidents and congresses sometime find ways to work together, in recent years *partisanship* has morphed into *hyper-partisanship* (see Table 6.1). Earlier key legislation was grounded in semi-partisan crossover voting. But in recent years, major legislation was almost exclusively passed along party lines, with virtually no Republicans crossing over to support Obama.

Even with divided control of the presidency and Congress (see Table 6.2), the two institutions must and do find ways to work together. Divided government, while sometimes leading to gridlock, may also lead to more moderate policies, an increased likelihood of executive-congressional negotiations and bargaining, and it may also keep the executive in check. At the same time, the opposition party in Congress often mounts its own programs. It will, when possible, defeat a president's policy initiative and substitute its own. This effort becomes all the

Table 6.1 The End of Bipartisanship[1]

REPUBLICANS WHO VOTED FOR . . .			
		HOUSE	SENATE
2010	Financial regulations	0	3
2010	Health care reform	0	0
2009	Economic stimulus	0	3
1965	Medicare	70	13
1965	Voting Rights Act	111	30
1964	Civil Rights Act	136	27
1935	Social Security	81	16
DEMOCRATS WHO VOTED FOR . . .			
		HOUSE	SENATE
2001	No Child Left Behind	197	43
2001	Bush tax cuts	28	12
1981	Reagan tax cuts	47	37

[1]Adapted from Bill Schneider, "Republican Revival?," *Inside Politics* Issue 5 (June 2010).

more troublesome, of course, for a president when Congress is controlled by the opposition party.

Note the contrast between the 111th Congress (2009–2011), in which the Democrats controlled the White House and both Houses of Congress, and the 112th Congress (2011–2013), in which the Republicans controlled the House of Representatives. The 111th was an especially activist Congress, passing a wide range of bills, including the president's $787 billion stimulus package, major health care reform, and the Dodd–Frank law (Wall Street banking regulation), approving a nuclear arms treaty with Russia, repealing "Don't Ask, Don't Tell," passing a tax bill compromise and food safety regulations, approving two Supreme Court nominees and new credit card consumer protections, extending homebuyer credits and student aid programs, extending the Patriot Act, and more. It was a truly impressive volume of activity.

However, after the Democrats got trounced in the 2010 midterm elections, losing sixty-three seats (and control) in the House, and six in the Senate, the Republicans flexed their new-found political muscle and blocked virtually all of the president's agenda. In this case, divided government meant divisive government and led to a mostly deadlocked government.

In addition to outspending Democrats heavily, Republicans were also aided by the rise of conservatives and libertarian Tea-Party activists who bolstered the ranks of the Republican Party. Intensely anti-Obama, these activists put pressure on party leaders to oppose virtually all of President Obama's legislative proposals in 2011 and 2012. The result? It was one of the least productive congresses in modern history, and Obama's second two years were a mirror opposite of his first two years.

Obama did win re-election in 2012, but this did not bring an improvement in legislative productivity. In fact, 2013 brought a government shutdown for the first time in nearly two decades (over the implementation of health care reform, or "Obamacare") and sequestration (mandatory cuts) of federal spending due to the failure to reach a budget agreement. The 113th Congress was one of the least productive in modern American politics (just slightly more so than the 112th), and it culminated with the president's party losing control of the Senate in the 2014 midterm elections.

Consequently, President Obama started his presidency with unified government and ended with divided government. Many of his second-term initiatives, such as gun control legislation and immigration reform, stalled in Congress or the courts. For example, Obama announced in late 2014 that illegal immigrant parents of American children would receive temporary work permits and a reprieve from deportation proceedings, but several states filed a lawsuit, and a deadlocked Supreme Court (with only eight justices after the death of Antonin Scalia) blocked the plan in 2016. Whether the Trump administration will achieve more results with Congress under unified government, with Republican majorities in the 115th Congress of 241-194 in the House and 52-48 in the Senate, remains to be seen.

Table 6.2 The Growth of Divided Government, 1928–2016

ELECTION YEAR	PRESIDENT	HOUSE OF REPRESENTATIVES	SENATE	DIVIDED/ UNIFIED
1928	R (Hoover)	R	R	u
1930	R (Hoover)	D	R	u
1932	D (Roosevelt)	D	D	u
1934	D (Roosevelt)	D	D	u
1936	D (Roosevelt)	D	D	u
1938	D (Roosevelt)	D	D	u
1940	D (Roosevelt)	D	D	u
1942	D (Roosevelt)	D	D	u
1944	D (Roosevelt)	D	D	u
1946	D (Truman)	R	R	d
1948	D (Truman)	D	D	d
1950	D (Truman)	D	D	d
1952	R (Eisenhower)	R	R	u
1954	R (Eisenhower)	D	D	d
1956	R (Eisenhower)	D	D	d
1958	R (Eisenhower)	D	D	d
1960	D (Kennedy)	D	D	u
1962	D (Kennedy)	D	D	u
1964	D (Johnson)	D	D	u
1966	D (Johnson)	D	D	u
1968	R (Nixon)	D	D	d
1970	R (Nixon)	D	D	d
1972	R (Nixon)	D	D	d
1974	R (Ford)	D	D	d
1976	D (Carter)	D	D	u
1978	D (Carter)	D	D	u
1980	R (Reagan)	D	R	d
1982	R (Reagan)	D	R	d
1984	R (Reagan)	D	R	d
1986	R (Reagan)	D	D	d
1988	R (G. H. W. Bush)	D	D	d
1990	R (G. H. W. Bush)	D	D	d
1992	D (Clinton)	D	D	u
1994	D (Clinton)	R	R	d
1996	D (Clinton)	R	R	d
1998	D (Clinton)	R	R	d

ELECTION YEAR	PRESIDENT	HOUSE OF REPRESENTATIVES	SENATE	DIVIDED/ UNIFIED
2000	R (G. W. Bush)	R	D*	d
2002	R (G. W. Bush)	R	R	u
2004	R (G. W. Bush)	R	R	u
2006	R (G. W. Bush)	D	D	d
2008	D (Barack Obama)	D	D	u
2010	D (Barack Obama)	R	D	d
2012	D (Barack Obama)	R	D	d
2014	D (Barack Obama)	R	R	d
2016	R (Donald Trump)	R	R	u

SOURCE: Harold W. Stanley and Richard G. Niemi, *Vital Statistics on American Politics*, 2001–2002 (Washington, D.C.: CQ Press, 2001). Updated by authors.

*Democrats gained control of the Senate after Vermont senator James Jeffords switched from Republican to Independent (voting with the Democrats) in May of 2001, breaking the 50-50 tie left by the 2000 election.

THE PRESIDENT IN THE LEGISLATIVE ARENA

Members of Congress quickly take the measure of a new president. Will the president stand firm? Will the president bend? Will the new president work with us or act independently of Congress? Will the president be highly partisan or bipartisan? Will the president be able to intimidate us, or can we lead the White House? Who will set the tone?

While the separation of powers and divided government are obstacles, they are not insurmountable barriers to cooperation. Presidents and Congress can legislate when the leaders of both institutions engage in bargaining and compromise.

Ever since the publication of Richard Neustadt's *Presidential Power* in 1960, presidency scholars have argued about just how much influence a president can exert over Congress. As discussed in Chapter 4, Neustadt famously portrays presidents as lacking the power to command Congress to pass their preferred legislation because ours is a system with separated institutions sharing power. Consequently, presidents are compelled to persuade, bargain, and negotiate.

In attempting to persuade Congress, presidents can employ an *inside* or *outside* strategy. The inside strategy—going Washington—calls for a president to bargain, make deals, compromise, and engage in coalition-building. Such face-to-face lobbying, some argue, yields benefits as presidents and members of Congress find some common ground, and presidents cajole, coax, or pressure Congress to act. The outside strategy—going public—argues that the president influences Congress first by going over the heads of Congress and making direct appeals to the public.[9] Presidents lobby the people; then, armed with popular support, they lobby Congress from a stronger political position.

Is there empirical support for the going-public approach to leadership? Certainly, presidents act as if this approach yields results—that is, they repeatedly do go public. Yet, rarely are their efforts are rewarded. George Edwards argues that such efforts are largely a waste of time, and may even be counterproductive.[10] Edwards suggests that presidents usually get more mileage by "staying private." While Edwards makes a powerful case, other scholars see presidents—at times and under certain conditions—successfully employing a going-public strategy. These studies assert that the bully pulpit can be employed as an agenda setter, and that if properly utilized the public strategy pays dividends.[11]

The reality is that presidents have to employ creatively both inside and outside strategies. They have to work tirelessly on what might be called the Washington, D.C., "ground game" of building alliances and coalitions among congressional and interest-group constituencies. Yet every effective president also has learned to speak to national and even international audiences to promote their policy priorities.

Under what conditions are presidents likely to establish their agendas and get congressional support? When is the Congress most likely to follow a president's lead? And when is it likely that a president will follow the lead of Congress?

While there is no magic key to unlocking the door to cooperation, a number of factors lend themselves to presidential success when dealing with Congress. First, in crisis situations, presidents are accorded additional deference, and Congress usually supports the president. Second, if presidents have a clear electoral mandate (when the campaign was issue oriented, a president won by a significant margin, and the president's party has a majority in Congress), then Congress may follow. Third, presidents may exert pressure on members of Congress if they won election by a landslide and ran ahead of members in their own districts (this is usually referred to as "presidential coattails").

Fourth, presidential popularity is a source of power over Congress. But social scientists disagree about how readily presidents may translate popularity into power. Fifth, skill can make a difference, but again, the degree of difference is difficult to identify. Skills such as agenda setting, knowledge of the legislative process, appreciation of timing, bargaining, persuasion, and public mobilization all can be used to advance the president's goals.

Partisan support in Congress is the sixth (and many believe the most important) major factor shaping presidential success with Congress. Parties sometimes serve as a bridge linking the institutional divide between the president and Congress. Lyndon Johnson had such a large majority of party members in Congress (especially in 1965–1966) that even if several dozen Democrats abandoned the president, he could still get his majority in Congress. In the past two decades, though, the two political parties have become more ideologically polarized. This, plus the persistence of divided government, has made bargaining and compromise more necessary *and* more difficult. It has also contributed to the decline of civility in politics.

President Lyndon B. Johnson's political skill was instrumental in enacting monumental legislation such as the Civil Rights Act of 1964. Cecil Stoughton, White House Press Office (WHPO).

Linked to this decline are the seventh and eighth factors that shape presidential success or failure in Congress: the nature of the opposition in Congress and the nature of consultation between the two branches. The opposition's number of votes, ideological commitment, and cohesiveness all affect its willingness to work with the White House. Additionally, presidents soon learn that they must consult not only with the president's own partisans but with the opposition as well. Attempting to gain cooperation and agreement is the first step. A president also needs an effective legislative liaison office that listens and works closely with the leadership on Capitol Hill. Then, too, a president needs to appreciate the policy values and political needs of members of Congress. Presidents sometimes need to follow as well as lead, especially when better ideas may be found in Congress.[12]

Finally, the size and type of agenda a president pursues needs to match the opportunities and constraints of the political environment. An ambitious agenda is difficult to pass even in good times; in tough times, tough choices may turn into impossible choices.[13]

Congress can, of course, play a major role in setting and sometimes shaping the national public policy agenda. It may be difficult for a plural institution to lead, yet Congress sometimes acts as a leadership and law-making as well as a representative institution. This happens when a party enjoys strong majorities in both chambers, when a president is vulnerable, such as at the end of a term, or

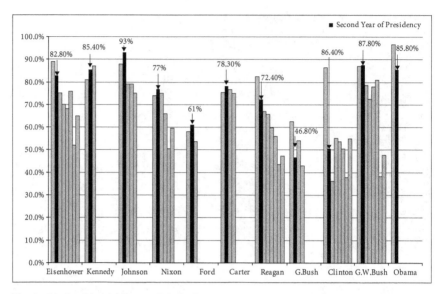

Figure 6.2 Presidential Success Rate in Congress.
SOURCE: Created by the authors using data from *CQ Weekly*.

is politically wounded (as Nixon was in 1973 and 1974), and when Congress has strong leaders, as when Sam Rayburn and Lyndon Johnson exercised impressive leadership toward the end of the Eisenhower presidency (see Figure 6.2).

But the central question here is whether a president can lead Congress. The answer remains: Yes, yet not often, and not usually for long. A mix of skill, circumstances, luck, popularity, party support, timing, and political capital needs to converge if effective collaboration of these two highly political branches is to occur.

The Presidential Veto

While leading Congress requires political skill, a president constitutionally can veto a bill by returning it, together with specific objections, to the house in which it originated. Congress, by a two-thirds vote in each chamber, may override the president's veto. Another variation of the veto is known as the pocket veto. In the ordinary course of events, if the president does not sign or veto a bill within ten weekdays after receiving it, it becomes law without the chief executive's signature. But if Congress adjourns within the ten days, the president, by taking no action, can kill the bill.

The President's veto strength lies in the usual failure of Congress to get a two-thirds majority of both houses. Historically Congress has overridden less than 7 percent of presidents' vetoes. Yet a Congress that could repeatedly mobilize a two-thirds majority against a president can almost take command of the government. This is a rare situation, yet such was the fate of Andrew Johnson in the 1860s.[14]

Presidents can also use the veto power in a positive way. They can threaten that bills under consideration by Congress will be turned back unless certain changes are made. They can use the threat of vetoes against some bills Congress wants badly in exchange for other bills that the president may want. A presidential veto can also protect a national minority from hasty, unfair legislation passed in the heat of the moment. But the veto is essentially a negative weapon of limited use to a president who is pressing for action.

In short, there is little Congress can do when confronted with a veto. It must either get enough votes to override the veto or modify the legislation and try again. Presidents are able to make the vast majority of their regular vetoes stick.[15] Proponents of a stronger presidency support what is called the "item veto," which would allow presidents to reject specific appropriations items in a bill but still sign the legislation. There is considerable support for this reform, and we discuss it in the concluding chapter.

While the veto power is important for presidents, they also must develop political resources to turn their policy agendas into programs. To do so, political parties can be instrumental.

Parties and Presidents: An Awkward Alliance

As discussed earlier, the Constitution deliberately created a separate legislative branch and a separate executive. Yet making our Madisonian system of separate powers work effectively requires some help to encourage meaningful cooperation between the branches. One of the devices that often serves this intermediary function is the American political party.

A political party at its best brings like-minded people together, that is, people who share similar policy perspectives. Thus members of Congress and a president

Barack Obama won the White House in 2008 with a compelling campaign message of changing the political process, but doing so in practice proved difficult. Photo by Tim Bekaert.

who are members of a common party not only can talk more easily across the branches, but can devise collaborative mechanisms to produce agreed-on legislation, treaties, budgets, and similar political decisions. One of the paradoxes of the president–party relationship is that while the party can be one of the useful tools of presidential leadership, it is less developed and less appreciated than should be the case.

It is often said that presidents are leaders of their political parties. In fact, however, a president has no formal position in the party structure. In theory, the supreme authority in our parties is the national presidential convention. More directly in charge of the national party, at least on paper, is the national committee (and each committee has a national chairperson). In practice, successful presidents control their national committees and, often, their national conventions as well. Although the national committee picks the party chair, nowadays presidents almost always inform the committee whom they want.

Political parties once were a defining source of influence for a president. It used to be said, for example, that our most effective presidents were effective in large part because they had made use of party support and took seriously their party leadership responsibilities. Today, the presidential–party relationship is more strained. President and party need each other, yet their sometimes competing interests, and sources of public support, create friction that can impede policy making.

Our earliest presidents vigorously opposed the development of political parties. They viewed them as factions and divisive—something to be dreaded as a political evil. The Constitution makes no mention of political parties. In his Farewell Address of 1796, George Washington warned against the "spirit of party generally" and said that the nascent parties were "the curse of the country." But if the inventors of the presidency bemoaned the emergence of parties, they soon came to accept them as inevitable, and many even attempted to use parties to their advantage.

Historically, political parties have enabled officeholders to overcome some of the limitations of our formal constitutional arrangements. Political parties facilitate coordination among the separated branches. President Andrew Jackson especially used his resources to promote partisan control of government, and his achievements as party leader transformed the office. With Jackson, the president became both the head of the executive branch and the leader of the party.

The first six presidents usually acted in a manner that accorded Congress an equality of power. However, starting with Andrew Jackson, presidents began more and more to assert their role not simply as head of the executive branch but as leader of the government. By skillfully using their position as head of their party, presidents persuaded Congress to follow their lead, thereby allowing them to assume greater control of the government and to direct and dominate public affairs.[16]

Many scholars believe that the effective presidents have been those who, like Jackson, strengthened their position by becoming strong party leaders. Cooperation and progress can be achieved through party alliances. Yet few presidents have been able to duplicate Jackson's success. Most have found it exceedingly difficult to serve as an activist party builder and party leader while trying to serve also as chief of state and national unifier. President William Howard Taft lamented that the longer he was president, "the less of a party man I seem to become."[17] President William McKinley said he could no longer be president of a party, for "I am now President of the whole people."[18]

Once in office, presidents often bend over backward in an attempt to minimize the partisan appearance of their actions. This is in part because the public yearns for non-partisan White House governance, for a president who is above politics. We, the public, don't want presidents to act with their eyes on the next election. And we don't want them to favor any particular group or party.

Herein lies another of the enduring paradoxes of the presidency. On the one hand, presidents are expected to be neutral public servants, avoiding political and party considerations. On the other hand, they are supposed to work closely with party leaders. Also, they must build political coalitions and drum up support, especially party support, for what they believe needs to be done.

To take the president out of partisan politics, however, is to assume incorrectly that the president will be so generally right and the leaders and rank and file of their party so generally wrong that the president must be protected from the push and shove of political pressures. But what president has always been right? Having a president constrained and informed by party platforms and party leaders is what was intended when our party system was developed.

Presidents and Use of Party Appeal in Congress

Presidential control of party support in Congress varies a lot, in part on whether a president enjoys large working party majorities in Congress, in part due to whether the president enjoys high popularity, and in part on what time it is in a presidential term. Presidential coattails, once thought to be a significant factor in helping elect members of a president's party to Congress, have had little effect in recent years. Members usually get reelected because of the partisan makeup of their districts and the fact that they can take advantage of incumbency or that they have a large war chest of campaign money, not on whether they have worked cooperatively with the White House. Congressional races are less affected by national issues or national trends. Time and again, presidents have found in midterm congressional elections, as was the case in 2006 and 2014, that they can do little to help members of their own party who are in trouble.

Presidential attempts to unseat or purge disloyal members of Congress in the president's party have not worked. Roosevelt's celebrated "purge" of non-supportive Democrats in the congressional elections of 1938 was mainly in vain. Anti–New Deal Democrats won reelection or election for the first time in most of the places where he tried to wield his influence.

Presidents today have little retaliatory leverage to apply against uncooperative legislators. Members of Congress, as a result of various congressional reforms, have more and more resources (trips home, large staffs, more research facilities, more home offices and staffs in their districts) to help win reelection. With the dramatic growth of government programs and governmental regulation, members of Congress are in a good position to make themselves seem indispensable to local officials and local business people, who need to have a Washington "friend" to cut through the red tape and expedite government contracts or short-circuit some federal regulation. These kinds of developments have enhanced reelection chances for most members while at the same time making them less dependent on the White House and less fearful of any penalty for ignoring presidential party appeals.

A president's appeal to fellow party members in Congress is effective only some of the time. President George W. Bush won strong Republican congressional support for his Iraq war policies yet failed to win support for his "reform" initiatives on social security and immigration policies. And a fair number of Republicans wound up actively opposing Bush on such issues as torture, stem cell research, and some of his economic "bailout" initiatives.

Party caucuses may be stronger in Congress, yet legislators know that neither the White House nor fellow members in Congress will penalize them if they can claim that "district necessities" forced them to differ with the party on a certain vote—even a key vote. Presidents doubtless will contrive to encourage party cohesion, but just as clearly, party support will vary with the kinds of measures for which the president is requesting approval.

EXECUTIVE-LEGISLATIVE POLICY MAKING: FOREIGN AFFAIRS AND CONFIRMATION POLITICS

Two areas where the president and Congress constitutionally are required to cooperate are foreign policy and federal appointments in the executive branch and the courts. In foreign policy, Congress has to declare war (though this has not happened since World War II, despite numerous extended military conflicts since then) and approve spending, but the president is commander-in-chief of the armed forces and the chief representative of the United States abroad. The president also must negotiate treaties, which require two-thirds Senate approval. All federal executive and judicial nominations additionally come from the White House and require majority Senate approval. Presidents generally have broad executive discretion in foreign affairs, but they face more challenges with getting the Senate to approve their nominees.

Foreign Affairs

Although foreign affairs in the eighteenth century were generally thought to be an executive matter, the framers did not want the president to be the only or even the dominant agent. Various powers vested in Congress by the Constitution were explicitly designed to bring the national legislature into the making of foreign and military policy. Indeed, a good part of the Constitution was written to deprive the executive of control over foreign policy and foreign relations, which under the English system were so dramatically vested in the king.

Thus the framers gave Congress as a whole the sole power to declare war, and they plainly intended the Senate to serve as a partner in the shaping and making of foreign policy. Constitutional scholar Leonard W. Levy goes even further: "The framers meant, at the most, that the president should be a joint participant in the field of foreign affairs, but not an equal one."[19]

But as the United States's world leadership role has increased, particularly after World War II, so have the president's foreign policy role and power. As foreign-policy successes from the 1940s to the present indicate—from the Marshall Plan and Truman Doctrine to the Camp David Accords and the first Iraq War—when presidents involve Congress and the people in shaping new foreign policies, those policies generally win legitimacy and work.

During war or crisis, presidential leadership matters, and a president's choices can have significant consequences. In normal times, presidents face an array of constraints that usually force them to bargain, compromise, settle for less, and make deals. In times of crisis, those constraints often, though not always, are removed. Thus, while presidential leadership is always important, it is most consequential—for good or ill—in time of crisis.

Presidential War-Making Powers Before 1974

No matter what the circumstances, most people expect Congress to fully exercise the system of constitutional checks to rein in the president, and vice versa. The Constitution delegates to Congress the authority to declare the legal state of war (with the consent of the president), but in practice the commander-in-chief often starts the fighting or initiates actions that lead to war. This power has been used by the chief executive time and again.

In 1846, James K. Polk ordered American forces to advance into disputed territory. When Mexico resisted, Polk informed Congress that war existed by act of Mexico, and a formal declaration of war was soon forthcoming. William McKinley's dispatch of a battleship to Havana harbor, where it blew up, helped precipitate war with Spain in 1898. The United States was not formally at war with Germany until late 1941, but prior to the Japanese attack on Pearl Harbor, Franklin Roosevelt ordered the navy to guard convoys to Great Britain and to open fire on submarines threatening the convoys. Since World War II presidents have sent military forces without specific congressional authorization to Korea, Berlin, Vietnam, Lebanon, Grenada, Cuba, Libya, Panama, Kuwait, Haiti, and Syria—in short, around the world.

From George Washington's time until today, the president, by ordering troops into battle, has often decided when Americans will fight and when they will not. When the cause has had political support, the president's use of this authority has been approved. Abraham Lincoln called up troops, spent money, set up a blockage, and fought the first few months of the Civil War without even calling Congress into session.

Congress was angered when it learned (several years after the fact) that in 1964 President Johnson won approval of his Vietnam initiatives on the basis of misleading information (similar to public and congressional anger that the Iraq War began in 2003 on the basis of misleading information as well as a lack of detailed post-invasion planning). Under Nixon in 1969 and 1970 a secret air war was waged in Cambodia with no formal congressional knowledge or authorization. The military also operated in Laos under Nixon without formally notifying Congress. It was to prevent just such acts as these that the framers of the Constitution had given Congress the power to declare war; and many members of Congress believed that what happened in Indochina in the 1960s and 1970s was the result of the White House's bypassing the constitutional requirements. They also agree, however, that the presidential excesses came about because Congress either agreed too readily with presidents or did little to stop them.

In the early 1970s, the Vietnam War was finally winding down, but not without leaving the nation reeling from the protests, civil unrest, and loss of lives associated with that unpopular and largely unsuccessful war. The nation's grief and outrage were fueled, too, by revelations that both Johnson and Nixon had misled Congress and acted in some instances without congressional approval in making and conducting the war. These disconcerting events were compounded by the Watergate scandals and the growing realization that a president of the United States had acted to obstruct justice. These developments led Arthur M. Schlesinger, Jr., a historian and former adviser to John F. Kennedy, to write *The Imperial Presidency*, charging that presidential powers were so abused and expanded by 1972 that they threatened our constitutional democracy.[20]

Schlesinger and other proponents of the "imperial presidency" view contend that the problem stems in part from ambiguity concerning the president's power as commander-in-chief; it is a vaguely defined office, not a series of specific functions. Schlesinger and others acknowledged that Johnson and Nixon did not create the imperial presidency; they merely built on some of the questionable practices of their predecessors. But some observers contend that there is a distinction between the abuse and the usurpation of power. Abraham Lincoln, Franklin Roosevelt, and Harry Truman temporarily usurped power in wartime. Johnson and Nixon abused power, deceiving Congress, misusing the Central Intelligence Agency, and manipulating public opinion and the electoral process.

The end of the Vietnam War, the 1974 impeachment hearings, and the resignation of President Nixon gave Congress new life. It set about to recover its lost authority and discover new ways to participate more fully in making national policy. We now examine Congress's more notable efforts to reassert itself.

The Continuing Debate over War Powers

The dispute over war powers arises because of some seemingly contradictory passages in the Constitution, which state that Congress has the power to declare war, and that the executive power shall be vested in the president, and that the president shall be the commander-in-chief of the army and navy.

During hostilities, especially if the military action is not an all-out war with the nation's vital interests clearly at stake, such as World War II, the country and

Congress typically rally behind a president. As casualties mount and fighting continues, support usually falls off. In both Korea and Vietnam, presidential failure to end the use of American ground forces led to increased political trouble.

There are several reasons why no formal congressional declaration of war has been issued since 1941. During a state of war, the president assumes certain legal prerogatives that Congress might not always be willing to grant. There are also international legal consequences of a formal declaration of war regarding foreign assets, the rights of neutrals, and so on, which our allies would not always be willing to recognize and which would be difficult to insist upon. Moreover, there is the psychological consequence of declaring war, compounded by the fact that, according to Article II, Section 2, of the United Nations Charter, war is illegal except in self-defense.

As discussed briefly in Chapter 5, in 1973 Congress overrode Richard Nixon's presidential veto and enacted the War Powers Resolution, which declared that henceforth the president can commit the armed forces of the United States only:

1. after a declaration of war by Congress
2. by specific statutory authorization from Congress; or
3. in a national emergency created by an attack on the United States or its armed forces.

After committing the armed forces under the third circumstance, the president is required to report to Congress within 48 hours. Unless Congress declares war, the troop commitment must be ended within sixty days. The president may have another thirty days to bring U.S. military forces home if their safety requires their continued use. A president is also obligated by this resolution to consult Congress "in every possible instance" before committing troops to battle.

Moreover, at any time, by concurrent resolution not subject to presidential veto, Congress may direct the president to disengage such troops. A concurrent resolution is passed when both chambers of Congress wish to express the "sense" of their body on some question. Both houses must pass it in the same form. These resolutions are not sent to the president and do not have the force of law. Because of a 1983 court ruling, the question of whether Congress can remove the troops by concurrent resolution or legislative veto is now in doubt.

Few people were satisfied with the War Powers Resolution of 1973. Nixon vetoed it because he said it encroached on presidential powers. Purists in Congress and elsewhere said it was clearly unconstitutional, yet cited reasons different from Nixon's. They said it gives away a constitutional power plainly belonging to Congress, namely, the war-making or war-declaring power, for up to 90 days.

All recent presidents have opposed the War Powers Resolution as unwise and overly restrictive. They claim it gives Congress the right to force them to do what the Constitution says they do not have to do: withdraw American forces at some arbitrary moment. The War Powers Resolution has not really been tested in the courts because it raises political questions which judges generally seek to avoid. And while Presidents typically avoid direct conflict with Congress over sending U.S. troops abroad, decision-making leadership still comes from the White House.

George H. W. Bush secured a UN Security Council resolution in November 1990 to authorize the use of force to repel Iraq's invasion of Kuwait, and then won a congressional joint resolution authorizing the use of military force just days before the Persian Gulf War began. Bill Clinton sent U.S. troops to Somalia, Haiti, and, under NATO auspices, to Bosnia, and in each case American soldiers were placed in danger of attack by adversaries. But President Clinton acted on his own, without direct congressional authorization, although Congress rather grudgingly did pass both supportive and restricting resolutions with respect to Clinton's sending troops on a Bosnian peacekeeping mission.

In the early months of the War on Terror, in 2001 and 2002, President George W. Bush acted unilaterally in a number of areas, including the arrest, without recourse to legal counsel, of U.S. citizens. In response to judicial rulings, Congress passed legislating detailing the extent and limits of executive authority over detention and treatment of suspected terrorists. Further, Bush was able to prosecute the war in Afghanistan with little congressional oversight, and he secured both congressional and UN Security Council resolutions authorizing action against Iraq if it refused to comply with weapons inspections. Despite strong disagreement over whether the UN resolution authorized military action, the Bush administration moved forward with the Iraq invasion in the spring of 2003, claiming that the two resolutions provided sufficient authorization. Furthermore, the administration's 2002 National Security Strategy asserted the right to engage in a preemptive strike against presumed threats. Such claims, rather than reviving accusations of an imperial presidency, were mostly ignored in Congress.

Candidate Obama criticized the Bush administration for claims of independent authority to launch military attacks. Yet as president, Obama did not consult seriously with Congress, nor did he seek supporting legislation or start the clock on the sixty-day War Powers Resolution for the 2011 bombing of Libya. Citing a United Nations Security Council resolution as authorization (which has no binding legal authority in the United States), the president argued that the military mission had a clear, narrow focus: saving lives. In June 2011, the administration released a report stating that U.S. air strikes did not "involve sustained fighting" or U.S. ground troops, and therefore, the War Powers Resolution did not apply.[21]

Backlash to Obama's bombing in Libya led to an odd coalition of House Democrats and Republicans bringing the legitimacy of the president's actions to a vote. On June 24, the House voted 295–123, with seventy Democrats voting with the majority, refusing to sanction the Libyan bombing missions. Shortly thereafter, the House voted 238–180 *not* to cut out funding for the mission. It was a stunning rebuke of a commander-in-chief in the middle of a military action. And while it was a largely symbolic act—had they truly been serious they would have cut funding—it did send a powerful message. Was this an empty gesture or a serious warning shot?

In 1999 a Republican-led House had voted against President Clinton's use of U.S. forces in Kosovo. Again, however, while refusing to authorize the military mission, they did not cut off funding. Fourteen years later, Congress refused to authorize military action and the president did not send troops abroad: In the summer of 2013, President Obama said he would not conduct military strikes against Syria for using chemical weapons against rebels unless Congress endorsed such action, even though he had pledged a year earlier that use of chemical weapons would not be tolerated. When Congress did not act, neither did the White House, prompting charges that the president had failed to exercise leadership responsibilities.

Such mixed messages send both a partisan and an institutional message. The partisan message is that political opponents may criticize their commander-in-chief as military action is debated, or even in progress. The institutional message is that Congress will, at times, attempt to assert its rights even when confronting a president over acts of war, but will go only so far.

In 2007, the National War Powers Commission, chaired by two former secretaries of state, James A. Baker and Warren Christopher, attempted to revisit the question of war powers in the United States. Their report, issued in 2008, called for the repeal of the War Powers Resolution of 1973, hoping to replace it with a proposed War Powers Consultation Act. A proposed War Powers Consultation Act called for greater consultation between the president and Congress when armed conflict seemed likely, creating a new Joint Congressional Consultation Committee to help streamline the process, and requiring Congress to vote up or down on war within a thirty-day time period. But the proposal was largely ignored.

So what is to be done? Why not scrap the War Powers Resolution and go back to the framers' understanding of the war powers? Congress has the Constitutional authority to declare war. If a president wants to engage American forces in armed conflict he must, unless he is confronting a direct attack on the United States, go to Congress and, in effect, ask for permission. Period.

What are the lessons of the War Powers Resolution of 1973? On the one hand, Congress tried to reassert itself, and tried to get tough about unilateral presidential war making. On the other hand, presidents have mostly ignored the resolution and viewed it as a nuisance. In the 1990s many members of Congress recognized that the 1973 approach was not effective and perhaps not wise. Those who want to strengthen the resolution and force presidents to comply with it to the letter do not have the votes to get their colleagues to confront the White House. Many Republicans would prefer to scrap the resolution altogether, saying it has not worked and it is not proper for Congress to undermine a president who has to act quickly in today's military emergencies, never mind what the Constitution may imply on the matter.

Constitutional and political questions will continue to surround the war-making powers as long as our constitutional democracy survives. The constitutional debate over the precise character of this power continues even as practical accommodations in our constitutional system evolve.[22]

Confirmation Politics

Another area in which executive-legislative cooperation is required constitutionally and has sparked contentious conflict in recent years is the federal confirmation process for executive and judicial nominations. The framers regarded this process and the Senate's advice-and-consent responsibility as an important check on executive power. Alexander Hamilton viewed it as a way for Congress to prevent the appointment of "unfit characters."

Presidents have never enjoyed exclusive control over hiring and firing in the executive branch. The Constitution leaves the question somewhat ambiguous: "The President . . . shall nominate, and by and with the Advice and Consent of the Senate, shall appoint Ambassadors, other public Ministers and Consuls, Judges of the Supreme Court, all other officers of the United States." The Senate jealously guards its right to confirm or reject major appointments. During the period of congressional government after the Civil War, presidents had to struggle to keep their power to appoint and dismiss. Presidents in the twentieth century gained a reasonable amount of control over top appointments.[23]

Today the U.S. Senate and the president often struggle over control of top personnel in the executive and judicial branches. Time spent evaluating and screening presidential nominations has increased. Senators are especially concerned about potential conflicts of interest and about related character and integrity concerns. In the Clinton administration, for example, nominations for attorney general, CIA director, surgeon general, and judgeships and ambassador positions were derailed due to stiff opposition in the Senate. Presidents George W. Bush and Barack Obama faced similar challenges with some nominations. In the early weeks of the Trump presidency, some Cabinet nominations sparked controversy because of questions about potential conflicts of interest or lack of political expertise. Still, with a Republican majority of 52 senators—and 51 votes required for confirmation (without a filibuster possibility for appointments, due to a 2013 rule change by the then-Democratic-led Senate)—confirmation of the president's nominees seemed likely, if Republican senators maintained party unity.

The Senate's role in the confirmation process was never intended to eliminate politics but rather to use politics as a safeguard. Some conservatives in recent years object that the Senate has rejected occasional nominees because of their political beliefs and thus interfered with the executive power of presidents. In such instances, so this complaint goes, the Senate's decision is not a reflection of the fitness of a nominee but rather of the political strength of the president.

Because of a tradition called senatorial courtesy, a president is unlikely to secure Senate approval for judicial nominations against the objection of the senators from the state where the appointee is to work, especially if these senators see members of the president's party, even if his party does not control the Senate. Thus, for nearly all district court judgeships and many executive appointments, senators can exercise what is in fact a veto. This veto can be overridden only with great difficulty. Further, it is usually exercised in secret and is subject to little accountability. But this form of patronage is sufficiently important to senators that senatorial courtesy is likely to continue.

There is a difference between judicial appointments, especially those to the Supreme Court, and administration appointments. The Senate plays a greater role in judicial appointments because of the life terms judges and justices serve, and because they constitute an independent and vital branch of the government, as we discuss in Chapter 8. The political nature of senior executive appointments in the federal bureaucracy is generally accepted; a president ought to be able to choose top appointees who share the president's views and will follow direction from the White House.

In contrast, a president is not expected to have or to enjoy partisan loyalty from those nominated to the bench. Thus presidents often have more difficulty in winning confirmation for their nominations to the Supreme Court than they have with their cabinet nominations.[24] But even Supreme Court nominations have become polarized in recent years. After Justice Antonin Scalia's unexpected death in early 2016, for example, Majority Leader Mitch McConnell declared that the Republican-controlled Senate would not hold hearings for President Obama's nominee, but instead would wait until after the presidential election—presumably in hopes of having a Republican president make the nomination. Less than two weeks after taking office, President Donald Trump did just that.

Despite the stalemate between the White House and the Senate over the Supreme Court vacancy in 2016, the confirmation provisions in the Constitution have fulfilled most of the intentions of the framers. The Senate has been able to use its power to reject unqualified nominees. It has sometimes also been able to prevent those with conflicts of interest from taking office. In addition, senators have been able to use the confirmation process to make their views known to prospective executive officials. Indeed, the very existence of the confirmation process generally deters presidents from appointing weak, questionable, or "unfit characters." Yet, by and large, presidents have still been able to appoint the people they want to important positions.

THE CONTINUING STRUGGLE

Congress has not won back much of its allegedly lost powers, and most observers are skeptical of Congress's ability to match the president's advantages in setting the nation's long-term policy direction over the long run. Ronald Reagan demonstrated that a popular president who knew what he wanted could influence the national policy agenda and also win considerable cooperation from Congress. George W. Bush and his father demonstrated that a president could win public and congressional support for foreign policy and military initiatives even with Congress controlled by the opposition party.

The American public may be skeptical and critical about its political leaders, yet it has not really lost the belief that presidents matter. Most Americans want presidents to be effective, especially in international and economic leadership. Whether or not people believed in Ronald Reagan's policy priorities, many supported his view that the country needed a strong president who would strengthen the presidency and make the office a more vital center of national policy than it had been in the years immediately following the Watergate scandals. Whether people were critical of Clinton's character or not, Americans generally recognized his leadership efforts to encourage trade, promote new jobs, and advance the cause of civil rights and environmental protection.

A central question during the 1970s was whether, in the wake of a somewhat diminished presidency, Congress could furnish the necessary leadership to govern the country. Most people, including many members of Congress, did not think Congress could play that role. The routine answer in the twenty-first century is that the United States needs a presidency of substantial power if we are to solve the financial trade, deficit, productivity, and other economic and national security problems. We live in a continuous state of severe challenges, if not emergencies. Terrorism or nuclear warfare could destroy our country. Global competition of almost every sort highlights the need for swift leadership and a certain amount of efficiency in government. Many people realize, too, that weakening the presidency may, as often as not, strengthen the vast federal bureaucracy and its influence over how programs are implemented more than it would strengthen Congress.

Congress fundamentally is not structured for sustained leadership and direction. Power in Congress is too fragmented and dispersed, and parochial interests often are privileged over trying to devise coherent long-term policy solutions. Congress can, on occasion, provide leadership on various issues, yet it is far less able to adapt to changing demands and national or international crises that arise than is the presidency. The presidency is a more fluid institution and thereby can usually more quickly adjust and adapt.

From time to time, as we have seen, Congress has tried to reframe itself as a more effective institution, both to check presidents and to serve as a national policy-making branch. Congress performs representational responsibilities well, and it is a place where new ideas can be incubated and championed. It also performs important oversight hearings and investigations. But major national policy decisions and coherent national planning typically come from leadership in the executive branch. Examples include the Manhattan Project, the Marshall Plan, civil rights legislation, cyber-security policy, and so on.[25]

In the twenty-first century, our complicated Madisonian system, the new forces of globalization, and the realities of hyper-partisanship place huge burdens on leaders in both Congress and the presidency. The challenge of working out ways to find common ground and serve the exalted shared aspirations of the American republic is greater than ever before, and ever expected.

FURTHER READINGS

Cameron, Charles M. *Veto Bargaining: Presidents and the Politics of Negative Power*. New York: Cambridge University Press, 2000.

Howell, William G., and Terry M. Moe. *Relic: How Our Constitution Undermines Effective Government—And Why We Need a More Powerful Presidency* (New York: Basic Books, 2016).

Kernell, Samuel. *Going Public: New Strategies of Presidential Leadership*. 4th ed. Washington, D.C.: CQ Press, 2006.

Krehbiel, Keith. *Pivotal Politics: A Theory of U.S. Lawmaking.* Chicago: University of Chicago Press, 1998.

Mann, Thomas E., and Norman J. Ornstein. *It's Even Worse Than It Looks: How the American Constitutional System Collided with the New Politics of Extremism.* New York: Basic Books, 2012.

Mayhew, David. *Divided We Govern.* New Haven, Conn.: Yale University Press, 1991.

Rudalevige, Andrew. *Managing the President's Program: Presidential Leadership and Legislative Policy Formulation.* Princeton, N.J.: Princeton University Press, 2002.

CHAPTER 7

Presidents As Chief Executives

The U.S. Constitution put the president in charge of the day-to-day operation of the federal departments and agencies. Article II, Section I opens with "The executive power shall be vested in a President of the United States of America." The Constitution further gives the president the power to require the opinion of the principal offices in the departments "upon any subject relating to the duties of their respective offices." Presidents are also charged "to take care that the laws be faithfully executed."

Being put in charge, however, is a far cry from making the executive branch work efficiently and effectively. In the beginning, presidents didn't have or didn't need much administrative help. For a while, newly elected President George Washington had just one aide, his nephew, whom Washington paid out of his own pocket. Today a president has a White House staff of 400 to 500, fifteen cabinet secretaries with nearly as many advisers with cabinet status, thousands of Executive Office of the President staffers, and at least four million others scattered in the civilian and military services of the executive branch. There are over two million federal civil servants (not counting the 600,000 in the U.S. Postal Service). There are at least 1.3 million serving in active military duty, with another 800,000 in the military reserve.

But every president learns that, though they may be atop this now sprawling executive branch, they are not always in charge of everything. Hurricanes, oil spills, terrorist attacks, cyberhacking, and emergencies occur without warning. Moreover, some agencies and officials seem to have plans or policies and priorities of their own. President John Kennedy, for example, was inadequately informed about the "Bay of Pigs" CIA operation that imploded on him in his early months at the White House. A few presidents, including Lincoln and Truman, have had to fire military commanders for actions in conflict with White House priorities.

Sometimes presidents lack the skill or experience to manage effectively. Yet inattention to matters of personnel and implementation cause considerable problems. Indeed, many of the mistakes or blunders of recent presidencies can be traced to lack of attention to the administrative responsibilities that are critically important to a successful presidency.

This chapter examines how both the cabinet and an extensive administrative presidency consisting of an Executive Office of the President have developed to help presidents become better managers. We consider both the frustrations presidents face and the various strategies or tools president try to use to influence executive branch performance.

The paradox of the presidency–executive branch relations is that presidents are thought to be atop and "in charge" of the federal bureaucracy, but, in practice, a president sometimes finds bureaucratic resistance, gets in conflict with an occasional cabinet member, and must regularly contend with congressional and interest groups lobbying within federal agencies. Then, too, some civilian and military federal employees have their own ideological or partisan views to the right or the left of a particular White House. Further, federal employees, as we will discuss, sometimes feel more of an allegiance to the Congress or to the law (as they perceive it) than to the wishes of a president or White House aides. In short, presidents have to work hard to lead, inspire, manage, and regularly negotiate with countless members of their own branch of government.

The Executive Office of the President is the institutional home for the White House staff and about two dozen staff agencies established to help presidents coordinate with the cabinet and the operation of the executive branch. (See Table 7.1.)

Let's first examine the complex political history of presidents and their cabinets.

PRESIDENTS AND THE CABINET

The presidential cabinet in America is a misunderstood political institution. This is in part because the cabinet in some parliamentary systems has more influence as a policy-making group. This is not the case in the United States.

The American cabinet is too diverse a group to function effectively as a policy-deciding group. Some cabinet members are appointed as much for their representativeness as for their policy or managerial expertise.

Cabinet members serve mainly as presidential emissaries to a department and as policy advisers to the president singly or as part of a selective team, for example as a member of the national security or economic policy team.[1]

President Jimmy Carter, an engineer and more of a manager than most presidents, acknowledged that he used his cabinet less and less as his four years wore on. "After a few months, the cabinet meetings became less necessary," Carter wrote. "As a result, in the first year we had thirty-six sessions with the full cabinet, then, during the three succeeding years, twenty-three, nine and six such meetings respectively."[2] Presidents have held fewer cabinet meetings the longer they were in office, usually preferring to rely on political advisers whose loyalties are clear.

The framers discussed at length the possibility of creating some form of executive council that would comprise the president, heads of the departments, and the chief justice of the Supreme Court, yet decided to leave things flexible. Indeed,

TABLE 7.1

The Institutional Presidency

President

The Cabinet
State
Treasury
Defense
Justice
Health and Human Services
Labor
Commerce
Transportation
Energy
Housing and Urban Development
Veterans Affairs
Agriculture
Interior
Education
Homeland Security

Others with Cabinet Rank
U.N. Ambassador
CIA Director
Environmental Protection Agency Administrator
Director, Office of Management and Budget
U.S. Trade Representative
Chair, Council of Economic Advisors

White House Staff
Chief of Staff
Press Secretary
Legislative Affairs
Political Affairs
Public Liaison
Communications Director
White House Counsel
Intergovernmental Affairs
Policy Planning and Development
Cabinet Liaison
Domestic and Economic Affairs
Science and Technology Policy
National Security Affairs

Executive Office of the President
Council of Economic Advisers
Office of Management and Budget
Office of National Drug Control Policy
U.S. Trade Representative
Council on Environmental Quality
National Security Council
Domestic Policy Council
National Economic Council
Office of Administration
Office of Science and Technology Policy
President's Foreign Intelligence Advisory Board
Privacy and Civil Liberties Oversight Board
White House Military Office
White House Office of Health Reform

the U.S. Constitution makes no provision for a cabinet. It merely states there are to be principal offices of the executive departments. The first Congress passed statutes that provided for the creation of three departments: State, War and Treasury. An attorney general was also authorized, yet this was a part-time adviser.

From the outset, President George Washington regarded his department heads as assistants and advisers. "He began the practice of assembling his principal officers in council. And this practice became in the course of time a settled custom. The simple truth is, however, that the cabinet is a customary, not a statutory body."[3] The term *cabinet* was probably first used in 1793, but mention of it in statutory language did not occur until 1907.

President Andrew Jackson did not even convene his cabinet as a group during his first two years in office, often relying instead on a "kitchen cabinet" of staffers and newspaper friends. President James Polk held at least 350 cabinet sessions during his four years. But, with the growth in the size of the cabinet, and the expansion of the White House and its advisory units, modern presidents only rarely call their cabinets together for decision-making purposes.

SELECTING CABINET OFFICERS

Few acts of a newly elected president are as important as the appointment of cabinet members and senior advisers. Presidents are thought to have a free hand in choosing their cabinet members, yet this is not exactly the way it works. In addition to administrative competence and experience, loyalty and congeniality are basic considerations in selections. Also, party rivals often have to be placated either with an appointment to the cabinet or selection as the vice presidential running mate.

Regional, ethnic, gender, and geographical considerations are important. Thus, the Agriculture post is traditionally given to a Midwesterner, and the Secretary of the Interior is almost always a Westerner. After capturing the presidency, a president usually goes about selecting the cabinet in such a way as to try to win the confidence of major sections and sectors of the nation.

Each cabinet member of the now fifteen official cabinet departments has to be confirmed by a majority in the U.S. Senate. Nominees are examined carefully at both ends of Pennsylvania Avenue and by interest groups and the media.

Today it has become harder to attract many talented individuals to cabinet-level positions due to the media culture of "gotcha" politics in Washington, D.C.

A president has to select certain cabinet officers because of the needed expertise they will bring to the administration and the policy needs of certain departments. Typically, for example, the secretary of defense is someone who has worked closely with that department in some previous capacity. A treasury secretary is traditionally viewed as, at least in part, the financial community's representative in the cabinet. In selecting a treasury secretary a president-elect usually wants someone who can simultaneously serve as a "spokesperson" to the financial world and as a "spokesperson" for those interests.

Generalists are often appointed to head up some of the domestic departments such as Commerce, Transportation, and HUD, while politicians especially close to clientele groups are often appointed heads of Agriculture, Interior, and Labor.

Cabinet picking invariably entails guesswork. Most presidents become aware after a while that some of their cabinet choices as well as some of their top White House aides were a mistake. Jimmy Carter and George W. Bush both wound up firing at least a handful of their cabinet members. Obama nudged out several aides and at least a few cabinet members.

President Clinton's first labor secretary, Robert B. Reich, shared this view about staffing a new administration:

> No other democracy does it this way. No private corporation would think of operating like this. Every time a new president is elected, America assembles a new government of 3,000 or so amateurs who only sometimes know the policies they're about to administer, rarely have experience managing large government bureaucracies, and almost never know the particular piece of it they're going to run. These people are appointed quickly by a president-elect who is thoroughly exhausted from a year and a half of campaigning. And they remain in office, on average, under two years—barely enough time to find the nearest bathroom. It's a miracle we don't screw it up worse than we do.[4]

THE JOB OF A CABINET MEMBER

Defining the job of a cabinet member depends on one's vantage point. Members of Congress believe a cabinet officer should communicate often and well with Congress and be responsive to legislators' requests. Reporters want a cabinet officer to be accessible, to make news; they applaud style and flair as well as substance. Interest groups want a cabinet member who can speak out for their interests and carry their messages to the White House and Congress. Civil servants in a department are generally looking for a cabinet leader who will boost departmental morale and appropriations. White House aides are concerned about a cabinet officer's loyalty to the president in addition to their ability. Presidents want a cabinet member who will enhance their administration's reputation without embarrassing or overshadowing them.

Presidents and senior White House aides expect cabinet officers and related agency heads to creatively manage their bureaucracies and to be responsive yet not overly responsive to their departments' natural client interest groups. White House staffers are well aware of the "iron triangles" that form enduring issue networks involving outside interest groups, likeminded members of Congress and their staffs, and veteran career federal employees. An example would be the generally strong ties between the Agriculture Committees in Congress, farmers and agri-business interests, and the Secretary of Agriculture. These networks are well known for being able to block presidential priorities or to merely promote their own alternative public policy initiatives. These triangular interests pre-exist every new presidential administration.

Presidents and their aides repeatedly say the last thing they want to see is a cabinet member who has become a special pleader at the White House for some of the special-interest groups. "The cabinet officer must certainly be attentive to his departmental business, and he should seek to ensure that the president has timely notice of the impact of policies on his department's specific interests," a former White House aide writes. "But a Secretary should never choose his departmental interest against the wider interest of the Presidency."[5]

The greatest test of cabinet members arises from the fact that they risk becoming tied almost as closely to Congress as they are to their president. Indeed, cabinet officers are legally obligated to obey Congress and the courts as well as the president—even though the various branches may hold contradictory views. In the perpetual tug-of-war between the branches, the cabinet officer is often like the knot in the rope.

"His or her appointment is subject to Senate confirmation. Every power a cabinet officer exercises is derived from some Act of Congress; every penny he or she expends must be appropriated by the Congress; every new statutory change the cabinet officer desires must be submitted to the Congress and defended there," writes Bradley Patterson. "A cabinet officer's every act is subject to oversight by one or more regular or special congressional committees, much of his or her time is accordingly spent at the Capitol and, with few exceptions, most of the documents in his or her whole department are subject to being produced at congressional request."[6]

When a president makes a decision, a cabinet officer is expected to carry it out. In fact, however, it is inevitable that after a person has been in the cabinet for a time and has become enmeshed in the activities and interests of a department, he or she develops certain independent policy views. A certain hardening of view may set in as the cabinet secretary gets pushed by subordinates, interest-group leaders, or others in a direction that makes it likely that he or she will at least occasionally come into conflict with the president. When this happens, the White House typically complains that the cabinet member has "gone native"—he or she has been captured by the interests native to that department. Often, the cabinet officer wants to extract more money out of the president's budget for the department. A budget director once complained, "Cabinet members are vice presidents in charge of spending, and as such they are the natural enemies of the presidents."[7]

THE WEST WING WANTS LOYALTY ALONG WITH COMPETENCE

Firing cabinet members is the last thing presidents like to do. When it is done, it is usually only after it is "overdue." And they do it at the risk of political backlash. President Andrew Johnson's removal of Secretary of War Edwin Stanton contributed to Johnson's impeachment. President Nixon's removal of special prosecutor Archibald Cox and the related resignations of Attorney General Elliot Richardson and Deputy Attorney General William Ruckelshaus badly damaged what remained of Nixon's credibility. Ronald Reagan fired Secretary of State Alexander Haig, White House Chief of Staff Donald Regan, and Secretary of Health and Human Services Margaret Heckler and encouraged some others, such as Labor Secretary

Raymond Donovan, to resign. George W. Bush asked for Defense Secretary Donald Rumsfeld's resignation as the Iraq War became a political liability.

Nixon fired Interior Secretary Walter Hickel after a celebrated "personal letter" from Hickel to the president was leaked to the press. Hickel was especially frustrated because he only saw the president once or twice for policy discussions. His letter included these pointed sentences: "Permit me to suggest that you consider meeting, on an individual and conversational basis, with members of your cabinet. Perhaps," continued Hickel, "through such conversations we can gain greater insight into the problems confronting us all, and most important, into solutions of these problems."[8] Hickel was soon gone.

From the perspective of the West Wing, the questions asked about cabinet members are: Have they managed the department well? Do they recruit talented officials to the department? Are they loyal to the president? Can they "handle" the interest groups associated with that department? Have they brought prestige to the department and to the administration? Have they come up with fresh and innovative ideas? Have they been able to implement the administration's programs in their department? This is a lot to ask, and it explains why White House–cabinet relations can often lead to so much frustration.

THE ROLE OF THE CABINET IN POLICY MAKING

A romantic view of the mythical American cabinet is encouraged in part by presidents themselves. Reagan, Clinton, and Obama all emphasized the importance of the cabinet when they picked their original teams. Reagan, early in 1981, told his cabinet nominees that he intended the cabinet to function much like a board of directors in a corporation, the president deliberating with them often and offering input before decisions. Trump boasted his cabinet would be the best and have the highest IQ of any cabinet ever.

A consistent pattern seems to characterize president–cabinet relations over time. Just as most presidents enjoy a distinctive honeymoon with the press and partisan officeholders, White House–cabinet ties are usually the most cooperative during the first year of an administration. A newly staffed executive branch, busily recasting the political agenda, seems to bubble over with new possibilities, proposals, ideas, and imminent breakthroughs. Ironically, White House staff, which soon will outstrip most of the cabinet in power and influence, receives somewhat less publicity at this time. In the immediate post-inaugural months, the Washington political community, and the executive branch in particular, becomes a merry-go-round of cheerful open doors for the new team of cabinet leaders.

But this ends soon. After little more than a year in office, Reagan's White House aides developed a distrust for many of their departmental secretaries, saying they had generally become advocates of their own constituencies. "Cabinet government is a myth," said a Reagan staffer. "I'm not sure it has dawned on the [cabinet] members yet that they have been cut out of the decision making process."[9] Obama cabinet and agency heads complained that the president and his staff quickly became isolated and developed a hard-to-penetrate "fortress."

Ambitious, expansionist cabinet officers become painfully familiar with various refrains from executive office staff, usually to the effect that there just isn't any more money available for programs of that magnitude; or that budget projections for the next few years require more spending cuts; and, perhaps harshest of all, that a proposal is excellent but will just have to wait.

After the first year or so, presidents become increasingly concerned with leaks from their administration. They worry about saying things or having key decisions made in large groups. They also believe their time is too precious to waste on many bull sessions among those who have little or nothing to contribute. So what do they do? They begin to hold fewer cabinet meetings and hold smaller sessions with a few cabinet members and with their own White House inner circle.

Why are more spirited and substantive discussions absent from the modern-day cabinet? The number of people attending cabinet sessions is too large. Recent presidents have often had nearly thirty people crowded in their cabinet meetings—this includes the president, vice president, the fifteen regular cabinet members, and a dozen key advisers such as CIA director, UN ambassador, and top budget, economic, and political advisers. Most cabinet members are unlikely to talk about their troubles or highly sensitive topics in a group that large. Thus both presidents and cabinet members become disillusioned with government by cabinet meeting.

One of the president's dilemmas is that a fundamental separation of policy formulation and its implementation often develops. Whereas most major policy decisions are made by the president and a smaller number of personal aides, responsibility for enacting these programs rests, for the most part, with the cabinet officers and their departments. The gap between these two functions of the executive branch has been widening, a result of the transference of power from the somewhat more public institution of the cabinet to the relatively hidden offices of the White House staff.

The very character of the cabinet—a body with no constitutional standing, members with no independent political base of their own and no requirement that the president seek or follow their advice—helps contribute to its lack of influence as a collective body. Ultimately, the influence of the cabinet rests essentially on the role a president desires for it. Recent presidents have made that role a limited one.

Cabinet roles and influence with the White House differ markedly according to personalities, the department, and the times. Each cabinet usually has one or two members who become the dominant personalities. Herbert Hoover's performance as secretary of commerce under Harding and Coolidge was of this type. Robert McNamara enjoyed especially close ties with both Kennedy and Johnson. And James Baker, George Shultz, and Edwin Meese all carried special weight with Ronald Reagan. Secretary of State John Kerry and Secretary of the Treasury Jack Lew served inner cabinet roles for Obama.

Certain departments and their cabinet officers have gained prominence in recent decades because every president has been deeply involved with their priorities and missions—Defense and State in the Cold War as well as in the war on terrorism, for example. Other departments may become important temporarily in the president's eyes, sometimes because of a prominent cabinet secretary who is working in an area in which the president wants to effect breakthroughs: for example, John Kennedy's Justice Department headed by his brother Robert. The Treasury Department has become a central player in exacting economic times, such as the Bush and Obama eras.

Vast differences exist in the scope and importance of cabinet-level departments. The huge Defense Department and the smaller departments of Labor, Housing and Urban Development, and Education are not at all similar. Certain agencies not of cabinet rank—the Central Intelligence Agency and the National Security Agency, for example—may be more important, especially in a post-9/11 and potential cyberwar-era world, than certain cabinet-level departments. Conventional rankings of the departments are based on their longevity, annual expenditures, and number of personnel.

Rankings according to these indicators can be seen in the first three columns of Table 7.2. A quick comparison of these columns reveals unexpected

TABLE 7.2 Ways of Looking at the Traditional Executive Departments

SENIORITY	EXPENDITURES	PERSONNEL	INNER AND OUTER CABINETS
1. State	1. Defense	1. Defense	*Inner:*
2. Treasury	2. Treasury	2. Veterans' Affairs	1. State
3. War/Defense	3. HHS†	3. Homeland Security	2. Defense
4. Interior	4. Agriculture	4. Justice	3. Treasury
5. Justice	5. Veterans' Affairs	5. Treasury	4. Justice*
6. Agriculture	6. Labor	6. Agriculture	*Outer:*
7. Commerce	7. Transportation	7. Interior	5. Agriculture
8. Labor	8. Education	8. HHS†	6. Interior
9. HHS†	9. HUD‡	9. Transportation	7. Transportation
10. HUD‡	10. Energy	10. Commerce	8. HHS†
11. Transportation	11. Homeland Security	11. Labor	9. HUD‡
12. Energy	12. Justice	12. Energy	10. Labor
13. Education	13. Interior	13. State	11. Commerce
14. Veterans' Affairs	14. State	14. HUD‡	12. Energy
15. Homeland Security	15. Commerce	15. Education	13. Education
			14. Veterans' Affairs
			15. Homeland Security

SOURCE: www.white.gov/omb/budget and Statistical Abstract of the United States.

NOTE: Some expenditures, such as for wars, are not easily traced to certain departmental outlays.

*Sometimes inner, sometimes outer: "Inner" and "Outer" cabinet is our classification done according to the counseling-advocacy departments and based on our research interviews.

†HHS: Health and Human Services

‡HUD: Housing and Urban Development

characteristics. Thus, although the State Department is more than 200 years older than some of the newer departments, its expenditures are among the lowest. On the other hand, the much younger Department of Human Services ranks rather high in expenditures.

The contemporary cabinet can be differentiated also into "inner" and "outer" cabinets, as shown in the fourth column in Table 7.2. This classification, derived from interviews, indicates how White House aides and cabinet officers view the departments and their access to the president. The occupants of the inner cabinet generally have maintained a role as counselor to the president; the departments all include broad-ranging, multiple interests. The explicitly domestic policy depart-ments, with the exception of Justice, comprise the outer cabinet. By custom, if not by designation, these cabinet officers assume a relatively straightforward advocacy orientation that overshadows their counseling role.

THE INNER CABINET

A pattern in recent administrations suggests strongly that the inner, or counseling, cabinet positions are vested with high-priority responsibilities that usually bring their occupants into collaborative relationships with presidents and their top staff. Certain White House staff counselors also have been included in the inner cabinet with increasing frequency. The secretary of defense was one of the most prominent cabinet officers during all recent administrations, for each president recognized the centrality of national security issues. The defense budget and the Department of Defense personnel make it imperative for presidents to work closely with de-fense and top military chiefs. Recent treasury secretaries also have played impres-sive roles in presidential deliberations on financial, business, and economic policy.

The inner cabinet, as discussed here, corresponds to George Washington's ori-ginal foursome. The status accorded these cabinet roles is, of course, subject to ebb and flow, for the status is rooted in a cabinet officer's performance and relationship with the president as well as on the crises of the day.

A National Security Cabinet

Military and trade challenges have made it mandatory for recent presidents to maintain close relations with the two national security cabinet heads. Just as George Washington met almost every day with his four cabinet members during the French crisis of 1793, so also all of our recent presidents have been likely to meet at least weekly and be in daily telephone communication with their inner cabinets of national security advisers.

Attorneys General

The Justice Department is often identified as a counseling department, and its chiefs usually are associated with the inner circle of presidential advisers. That Kennedy appointed his brother, Nixon appointed his trusted campaign manager and law partner, Carter appointed a personal friend, and Reagan appointed his personal attorney and later one of his campaign managers to be attorneys general indicates the importance of this position, although extensive politicization of the department has a long history. The Justice Department traditionally serves as the president's attorney and law office, a special obligation that brings about continuous and close relations between White House domestic policy lawyers and Justice Department lawyers. The White House depends on the department's lawyers for counsel on civil-rights developments, presidential veto procedures, tax prosecutions, antitrust controversies, presidential pardons, oversight of regulatory agencies and separation-of-powers questions. Its Office of Legal Counsel has close ties to the White House.

Trump appointed conservative U.S. senator Jeff Sessions from Alabama as his attorney general. Sessions was the first U.S. senator to endorse Trump for president, and he did so because he admired Trump's anti-immigration and protectionist trade policies. Session had sixteen years of experience as a prosecutor and two years of service as Alabama's attorney general.

Treasury Secretary

The secretary of the treasury is a critical presidential adviser on both domestic and international fiscal and monetary policy, but this person also plays somewhat of an advocate's role as an interpreter of the nation's leading financial interests. Treasury has become a department with major institutional authority and responsibility for income and corporate tax administration, currency control, public borrowing, and counseling of the president on such questions as the price of gold and the balance of payments, the federal debt and international trade, development and monetary matters. In addition, the treasury's special clientele of major and central bankers has unusual influence. The treasury secretary is also a pivotal figure in crucial negotiations with Congress on tax and trade matters.

Reagan's second-term treasury secretary, James A. Baker, was regarded as one of the most important individuals in government for several reasons. He had served as Reagan's chief of staff and had the confidence of the president, he enjoyed a reputation for competence, and he was nearly always a central player in policy decisions concerning the dollar, trade and tariff legislation, tax reform, and our economic relations with key allies.

THE OUTER CABINET

The outer cabinet positions deal with strongly organized and more particularistic clientele, an involvement that helps to produce an advocate relationship with the White House. These departments—Health and Human Services, Housing and Urban Development, Labor, Commerce, Interior, Agriculture, Transportation, Energy, Education, and Veterans' Affairs—are considered the outer-cabinet departments. The newer department of homeland security is harder to locate because of its many diverse responsibilities. Because most of the president's controllable expenditures, with the exception of defense, lie in their jurisdictions, they take part in the most intensive and competitive exchanges with the White House and the Office of Management and Budget (OMB).

These departments experience heavy and often conflicting pressures from clientele groups, from congressional interests, and from state and local governments. These pressures sometimes run counter to presidential priorities. Whereas three of the four inner-cabinet departments preside over policies that usually, though often wrongly, are perceived to be largely nonpartisan or bipartisan—national security, foreign policy, and the economy—the domestic departments almost always are subject to intense crossfire between partisan and domestic interest groups.

OUTER-CABINET ISOLATION

As tensions build around whether, or to what extent, domestic policy leadership rests with the departments, with the OMB, or with the White House, and as staff and line distinctions become blurred, the estrangement between the domestic department heads and the White House staff deepens. White House aides often grow to believe they possess the more objective understanding of what the president wants to accomplish. At the same time, the cabinet heads, day in and day out, must live with the responsibilities for managing their programs, with the execution of laws Congress delegates to them, and with the multiple claims of interest groups.

John Ehrlichman, one of President Nixon's senior West Wing aides, wrote that Nixon viewed many of his domestic cabinet officers as "crybabies" and would often threaten to fire them or transfer them to some more remote position. Nixon, said Ehrlichman, disliked meeting with them, disliked their demands on his time, and disliked their constant efforts to increase their budgets.

The size of the bureaucracy, distrust, and a penchant for the convenience of secrecy lead presidents to rely heavily on senior White House staffers and, in more recent administrations, White House policy czars. The White House and executive office aides increasingly become involved not only in gathering legislative ideas but also in getting those ideas translated into laws or executive orders and then into programs. Program coordination and supervision, although often ill managed, also become primary White House interests. To an extent, these additional responsibilities transform the West Wing and the nearby Eisenhower Executive Office Building into an administrative rather than a staff agency. Outer-cabinet departments, understandably, begin to lose the capacity to shape their programs, and the department heads feel uneasy about the lack of close working relations with the president.

President Obama, perhaps reflecting his limited administration experience or possibly his distrust of the bureaucracy, appointed nearly a dozen White House–level policy czars to help him coordinate or implement his priorities. He initially had them for economic recovery, for the Middle East, for Afghanistan-Pakistan, for health care reform, for regulatory reform, for energy and climate change, and for terrorism; he even had a "car czar" to help oversee the bailout and recovery of General Motors and Chrysler.

A few years later, most of these policy czars had quit or had become mini-mized in the policy-making process. Moreover, Obama's White House staff experi-enced considerable turnover and an image of being dysfunctional. White House relations with regular cabinet members were often strained. Top Obama advisers, however, praised him for his way of asking them to devise what they believed were the right policies, such as on economic recovery, and for them to leave the politics and political strategy to him.

Obama campaigned as a transformational leader, but in large part because of the institution, he governed as a transactional politician. He was an inspiring speaker, yet he could also be distant, stoic, insular, and instinctively deliberate. He campaigned advocating a major overhaul of how government and politics in Washington work, yet except for health care, the Iran nuclear treaty, and perhaps also consumer protection issues, he became preoccupied with incrementalism and trying to find common ground.

THE RISE OF THE ADMINISTRATIVE PRESIDENCY

As presidents fail to get Congress to respond favorably to their legislative propos-als, ways are sometimes found to "go around" Congress. Frustrated by congres-sional delays and nay-saying, presidents look for ways to achieve their policy goals without going through the difficult and cumbersome legislative arena. One stra-tegic approach popular with recent presidents is to use various unilateral powers to slow or accelerate the implementation of laws.

Every president has relied on certain administrative discretionary authority they believe is appropriately theirs. Thomas Jefferson purchased the Louisiana Territory this way. Lincoln issued his famous Emancipation Proclamation this way. Kennedy created the Peace Corps by executive order. But not all executive decision-making goes uncontested. Thus, FDR's internment of thousands of Japanese Americans during World War II, even though it initially won support from a majority in the Su-preme Court, was later viewed as a mistake. Some of George Bush's early post-9/11 decisions on warrantless wiretapping and treatment of enemy combatants were over-ruled by the courts or Congress or both. And some of Obama's executive decisions about whether to deport illegal aliens were ruled unconstitutional by the court.

Presidents may encounter a fair amount of bureaucratic as well as congres-sional resistance. But they employ a variety of administrative tools to influence how government works.

Among these resources or devices are:

- executive orders
- executive agreements
- national security directives
- reorganizations or restructurings
- bill signing statements, or veto signing statements
- presidential memorandums to agency heads
- presidential proclamations

An *executive order* is a directive a president issues to provide guidance that laws are fruitfully and properly executed. It is an implied power, not specifically described in the Constitution yet deemed essential for the functioning of government. Over the years, presidents have used executive orders and similar administrative devices to exercise their influence in the way the bureaucracy performs. President Reagan issued 381 executive orders; President Clinton issued 364. In most instances, Congress and the courts go along with the use of these mechanisms, but their increased use—and occasional misuse—have invited increased analysis.[10]

Executive agreements are a pact, or informal treaty, made by a president with a foreign government. The ability to use this instrument is generally derivative from some broader treaty or general congressional delegation of power to a president; yet, unlike treaties, they do not require the advice and consent of the U.S. Senate.

A *National Security Directive*, or action memorandum, is a formal notification to a department or agency head clarifying a presidential decision in national security policy and generally requiring a follow-up by the agencies involved. They are similar to executive orders, but many of them are treated as "classified" and are not immediately shared with the public or even with Congress.

These and similar devices, strategically deployed, can enhance the power of a president. Using executive orders, memoranda, and a variety of other administrative devices, presidents have been able to make policy without legislative approval and sometimes even against the will of Congress. The Supreme Court has held that executive orders have, under most circumstances, the full force of law.[11]

Originally, the executive order was intended for rather minor administrative and rule-making functions, to help the nation's chief administrative officer administer the laws more efficiently and effectively. Gradually, however, the executive order has become an important and sometimes controversial tool for a president to make policy.

Both the Bush and Obama presidencies were faulted for so-called warrantless wiretapping, widespread data surveillance, and droning programs. Debates over the legality of their activities have exploded as terrorism has put the United States into an omnipresent conflict with stateless actors. Some critics faulted the White House on civil liberties grounds while others faulted them on procedural or constitutional grounds. These debates will continue through the Trump presidency and beyond.[12]

As the nation's chief executive, the president has significant administrative and managerial responsibilities. To do the job, a president needs the power and authority to issue administrative orders and instructions. The executive order, like executive agreements and national security directives, is an "implied" power, not specifically mentioned in the Constitution but deemed essential for the functioning of government.

George Washington issued the first executive order on June 8, 1789. It instructed heads of departments (cabinet officers) to make a "clear account" of their departments. Under the National Administrative Procedure Act of 1946, all executive orders must be published in the *Federal Register*. Congress, if it wishes, can overturn an executive order. Executive orders can also be challenged in court on the grounds that they may violate the Constitution.

Over time, presidents have gone beyond the use of executive orders for merely administrative matters and have begun to use orders to "make law" on more substantive and controversial matters. Such efforts bypass Congress and sometimes overstep the bounds of what is an appropriate use of the administrative tools of the office. Presidents have been accused, with some justification, of "going around Congress" and "legislating" independent of Congress.

Signing statements are issued by presidents citing reasons why they were signing and not vetoing legislation submitted to them by Congress. But occasionally a president would note his differences with the legislation, indicating that some portion of it, in his view, may be unconstitutional. In effect, a signing statement can express a president's unwillingness to implement a part of a bill.

President Ronald Reagan issued dozens of signing statements noting his objections to contrarian opinions in legislation he signed. George W. Bush issued 161 signing statements challenging more than a thousand statutory provisions. Barack Obama, even though he had criticized this practice, continued it on a lesser scale.

Critics call its excessive use a threat to the rule of law, since presidents seem to be encouraging executive branch administrators to ignore policies enacted into law by the legislative branch.

The much-debated question here: When a president indicates that the executive branch will not enforce a provision of a law because that president regards it as unconstitutional, is it the same as a veto or item veto? Some scholars contend it is a necessary and justifiable presidential prerogative, while others say it is only appropriate in rare instances when the clear constitutional authority of a president is being challenged.

Presidents will continue to use as many administrative tools as they can to try to achieve and implement their priorities. Congress, the courts, and the public will sometimes push back or object to presidential misuse or excessive use of these implied or unilateral powers. Congress and the judiciary have only occasionally challenged these so-called "unitary execution" tools used by recent presidents, partly because there have been so many precedents and partly given the press of other business on their busy calendars.

In 2014, the U.S. Supreme Court ruled that President Obama had overstepped in his authority to make recess appointments to the National Labor Relations Board during a three-day break the Senate had taken. Congress and the American people challenged Obama's and the National Security Agency's alleged overreach in personal data collections. This was, in part, due to the Edward Snowden revelations.

Constitutional governments want to do whatever they can to protect their citizens and to make government effective—but they also have to follow the laws and the Constitution.

How one stands on these debates often depends on how much one believes in constitutional principles of separation of powers as well as on one's partisan support, or lack thereof, for the president using these devices.

THE EXECUTIVE OFFICE OF THE PRESIDENT, CONTINUED

An Executive Office of the President was created in 1939, as noted earlier, to provide a president more help in running the continually expanding federal departments and agencies. This EOP today comprises the White House Office, the Office of Management and Budget, the Council of Economic Advisers, the National Security Council, the Office of the Vice President (though there is also a vice president's office in the U.S. Capitol), and at least a dozen additional policy and advisory boards. We'll examine a few of these offices.

THE WHITE HOUSE STAFF

The post–World War II era has witnessed a rise in the size, importance, and power of the president's White House and Executive Office staff, and a corresponding decline in the importance and power of most of the cabinet. As discussed earlier, many functions once performed by the cabinet are now the responsibility of White House advisers.

Part of the reason can be traced to the failure of the cabinet and bureaucracy to supply presidents with the help they believe they need. As noted earlier, presidents come to question the loyalty of some cabinet officials, and the bureaucracy is often a creature of habit in which the president may want creatures of politics or at least political responsiveness. Then, too, bureaucracies move at a slower pace than most presidents prefer. The White House staff has emerged to fill this vacuum.

The way a president organizes his staff depends on *personality, experience,* and *circumstances.*

Experience plays a big role also in the choice of staffing structure. Eisenhower, accustomed to a hierarchical and formal command structure from his military career, chose a formal staffing system for his presidency. There is not one perfect staffing structure for all seasons. In a crisis, for example, presidents often abandon the more formal or customary staff system and rely on a select few close advisers, as Kennedy did during the Cuban missile crisis, and as George H. W. Bush did during the Gulf War.

Presidents must also decide how to organize their staff. There are a variety of possible models: FDR's competitive approach, which set some staff members against other staff members in a dynamic tension; JFK's collegial style, which sought a cooperative, bonding approach; Nixon's hierarchical model, with a closed, rigid pyramid of access and line of authority; and Reagan's delegating style, which transferred power and authority to key senior West Wing aides.

Each style of staff organization has costs and benefits. The key is for presidents to know themselves, their strengths and weaknesses, and to model the staff in such a way as to take advantage of their strengths while ensuring that their weaknesses do not lead to serious mistakes.

The most visible and often most important members of the White House staffs in recent presidencies are: the *chief of staff*, *the national security adviser*, the *chief political adviser* (or counselor as they are sometimes called), and the *White House press secretary*. Let's look at the central White House positions.

White House Chief of Staff

Each president must have an effective and trusted senior adviser to oversee the much larger White House and executive office staffs. That same person typically also becomes the chief gatekeeper, through whom cabinet members must go to have access to a president.

One of the first questions presidents must decide when putting together their administration is how strong a chief of staff he will have. James P. Pfiffner, an expert on presidential management, says there are "two firm lessons of White House organization that can be ignored by Presidents only at their own peril: No. 1, A chief of staff is essential in the modern White House; No. 2, a domineering chief of staff will almost certainly lead to trouble." Pfiffner concludes that "the preferred role for a chief of staff is that of a facilitator, coordinator, and a neutral broker."[13]

A president's chief of staff, unlike cabinet members, needs no confirmation by the U.S. Senate. Yet, in many ways, the chief of staff becomes more consequential than most of the cabinet.

Chiefs of staff, in effect, manage White House operations. Other key operatives such as national security and domestic and economic staffers report through the chief of staff to the president. Several recent chiefs of staffs have required cabinet officials and similar advisory staff organizations to prepare weekly reports for the president, but these come to the chief of staff.

Chiefs of staff in recent presidencies have usually become deeply involved in helping presidents shape policy priorities, political and legislation strategies, and public relations approaches. It is a challenging position and several chiefs of staff have become embroiled in controversial clashes with cabinet members, with presidential spouses, and with the laws.

President Eisenhower's long-serving chief of staff, former New Hampshire Gov. Sherman Adams, had to resign in a scandal over gifts he had received. President Nixon's chief of staff, H. R. Halderman, had to depart because of Watergate scandal cover-ups. One of Ronald Reagan's chiefs of staff was eased out in part because Nancy Reagan didn't like him.

Effective chiefs of staff help a president gain control over White House staff and cabinet. They manage, at least to some extent, the avalanche of intelligence and information that pours into the White House. They try to protect the president's time and strive to serve as both a part of the president's political brain trust and an honest broker so that alternative views receive attention.

Past presidential advisers caution that nothing is more important for chiefs of staff to remember than that their power derives only from the president they serve. "One who forgets this precept, who acts as if he were president, will get into trouble sooner than later."[14]

The challenges, and perhaps the paradox, of serving as a president's chief of staff is that one has to have an enormously strong ego and a strong sense of self-confidence as well as emotional security, yet not let this evolve into an intoxicating swollen ego or narcissistic personality disorder. Former Republican National Committee Executive Director Reince Priebus served as Donald Trump's initial staff chief.

National Security Adviser

Every president in recent decades has recruited experienced foreign policy veterans to head up their national security teams and coordinate the National Security Council (NSC). This council has grown to include cabinet officers from the state and defense departments, the intelligence agencies and others, usually including the vice president.

Today's national security assistants often have a staff of up to 100 or more. Henry Kissinger served, and in many ways defined this position, in the Nixon presidency. He gradually became Nixon's most senior foreign policy strategist and often, both because of proximity and skill, more of the administration's secretary of state than the real secretary of state.

The Chief White House Political Counselor

This is sometimes the least defined role. But every president since JFK has had one or a few political operatives who concentrated on explaining and promoting the president's political priorities.

Barack Obama, like many of his predecessors, brought several message managers and speechwriters to his staff who had successfully navigated him through the dozens of caucus and primary states and then through his second general election.

Obama's initial chief political guru at the White House, as he had been in the 2007–2008 campaign, was David Axelrod. He had worked as a news reporter and political columnist for the *Chicago Tribune* for several years before becoming a political consultant, specializing in media relations.

Axelrod's two years in the White House proved frustrating and, in many ways, is a case study of the challenge of being the top political guru in any White House. Governing proved to be much more complicated and, as it always is, harder than campaigning. Axelrod at the White House worked with the national party leaders, helped oversee media relations and polling, and was Obama's key aide in translating the president's campaign promises into programs. He also became Obama's main envoy to Sunday morning television talk shows and similar media outlets.

But as the economy went from bad to worse and an ugly polarization increased in response to Obama's proposed health care initiative, the president's popularity dropped—almost twenty points. Axelrod never lost his devotion to Obama, but he became somewhat of a scapegoat for Obama's failure to frame a coherent and convincing message.

Axelrod looked like a political genius in 2008. But by 2010 he found the media, and a few of his colleagues, pointing to him as a flawed message maven.

In his memoir, Axelrod said he became a White House "lame duck" even before two years had elapsed. He says he became soured on the partisan, intra-party, and ultra–White House blame game. He was frank that even some of his teammates would drive him nuts at times. An understanding Obama thanked him, yet said, "You have to get out of here early in the [coming] year. You need some time to clear your head. Hell, I'd like to do it myself, but I can't go. You can. And I need you rested and ready for the campaign. You're the closest to me, to how I think. I need you firing on all cylinders."[15]

Trump's chief political strategist has been Stephen Bannon, a former Wall Streeter, and head of conservative Breitbart news. He is credited with Trump's effective populist and nativist electoral strategies in the 2016 presidential campaign. Trump also relies heavily on his son-in-law Jared Kushner, a senior advisor for political and foreign policy counsel.

White House Press Secretary

"I have always thought that the job of the White House press secretary is the toughest position after the presidency itself," writes long-time White House correspondent Helen Thomas. "In fact, an *impossible job* might be a better description because the press secretary is caught between two worlds—an administration that wants to paint a rosy picture, no matter what the facts, and a skeptical perhaps cynical press corps that is seeking truthful answers." [16]

Both Bill Clinton and George W. Bush ran through four press secretaries. The job burns people out for the obvious reasons. Obama's first press secretary, Robert Gibbs, knew it was an all-consuming job and that, after a while, Obama's media coverage would become harsher than what he received in his campaign. Gibbs would have to take some of the blame, deserved or not. And that is just what happened. Obama ran through three press secretaries.

Presidents, not surprisingly, like getting favorable media stories, especially about the priorities they are promoting. Media representatives covering the White House are always on the outlook for things that are going, or could go, wrong, at the White House: conflict among aides or between the White House and a cabinet member, campaign promises being broken, hypocrisy, scandals, and gaffes.

All presidents and their media advisers market and "spin" their side of the story. Bush's "Mission Accomplished" speech on the USS Lincoln backfired on him, as did his administration's paying several conservative columnists more than $250,000 to write favorable stories about some of their domestic policy programs.

Many presidents have deceived the public, and the media know this, and that's why they often perform "watchdog" or even "attack dog" duties; this is what Americans want. In the process, however, the credibility of both presidents and the media typically suffer.

The Vice Presidency

To the founding fathers, the vice presidency was mostly an afterthought. To some scholars, it is one of our constitutional mistakes. To some modern-day presidents, it sometimes appears to be more of a headache or a threat than an asset. To some vice presidents, it is often a confusing and unhappy experience. Lyndon B. Johnson said that much of the unhappiness in the office stems from knowing you are on "a perpetual death watch."

John Adams, our first vice president, rightly understood the paradoxical nature of the job, saying, "I am nothing, but I may be everything."

A vice president's chief importance still consists of the fact, as Adams noted, that he or she may be elevated to the presidency. We yearn for someone to fill the post who has the competence and judgment to be president, yet it is typically an advisory and waiting post.

A prime paradox is how we select vice presidents. At least in modern times, we select our presidential nominees by a process of intense democratic exposure and deliberation that is long and grueling. But we leave the designation of the vice presidential running mate almost entirely to the judgment of the presidential nominee, a judgment sometimes made hastily or for politically expedient reasons, sometimes resulting in an inadequately vetted candidate who ends up embarrassing the presidential nominee.[17]

The main purpose of having such a position is to have a competent leader, who generally shares the president's views, available if ill fortune befalls the president. In the past, however, there has sometimes been the temptation to select a vice presidential nominee who might balance the ticket to help win electoral college votes. The selection of Richard Nixon in 1952, LBJ in 1960, and Lloyd Bentsen in 1998 were examples of this. These two needs, competence and electoral utility, need not be incompatible, yet they sometimes are. The question also used to arise: How can we get vice presidents of presidential quality if, once in office, they may have so little to do? Some presidents have primarily shared "dirty work," such as press bashing, attacking the opposition party, and funeral duty responsibilities, with their vice presidents. Some did not share much at all for fear of being upstaged. Other have, understandably, refused to delegate responsibilities.

One student of the office concludes there really can be no deputy or alternate president because of the "indivisibility of presidential leadership and the lack of place for tandem governance for two."[18]

Because vice presidents are always "a heartbeat away" from becoming president, there is sometimes a strain in relations between vice presidents and their bosses.

Another paradox of the vice presidency is that it is a constitutional hybrid of an office: part legislative and part executive in character. A vice president is, as the Constitution instructs, explicitly president of the U.S. Senate, yet the person in that office has now come to be viewed primarily as "standby equipment" if something happens to a president, as well as a presidential adviser and troubleshooter.

To the extent that the office was debated in the founding period, it was to argue that the vice president would be a "responsible" tiebreaker when the Senate was deadlocked. Yet for a couple of generations now, vice presidents have minimized their Senate duties and have made their home at the White House—generally as senior White House advisers.

What it takes to be an effective vice president is different from what it takes to be president. Foremost among the attributes of an effective president are independence and strength of character and skills as a national agenda setter and national unifier. A vice president, on the other hand, even while acting as an "understudy" for the president, must be loyal and self-effacing while trying to avoid being obsequious. A vice president is well-aware that the office and its influence are at least 90 percent dependent on the preferences, and even the whims, of the presidents. A president can bestow assignments on a veep, yet can remove these same assignments at will.

Originally, the person who received the second-highest vote in the presidential election became vice president. This was changed after a bitter dispute and intrigue over the 1800 election, when Thomas Jefferson and his presumed running mate, Aaron Burr, received equal votes. With the Twelfth Amendment to the Constitution (1804), the president and vice president were elected on separate ballots. Nowadays, however, presidents essentially dictate their choice of running mates and successors.

The vice presidency has been significantly affected by two post–World War II constitutional amendments. The Twenty-Second, ratified in 1951, imposed a two-term limit for the presidency, which means vice presidents have a somewhat better chance of moving up to the presidency.

The Twenty-Fifth, ratified in 1967, confirmed prior practice that, on the death or resignation of a president, the vice president becomes president, not just acting president. The Twenty-Fifth Amendment also provides a procedure, still somewhat ambiguous, to determine whether an incumbent president is unable to discharge the powers and duties of the office. Thus, the amendment allows an incapacitated president to lay aside temporarily the powers and duties of the office without forfeiting them permanently, as Reagan did for a few hours during a 1985 cancer operation.

The Twenty-Fifth Amendment also creates a mechanism through which a vice president, along with a majority of the cabinet, may declare a president incapacitated and thus serve as acting president until the president recovers. This procedure answers several problems yet also, as will be discussed, raises questions.

In addition, the Twenty-Fifth Amendment established procedures to fill a vacancy in the vice presidency (a procedure used when Richard Nixon selected Gerald Ford after Spiro Agnew's resignation and Gerald Ford selected Nelson Rockefeller after Nixon's resignation). In the event of such a vacancy, the president nominates a vice president, who takes office upon confirmation by a majority vote of both houses of Congress. This procedure should normally ensure the appointment of a vice president in whom the president has confidence. If the vice president, under these circumstances, has to take over the presidency, he or she can usually be expected to reflect most of the policies of the person the people had originally elected.

Dick Cheney was probably the most consequential vice president in American history. He had greater legislative and administrative experience than his boss, George W. Bush, who was one of the least experienced of modern presidents. Cheney had served in Congress for ten years, rising to a key party leadership position in the House of Representatives. He had served as White House chief of staff under President Ford and secretary of defense under President George H. W. Bush.

George W. Bush trusted the older Cheney in part because of his greater Washington experience and somewhat because Cheney made it clear he had no intention of running for president. Cheney, with Bush's encouragement, played a crucial role in recruiting dozens of personnel for the cabinet, subcabinet, and executive office of the president—including his one-time mentor, Donald Rumsfeld, to serve as secretary of defense.

Cheney brought with him a clearly honed view, essentially a theory, of presidential leadership. He had watched how Congress had reasserted itself during the Ford and Carter presidencies. He believed in a vigorous Congress, yet believed even more strongly that America needs a robust and assertive presidency, especially in foreign policy and national security matters.

Indeed, Cheney was a veritable crusader, well before his vice presidency, for restoring or expanding presidential power. For Cheney, this was a philosophical commitment: This is the way it should be, regardless of who was president or which party controlled the White House. In this, he may have differed from many traditional conservatives, yet he was not alone. He believed Congress was too unwieldy, leak-prone, and risk-averse to provide strategic and responsible national security leadership.[19]

Cheney, with a large staff of several dozen, played a key and often effective role in congressional relations and party fundraising. He regularly traveled abroad, and few people doubted he spoke for George Bush. There were times early in the Bush presidency that Cheney almost seemed the dominant partner, prompting satire about Cheney pulling the levers behind the curtain or serving as Bush's ventriloquist. Both Bush and Cheney worked hard to counter these depictions.

Dick Cheney gradually became a polarizing figure and earned the dubious distinction of being the most disapproved vice president since regular polling began in the 1940s. He was polarizing not only because he took strong positions on constitutional issues of separation of powers but also because he was unapologetically pro-business, pro-military, anti-UN, and a vigorous champion of American exceptionalism. Despite stalwart efforts to be a "behind the scenes" low-profile operative, his influence became increasingly apparent.

Cheney was blamed, rightly or wrongly, for misleading intelligence and "cheerleading" advice leading to the war in Iraq. He was faulted, as well, for the way the United States treated detainees and prisoners of war. He was accused of divisive partisanship.

The man who held decisive authority in the White House during the Bush years has so far remained unaccountable for the aggrandizement and abuse of executive power; for the imposition of repressive laws whose contents were barely known by the legislature that passed them; for the instigation of domestic spying without disclosure or oversight; for the design and conduct of what the constitutional framers would have called . . . a government within a government.[20]

Nobody faulted Cheney's patriotism or commitment to fighting terrorism. Strength and resolve were his mantras.

Cheney argued that the Bush White House had been justified in expanding executive authority over a broad range of matters. We had, Cheney contended, ample precedent dating back to Lincoln and FDR. Presidents, he explained, had Article II authority as commander-in-chief to put in place programs that would successfully defend the nation's security.

Cheney earned a long list of satirical nicknames, such as "Dark Side," "Big Time," and "Darth Vader," for both his and his staff's willingness to confront politicians, administration rivals, and the media for his "do whatever it takes" philosophy to protect America and defeat terrorists. "We also have to work . . . sort of the dark side, if you will. We've got to spend time in the shadows in the intelligence world," said Cheney after 9/11.

Cheney's vice presidency set a benchmark for its influence and for the degree to which he was praised, criticized, and caricatured.

George W. Bush agreed that Cheney "was very influential." Yet Bush held that Cheney was no more influential than Secretary of State Condi Rice, Secretary of Defense Bob Gates, or National Security Adviser Steve Hadley. Here, Bush may have wanted to set the record straight, at least from his standpoint, that Cheney was merely one among many top advisers and not the domineering "co-equal" partner of a feckless president who, some believed, was inexperienced. Bush didn't always take Cheney's advice, especially in the last few years of the Bush presidency. Thus, for one example, Bush fired Defense Secretary Rumsfeld over Cheney's objections. Cheney also argued on occasion for different foreign policy approaches in dealing with Iran and North Korea. He also wanted a full presidential pardon for one of his top aides.

President Obama and his political advisers wanted someone who would both help the ticket politically as well as be someone who could help him as an effective vice president. Joe Biden had more than three decades of service in the U.S. Senate, including leadership positions on both the Senate Judiciary and Foreign Relations Committees. He had some blue-collar political appeal and was generally well liked by both Democrats and Republicans in Congress. He had also handled himself well in the 2007 primary debate performances.

Obama and his aides worried that Biden was prone to making gaffes and had been dogged by plagiarism charges. "He was also known," wrote Obama campaign manager David Plouffe, "to test even the Senate's standard for windiness, taking an hour to say something that required ten minutes."[21]

But Obama went with Biden, who turned out to be an effective campaigner in 2008 and 2012 as well as a loyal and effective vice president.

Biden also played important roles in the Obama White House, yet his advisory roles were neither as consequential nor as controversial as Cheney's role had been in the G. W. Bush White House. This was, in part, because Obama and Biden shared, with few exceptions, the same policy and political views. They were ideo-logically mostly "on the same page," whereas Cheney's views sometimes sharply differed with more than a few cabinet and White House aides.

Biden was a frank adviser, yet also an unwaveringly loyal champion of Obama initiatives on the public stage. Obama trusted Biden with some of the most critical assignments, such as promoting a $787 billion Recovery Act, federal debt negotia-tions, and critical discussions in Iraq and Afghanistan.

Biden was viewed as a classic pragmatist who mostly avoided White House and cabinet infighting that had sometimes characterized the Cheney vice presi-dency and sometimes plagued the Obama executive office staff.

Biden briefly considered running for president in 2016, but decided not to contest Hillary Clinton. Obama praised him as "the greatest vice president you could ever want." But as *New York Times* writer Peter Baker noted, "Nearly every vice president dreams of being one of the great men in history, and in reality every one ends up being disappointed . . . especially when they don't become president."[22]

Donald Trump selected Indiana Governor Mike Pence as his vice president. Pence's selection probably helped Trump win crucial Midwestern states. Pence had served in the U.S. House of Representatives and was a reassuring stalwart Chris-tian Republican when both the Christian right and mainstream Republicans were puzzled by the outsider Trump. Plus, Pence had legislative and political governing experiences, which Trump lacked.

What of the vice presidency? Ambiguous and fragile though it may be, this office is here to stay, paradoxes, uncertainty, tensions, and all. The office "solves" our nation's succession problems and can be made into a relatively useful learning ad-visory and troubleshooting position. The job will remain attractive to many aspir-ing politicians precisely because it is one of the major paths to the presidency, and it can also, these days, be an attractive capstone to a distinguished political career.

Vice presidents will continue to have, and perhaps should have, a more or less undefined set of troubleshooting and advisory functions. Different incumbents will bring different skills and strengths to the office. Some will be astute policy-makers. Some will be better at diplomacy. Some will be gifted political negotiators or coalition builders. Flexibility is needed.

Although the office may remain puzzling, the person holding the office is usu-ally important, and the presidential–vice presidential partnership can be a critical one in the overall success of a presidency. Still, a central paradox remains: Nearly all the credit for a successful presidency goes to the president. Vice presidents almost always lose their independence and sometimes even their identity, if not their integrity.

ADVOCACY POLITICS IN THE EXECUTIVE BRANCH

Effective presidents must have the organizational and leadership ability to hear and balance the policy views of both their cabinet members and their White House pol-itical advisers. Political scientist Fred Greenstein writes that a "president's capacity as an organizer includes his ability to forge a team and get the most out of it, mini-mizing the tendency of subordinates to tell their boss what they sense he wants to hear."[23]

Political scientist Alexander L. George encouraged presidents to develop a multiple advocacy advising process that allows contrary and minority viewpoints to be weighed alongside conventional advice. His suggestions do not attempt to diminish partisanship, parochial viewpoints, and bargaining in the presidential advisory process. Instead, this system would seek to strengthen the analytical and rational components of advisory networks.[24] Multiple-advocacy systems that would enhance the constructive advice he might get cannot be imposed on a presi-dent. A president must find it compatible with his or her style.

MANAGING THE BUREAUCRACY

As the nation's chief executive officer, presidents are supposed to sit at the top of the bureaucracy and control its actions. But their control is incomplete at best. A president operates under a four-year time restraint; the bureaucracy has no such time constraint. The old saying, "Presidents come and go yet bureaucrats stay and stay," speaks volumes. The president is the temporary occupant of the White House; the bureaucracy is, at least in relative terms, the permanent government.

Donald Trump berated federal bureaucrats, including those in the intelligence agencies, before he was sworn into office. He pledged to "drain the swamp" saying, "I will be the voice of the people," and boasting, "I alone can fix it." Trump was not alone in criticizing the federal bureaucracy. Those who have studied the federal civil service system often conclude it is cumbersome in hiring, too lame in disciplining mistakes or poor performance, and too permissive in its promotion practices.

A fascinating question in the Trump years is whether it's possible to be an ef-fective chief executive while being openly hostile toward federal civil servants and many professional experts.

Cabinet members are temporary and often frustrated presiders over huge federal departments. Dr. Steven Chu, Obama's first secretary of energy, worried about the "glacial pace" of his department and wryly noted that Newton's first law of physics, that a body in motion tends to stay in motion, "does not apply" in Washington. Here, "if you start something in motion, it either stops or gets de-railed. You have to keep applying force."[25]

The federal bureaucracy, greatly swollen by New Deal and Cold War agencies, as well as by the Great Society and Homeland Security programs, can be one of the most visible constraints on a president. Presidents fault the bureaucracy for the many problems that beset the implementation and evaluation of presidential programs. Presidents and their aides begin to believe there are a lot of bureaucrats out there who function like those in "Dilbert" cartoons.

The problem of how to inspire, motivate, and manage the bureaucracy has become a major preoccupation for presidents. Even people who championed the New Deal grew to recognize that the executive bureaucracy can be a presidential curse.

Gaining control over existing bureaucracies and making them work with and for the White House is an enormous challenge for presidents. They constantly delegate, they must be most precise about what they delegate, and they must know whether and for what reasons the agencies to which they are delegating share their general outlook. They must be sensitive to bureaucratic politics, to the incentives that motivate bureaucrats, and to the intricacies of their standard operating procedures. They must have some assurance (and hence an adequate intelligence system) that what they are delegating will be carried out properly.

Recent presidents and their aides have sometimes misunderstood the workings of bureaucracy, mistakenly yet frequently looking upon the executive branch as a monolith. They are especially offended when senior bureaucrats differ with them or otherwise refuse to cooperate. Presidents too often become defensive and critical of the bureaucracy.

Bureau chiefs and career civil servants sometimes do avoid taking risks and responsibility, opting instead for routine and security. The bureaucracy has its own way of doing things, perhaps more conservative or more liberal than what a president wants. But the fact that bureaucratic and presidential interests often differ does not mean that the permanent employees of the federal executive branch constitute an enemy. Bureaucratic organizations generally act in rational ways to enhance their influence, budget, and autonomy. And they generally believe that in doing so they act in the nation's interest.

Of course, this sometimes means that bureaucrats will define the national interest differently from the way it is defined in the White House. But a close examination of the two definitions may reveal that both are valid and representative views of what is desirable. Properly understood, the bureaucratic instinct for competition, survival, and autonomy can be creatively harnessed by the White House both to educate itself and to develop cooperative alliances.

If presidents rarely control the bureaucracy, they still need the bureaucracy to take care that both the laws and their policies are implemented. But they are not helpless. Different presidents use different methods to move the bureaucracy. Some presidents do it by placing loyal followers in key positions, others assign a top White House aide envoy to ride herd; some try to circumvent an unresponsive agency, others create new agencies staffed by their hand-picked administrators. Other presidents devote their own time and effort to either persuade or negotiate with an unresponsive bureaucrat. Still others utilize the unilateral or unitary tools discussed earlier to influence bureaucracy to comply with their priorities.

Bureaucrats can frustrate a president's wishes in a variety of ways. Orders are never self-executing, and it may not be exactly clear what a president wants. Also, some members of the permanent government may disagree with the president's directives and may intentionally sabotage an order by ignoring it, altering it in its execution, or failing to pass it on to the operational level. Delay is the most common form of bureaucratic resistance.

CONCLUSION

Presidents are understandably expected to be good administrators—to see that the laws of the land are properly implemented. Traditional public administration ideas held that Congress would make the laws and the president, collaborating with cabinet heads, would impartially administer the laws. In practice, of course, presidents and their advisers promote a number of their own new policies and regularly push to get these adopted. Moreover, laws are often subject to interpretation as they are implemented, so presidents and executive branch officials are also regularly involved in policy making even as they administer the laws.

Presidents often come to office believing that their main challenge will be dealing with Congress. Although this is true, they also soon discover that dealing with the complex federal bureaucracy is often just as much of a challenge, and takes as much, or even more, of their time.

A president's ability to nominate the cabinet, subject to Senate confirmation, and appoint up to 4,000 officials to key executive branch positions is obviously one of their primary assets in trying to influence the executive branch.

Other resources for what is now called the administrative presidency include internal review of agency budgets, executive orders, national security directives, White House interpretation of new laws through signing statements, and various personnel and restructuring initiatives.

Even as modern presidents have been given numerous advisory and policy intelligence resources, presidents are paradoxically often constrained, if not overwhelmed, by what they, and we perhaps mistakenly assume is their own branch of government.

FURTHER READING

Dodds, Graham G., *Take Up Your Pen: Unilateral Presidential Directives in American Politics.* (Philadelphia: University of Pennsylvania Press, 2013).

Patterson, Bradley, *To Serve the President: Continuity and Innovation in the White House Staff* (Washington, D.C.: Brookings Institution Press, 2008).

Vaughn, Justin, *Czars in the White House: The Rise of Policy Czars as Management Tools* (Ann Arbor: University of Michigan Press, 2015).

Warber, Adam L. *Executive Orders and the Modern Presidency,* (Boulder, CO: Lynne Rienner, 2006).

Witcover, Jules, *The American Vice Presidency: From Irrelevance to Power* (Washington, D.C.: Smithsonian Books, 2014).

CHAPTER 8

Presidents and the Court

The rule of law or the rule of men? The ideal is that government is empowered and constrained by law and yet it is, and must be, men (persons) who make and implement laws. The central paradox reflects the tension between law—neutral, objective, blind—and politics—power, money, partisan, and personal. This tension has been especially visible in the war against terrorism, which we discuss later in this chapter.

The history of presidential–Supreme Court relations suggests that rather than limiting presidential power grabs, courts often allow for an expansive view of presidential power. Although the Supreme Court has occasionally halted presidential action or declared a presidential act unconstitutional, the Court has more frequently legitimized the growth of presidential power. However, in recent years, the Court has been more willing to step in and check presidential power, whether it is to declare acts of the George W. Bush administration in some anti-terrorism cases unconstitutional or to decide against the Obama administration in cases dealing with recess appointments or executive overreach. This has led some to applaud the assertiveness of the Court, and others to worry about a more openly partisan nature of the Supreme Court.

The framers of the Constitution intended the Court to serve, along with the presidency, as a check on the anticipated (or at least potential) excesses of the national legislature. The Court, they hoped, would comprise wise, virtuous, and well-educated statesmen who would preserve the Constitution, especially from legislative encroachment. Most framers believed the Court would work hand-in-hand with the executive. Some even viewed it as part of the executive department or at least engaged in the similar functions, namely executing, interpreting, and applying the laws.

Both president and Court have a national constituency. But where the president serves many masters, the court serves—or should serve—only one: the Constitution.

Presidents and the Court have had their share of clashes. This is to be expected. The Constitution stands as the supreme law of the land in a nation governed by laws, not men. The rule of law has a key limiting and empowering function for our government. Yet, the Constitution is sometimes ambiguous, sometimes silent on matters of grave concern; the law is flexible and changing, open to interpretation. Differences of opinion, interest, and interpretation are inevitable. In most yet by no means all encounters between presidents and courts, presidents emerge victorious. The exceptions are notable. Jefferson came into conflict with the Marshall Court. Lincoln, after his death, was rebuffed for using military courts in areas where they were not justified. FDR saw several early New Deal initiatives struck down by the Court as unconstitutional. Truman was ordered by the Court in 1952 to release steel mills from federal control. Richard Nixon's policy and political intentions were overturned by the federal courts on at least seventy-five occasions, most famously in the summer of 1974 when the Supreme Court directed him to release White House tapes for use in criminal investigations. Bill Clinton, in areas such as executive privilege and executive immunity, often found himself rebuked by the courts. George W. Bush suffered a series of judicial rebuffs in the War on Terror. And President Obama faced several rebuffs from the Court.

Here are some basic characteristics of 225 years of presidential–Supreme Court relations.

- There is no getting politics out of a nomination to the Supreme Court. Picking justices is a political act. Presidents want to shape the Court. Yet, they possess no special legal or constitutional right to impose their views on a whole branch for a generation. The Constitution entitles a president only to try, not necessarily to succeed.
- Presidents nominate Supreme Court justices, and their nominees are usually confirmed by the U.S. Senate. Most justices conform to the general intentions of the presidents appointing them. However, nearly 25 percent of the justices deviate enough that we call them "wayward justices." That is, they voted and wrote decisions contrary to the views and values of the president who appointed them. Several factors encourage justices, once on the bench, to grow independent from the presidents who nominated them.
- The Supreme Court is generally a friend of the presidency and supports the use of presidential power, especially in wartime or in the conduct of foreign affairs. Indeed, the judiciary has played a significant role in the trend toward executive primacy in foreign policymaking.
- The justices can thwart presidential initiatives and are most likely to do so if evidence exists that Congress would agree with the Court, and if there is clear absence of any authority for the presidential action either in the Constitution or in congressional statutes. They are also likely to weigh in against a president when a president's public approval is low, at the end of his term, or after the president has left office or died.
- Presidents take an oath of office, typically administered by the Chief Justice, pledging to uphold the Constitution and not necessarily what the Supreme Court says about the Constitution. Presidents reserve the right to interpret

the Constitution for themselves. They may, as they usually do, defer to the judgment of the Court, yet they do not have to accept or agree with the judicial reasoning. President Obama, for example, vigorously opposed the Court's ruling and reasoning in *Citizens United*.

This chapter explores these realities and seeks to answer the following questions and paradoxes. How do presidents select nominees for the Supreme Court? Why do some nominees get rejected? Why do some justices grow independent once on the Court? What were the Lincoln and FDR experiences with the Court, and why did Roosevelt try to "pack the Court?" When, and in what circumstances, has the Court acted to expand the prerogatives of the chief executive, and when has the Court restrained the presidency? Can we expect the judiciary to constrain a powerful and popular president bent on exercising his or her will? Finally, do national security considerations justify virtually any means, constitutional or otherwise, a president wishes to adopt to ensure U.S. security?

For this chapter, our lead paradox outlined in Chapter 1 is especially germane: We demand a powerful leader, yet we are suspicious of the potential to abuse power. We want our presidents to govern effectively and solve problems, yet sometimes we do not give them sufficient constitutional authority to meet these demands.

PRESIDENTIAL NOMINATIONS TO THE COURT

In nominating justices to the courts, we can see yet another Chapter 1 paradox at work: "We admire an 'above politics,' nonpartisan, bipartisan, or "post-partisan" style of leadership, and yet the presidency is perhaps the most political office in the

President Trump nominating Neil Gorsuch to fill the Supreme Court seat vacated due to the death of Justice Antonin Scalia. White House official photographer.

American political system, requiring an entrepreneurial master politician. Similarly, we want presidents who can both unify us and take the necessary bold and unpopular decisions that are likely to upset us."

Presidents have had to look at the judicial selection process as a partnership venture between the White House and the Senate. The Constitution provides for a number of occasions where *branches* share power. A judicial nominee must win a majority confirmation in the Senate. Presidents usually get their way with cabinet and top executive department nominations. The widely accepted view is that presidents are entitled to the assistance in the executive branch of people they respect and trust and whose views are compatible with their own. The Supreme Court, however, is different. It's a separate branch, and most members of the Senate nowadays think they have an equal responsibility for who should sit on the nation's highest court.

The U.S. Constitution is silent as to the criteria that should guide a president in selecting a Supreme Court nominee. As Terry Eastland, a former Reagan and Bush administration aide, writes: "This is a matter clearly within the president's discretion." However, "the considerations that have decisively influenced presidents in judicial selection have included political patronage, geographical balance, judicial philosophy, and—especially in recent years—race and gender."[1] Judicial philosophy is plainly now the dominant criterion.

Most presidents understandably seek to nominate to the bench persons who share their partisan and policy preferences. In effect, presidents make predictions about the likely future performance and policy opinions of their potential nominees. If a president can nominate two or three members to the Court, that president's political philosophy can extend beyond his or her term in office. Thus presidents pay a great deal of attention to who they shall nominate. In many instances this has led to nomination of friends, advisers, and loyal partisans. Yet party label alone is not enough. President Theodore Roosevelt wrote to his friend Henry Cabot Lodge and outlined some of his views about what was important as he considered the Massachusetts Chief Justice Oliver Wendell Holmes Jr. as a Supreme Court nominee. To Lodge he wrote, "I should like to know that Judge Holmes was in entire sympathy with our views, that is, with your views and mine . . . before I would feel justified in appointing him."[2]

In nominating someone to the Supreme Court, presidents adopt one or a combination of the following models. The merits model suggests that the president chooses the most qualified person he can find. Following the patronage model, a president nominates a person who he believes will carry out his agenda. The ideological model suggests that the president nominates someone whose ideological views mirror his or her own. Finally, the constituency model suggests that the president nominates someone who fills a regional, religious, racial, or ethnic category.[3]

In recent decades, presidents have been more partisan in judicial selection.[4] Jimmy Carter did not get the opportunity to nominate any justices to the Supreme Court, but Ronald Reagan was able to nominate three Republicans: Sandra Day

O'Connor, Antonin Scalia, and Anthony Kennedy. Reagan also elevated William Rehnquist to Chief Justice in 1986. George H. W. Bush nominated David Souter and Clarence Thomas. Bill Clinton nominated two justices to the Court: Ruth Bader Ginsburg and Stephen G. Breyer. George W. Bush nominated John Roberts as Chief and Samuel Alito as an associate justice. And Obama nominated Sonia Sotomayor, Elena Kagan, and Merrick Garland. President Trump nominated Neil Gorsuch. All these justices came from the nominating president's party. (See Table 8.1.)

The appointment of federal judges also reflects the partisan interests of the president and his party. Only 13 of over 100 members of the Supreme Court came from a party other than the president's. Republican presidents tend to appoint more white men to the bench than do Democrats, who appoint a higher percentage of women and minorities to federal judgeships.

Presidents have been influenced by a variety of factors when searching for potential Supreme Court nominees. First is finding someone who shares their ideological and philosophical views. Second, presidents are politicians, and they naturally want praise and political credit for their appointments. Reagan's first nominee, Sandra Day O'Connor, conveniently satisfied both of these standards. She was a strong Reagan supporter and her appointment won praise for the president.

Still other factors are at work. Nominees have to be confirmed by a majority of the U.S. Senate. Presidents or their aides consult leading senators. They often consult

TABLE 8.1 Party Affiliation of District Judges and Courts of Appeals Judges Appointed by Presidents

PRESIDENT	PARTY	APPOINTEES FROM SAME PARTY
Roosevelt	Democrat	97%
Truman	Democrat	92%
Eisenhower	Republican	95%
Kennedy	Democrat	92%
Johnson	Democrat	96%
Nixon	Republican	93%
Ford	Republican	81%
Carter	Democrat	90%
Reagan	Republican	94%
Bush, G. H. W.	Republican	89%
Clinton	Democrat	88%
Bush, G. W.	Republican	87%
Obama	Democrat	93%

sources: Sheldon Goldman, "Judicial Selection Under Clinton: A Midterm Explanation," Judicature (May/June 1995): 280; Sheldon Goldman and Elliot Slotnick, "Clinton's Second Term Judiciary: Selection Under Fire," Judicature (May/June 1999). Updated by authors.

with members of the Senate Judiciary Committee, the committee responsible for confirmation hearings. Presidents also take into account the wishes of public and private sector leaders and select groups who have a known interest in the nomination.

Who gets nominated and confirmed? They have been lawyers, and in recent years most have been graduates of distinguished law schools (see Table 8.2). Almost all have been active in politics in some way or another. Some have served in local or state elective office. Some have been party leaders. Some were actively involved in presidential campaigns. A few even ran for the presidency themselves (Taft, Hughes, and Warren). Almost a third served as executive branch officials in the national government before their appointment to the Court, as was the case with both George W. Bush's nominees. Nine were attorneys general, four were solicitors general, at least eighteen held cabinet-level posts, and over a dozen held various other Department of Justice positions.

Perhaps the most common background in the recent past has been some experience serving as a state or federal judge. Why? In part because it is believed this was ideal training for service on the nation's highest court. Presidents also recognized it was easier to discern the predictable future responses of a potential Court member if their decisions could be studied.

The Constitution nowhere stipulates that Court members must be lawyers. Nor is there any congressional statute insisting on judicial experience. Yet no

Table 8.2 Current Supreme Court Appointments

NAME	YEAR OF APPOINTMENT	LAW SCHOOL	APPOINTING PRESIDENT	PRIOR JUDICIAL EXPERIENCE	PRIOR GOVERNMENT EXPERIENCE
Anthony M. Kennedy	1988	Harvard	Reagan	U.S. Court Of Appeals	
Clarence Thomas	1991	Yale	Bush, G. H. W.	U.S. Court Of Appeals	Chair, Equal
Ruth Bader Ginsburg	1993	Columbia	Clinton	U.S. Court Of Appeals	
Stephen G. Breyer	1994	Harvard	Clinton	U.S. Court Of Appeals	U.S. Senate Committee
John Roberts	2005	Harvard	Bush, G. W.	U.S. Court Of Appeals	Department of Justice, Office of Legal Counsel
Samuel Alito	2006	Yale	Bush, G. W.	U.S. Court Of Appeals	U.S. Senate Aide
Sonia Sotomayor	2009	Yale	Obama	U.S. Court Of Appeals	Assistant District Attorney
Elena Kagan	2010	Harvard	Obama	N/A	Solicitor General

one disputes the need for *legal* experience. The desirability of *judicial* experience, however, is less clear. Several distinguished justices did not have prior judicial experience, including John Marshall, Earl Warren, Louis Brandeis, Robert Jackson, and Lewis F. Powell. Intelligence and temperament, as well as being well read, would seem to be just as important as lower court experience. However, most future court nominees are likely to come from the lower federal courts.

Future presidents will probably consider these political factors:

- whether the choice has won respect for their grasp of the Constitution
- whether their choice will render the president more popular among influential interest groups
- whether the nominee has been a loyal member of the president's party
- whether the nominee favors presidential programs and policies
- whether the nominee is acceptable to the home-state Senators
- whether the nominee's judicial record, if any, meets the presidential criteria of constitutional construction
- whether the president is indebted to the nominee for past political services

Ethnicity and gender considerations also play a role in presidential court nomination decisions.

On January 31, President Trump announced his first nomination to the Supreme Court, Neil M. Gorsuch. During the campaign, many Republicans said they voted for Trump only or primarily because of the Supreme Court. In nominating Gorsuch, Trump rewarded these voters with a very conservative nominee who has an elite background (degrees from Columbia University, Harvard University, and the University of Oxford), is a white male, and who comes from a prominent Republican family (his mother was the first female administrator of the Environmental Protection Agency during the Reagan presidency and in 1982 was cited for contempt of Congress for refusing to turn over documents relating to the mismanagement of Superfund monies). Gorsuch's nomination was widely hailed in conservative circles as a fitting replacement for the Scalia seat, but Democrats, still smarting from the Republican refusal to even hold hearings on President Obama's nominee Merrick Garland for nearly eleven months, decided to take a stand, making for yet another contentious battle.

CONFIRMATION BATTLES

Article II, Section 2 of the U.S. Constitution says the president shall have power to nominate and, "by and with the Advice and Consent of the Senate," place Supreme Court justices on the Supreme Court. If a president decides simply to assert his or her power to pack the court with good friends or unqualified or extremist persons, senators from the opposition party, or even from the president's own party, may try to use their constitutional power to defeat the president. Over the history of the Republic the Senate has rejected twenty-six presidential nominees to the Court. This amounts to 15 percent of those nominated. This rejection rate increases about 25 percent for presidents in their last year in office and when the Senate is controlled by the opposition party. This check on presidential power has forced presidents not to appoint persons who would fail to win Senate approval. In yet other instances, some potential nominees have taken themselves out of consideration precisely because they feared grueling confirmation hearings.[5]

Why are some nominees rejected? Sometimes it is because a president is highly unpopular in the country and in the Senate. President Andrew Johnson's stock in the Senate was so low he probably could not have had any nominee of his confirmed; his one nominee fell victim to Senate rejection.

On occasion a practice known as "senatorial courtesy" contributes to the rejection of a nominee. This occurs when both senators or the senior senator from a nominee's home state indicate(s) to the White House that they strongly oppose the proposed Court appointment. This practice is more common in cases of federal district judge appointments, yet it has in times past undercut a presidential Supreme Court appointment.

The political and philosophical views of a nominee can sometimes stir up the opposition of major interest groups and the opposition party, as was the case in Reagan's 1987 nomination of Robert Bork. This can especially doom a candidacy when the opposition party controls the U.S. Senate, as it did when Nixon, for example, tried to appoint Clement Hayworth in 1969. Many senators, especially Democrats, viewed Hayworth as too conservative. The senate rejected another of Nixon's nominees, Florida Judge G. Harrold Carswell, mainly on the basis of inadequate professional competence. Opposition to Carswell was fast and strong. One respected law school dean suggested this nominee presented more slender credentials than any other nominee for the Supreme Court put forth in the twentieth century, and after the confirmation hearings were completed, most senators agreed.

Sometimes the Senate rejects a nominee to signal its opposition to the policy or recent record of the incumbent Supreme Court. Sometimes senators are unsure of the political reliability of a nominee. And sometimes the Senate merely makes a mistake, as some observers believe it did when it rejected President Herbert Hoover's 1930 nomination of Judge John J. Parker of North Carolina.

Only in recent years has the confirmation process turned into a more openly partisan conflict. As the stakes for various interest groups grew, so too did partisan bickering, "gotcha politics," and televised hearings as theater. Early public hearings were a rarity. The first truly public hearing occurred in 1916 for nominee Louis Brandeis, and Brandeis didn't even show up for that. The first nominee to testify before the Senate Judiciary Committee was Harlan Fiske Stone in 1935, and it wasn't until the 1960s that it became customary for nominees to testify. Since 1955, every nominee has testified before the Senate.

In late 1987, Reagan's nomination of Robert H. Bork incited sharp differences of opinion about how much the Senate should take into account the philosophical views of a nominee. Some Democrats in the Senate, such as Ted Kennedy and Joe Biden, proclaimed that the framers had intended the broadest role for the Senate in choosing members of the Court and hence they had wide authority in checking into a nominee's constitutional views and values.

In 1991, George H. W. Bush nominated Clarence Thomas. This nomination fight was one of the most notable in U.S. history. Thomas barely won confirmation by a 52–48 vote, but both his nomination and especially his confirmation battle triggered a major political backlash for Bush and to some extent for the U.S. Senate.[6]

During the Clinton years, confirmation politics often were deeply partisan. While partisanship has always played a part in the process, an intense partisanship affected confirmation politics in the 1990s. Republicans blocked many Clinton nominees, delaying the holding of hearings on others, and refused to even deal with still others. It was as strategy designed to prevent the president from filling seats on the bench. When George W. Bush became president in 2001, and the Democrats controlled the Senate, they did much the same. And then, when Barack Obama became president, Republicans blocked his nominees. A frustrated Bush proposed process changes in the confirmation system, setting specific deadlines for the president and Senate to act on judicial nominations.[7] But such efforts went to the back-burner when Republicans regained control of the Senate in 2003, and Bush's judicial nominees fared somewhat better with their partisans in control of the process.

Justice Antonin Scalia died in 2016 at age 79. No one saw it coming. Scalia, a Ronald Reagan appointment, was one of the two most conservative Justices on the Court. President Obama would have the opportunity to make his third appointment to the Court. Article II, Section 2 of the Constitution states that the president "shall nominate, and by and with the advice and consent of the Senate. Shall appoint . . . Judges on the Supreme Court." But would the Republican-controlled Senate, with less than eleven months left in Obama's term, give the President's nominee a hearing or a vote? Within hours of the announcement of Scalia's passing, Senate Republican Majority Leader Mitch McConnell ruled out filling Scalia's Supreme Court seat until after the election, meaning that a vacancy would exist for over a year and a half, if not longer. Arguing that a seat on the Court should not be filled in the final year of a president's term, and that the next president should nominate a new Justice, the Republicans denied President Obama his constitutionally mandated right.

WAYWARD JUSTICES

Once confirmed, new members of the Court are in no way obliged to the president who appointed them. Indeed, there is an element of unpredictability in how justices will vote in future years. Loyalty to the president who appointed them is not considered a proper reason for judgment on the Court. Even justices who have "pleased" their sponsoring president acknowledge that they think and act differently once they join the Court.

How often do presidents fail to get what they want in the people they appoint to the Supreme Court? One student of the judiciary found that nearly 25 percent of the justices have "deviated" from the expectations presidents held for them.

In some instances, such as the Earl Warren case, we can relate judicial performance to presidential expectations with considerable precision. More often, assumptions have to be made based on the general political views of the presidents and on the situations in which they operated. In still other cases of short tenure, it is near impossible to discern the "loyalty" or "deviation" of a justice. Several years ago, political scientist Robert Scigliano examined the fit or lack of fit between justices and presidents and concluded:

> ... that about three-fourths of those justices for whom an evaluation could be made conformed to the expectations of the Presidents who appointed them to the Supreme Court. ...
>
> Our conclusion is an important one in that it indicates limitations upon the ability of Presidents to influence the policies of the court through appointments and assures us, retrospectively at least, of a certain, but crucial, measure of judicial independence from Presidential attempts to bring the Court closely into line with the executive branch of government.[8]

Why have so many justices disappointed the presidents who appointed them? Sometimes it is because the presidents and their advisors failed to examine closely the already known views of the prospective nominee. Woodrow Wilson apparently overlooked some of the doctrinal conservatism of McReynolds. Eisenhower apparently engaged in some wishful thinking in his selection of Earl Warren. Eisenhower was also in debt to Warren politically for his help at the last stages of the 1952 presidential nomination battle. Justice Salmon P. Chase rejected war-funding legislation sought by Abraham Lincoln, the president who appointed him. And Truman appointee Tom C. Clark voted against Truman in the Steel Seizure case.

The constitutional obligations of the court are different from those of being a friend or adviser to a president. The Court is not supposed to be a rubber stamp for anyone, and most justices come to view themselves as virtually a sovereign in their own right. The Court, moreover, decides when violations of the law, including violations by the executive branch, occur.

Life tenure adds an incentive to think, act, and decide independently. The framers knew that what Alexander Hamilton called "the least dangerous branch" would need to be at least somewhat free from the influences of ambition and interest if they were to perform their responsibility. This gives justices "high honor, high responsibility, and guaranteed tenure and salary, so that they need neither seek higher office nor worry about retaining the one they have. These conditions, at once emancipating and greatly demanding, result in judicial behavior which may not conform either to presidential expectations or to the views that the justices expressed before joining the Court."[9]

Once a justice is on the Court, a president cannot effectively threaten, intimidate, or retaliate against a wayward or hostile justice. There may be times and circumstances when presidential "jawboning" would sway a decision but, as the following examples suggest, they would be the exception to the rule. Jefferson tried in vain to have a justice impeached. FDR tried to pack the Court. Nixon, in a crucial case involving him, hinted he might not comply with the Court's decision. President Obama publically chided the Court in a State of the Union address over its' *Citizens United* decision. These presidential intrigues failed.

Thus there is, as there should be, a certain amount of unpredictability in the judicial appointment process. Presidents can never be certain their nominees will be approved by the Senate. Nor can a president ever be sure a justice will not "grow" or change after he or she dons the judicial robes.

THE TEMPTATION TO MOVE BEYOND THE LAW

Given the many roadblocks and agents that have a veto that may block the president's path, it is not surprising that the more ambitious presidents get frustrated as others block their way. Well-organized opposition in Congress, demanding special interests, an uncooperative business community, an adversarial press, and others can at times seem to gang up on the White House.

When faced with these multiple opposing forces, most presidents feel trapped. The choice may appear to be either to accept defeat or to take bold action on behalf of what presidents claim is the national interest. Making the complex separation of powers work is difficult under the best of circumstances; in normal times it may seem impossible to get the system moving. Thus, rather than accept defeat, some presidents are tempted to cut corners, act unilaterally, move beyond the law, and stretch constitutional limits.

Knowing they will be judged on how much they are able to accomplish, presidents, when faced with potential gridlock, look for ways to get around Congress. Sometimes presidents can exert unilateral authority, and at other times they may stretch the envelope and venture into areas of questionable legitimacy.

Presidents may see the system itself as the problem and thus feel justified in going beyond the law. Richard Nixon with Watergate and Ronald Reagan with the Iran-Contra scandal are two pronounced examples. Clinton, George W. Bush, and Obama in some of their antiterrorism initiatives also illustrate this.

Some presidents get away with it (e.g., Reagan); some do not (Nixon). But when the choice seems to be stay within the law and fail (Ford, Carter) or go beyond the law and maybe you will succeed and maybe you won't get caught, the temptation is great—too great for some leaders to resist.

Arrogance may overtake the president and his top staff. "We know best" and "they are blocking progress" leads to the belief that the "slight" abuse of power is being done for the greater good. But such an attitude leads to the Imperial Presidency, and to further abuses of power.

President Reagan was convinced that communism was an evil that had to be fought at all costs, that the Marxist government in Nicaragua was a serious and direct threat to the United States, that the Congress was soft on communism, and that public opinion, which opposed U.S. intervention, was uninformed in spite of Herculean efforts by the administration. Therefore, Reagan was faced with the difficult choice of either accepting the will of Congress, the voice of the people, and the law, or acting in what he believed to be the national interest. He acted. Likewise, George W. Bush engaged in domestic surveillance that was clearly illegal. He believed the law interfered with his responsibility as Commander-in-Chief, so he moved beyond the law . And President Obama likewise sought to move beyond what many believed were the constitutional limits of his office in his efforts to fight terrorism and protect some undocumented immigrants.

Must a president, in all circumstances and at all times, obey the law? And whose interpretation of the law must a president obey? May a president disregard a decision of the Supreme Court he finds legally objectionable? Some of our most famous presidents—Jackson, Lincoln, and Franklin Roosevelt—clashed with Congress and the Courts. Did they cross a line in doing so? Are presidents entitled to claim that their understanding of the Constitution should supersede that of Congress or decisions and precedents of the Courts?

No one is above the law. And yet, who—if anyone—has the "final word" on what the law means and how it is to be applied to the separate branches?

Conventional wisdom as well as constitutional design suggest that Congress *makes* laws, the Executive *implements* laws, and Courts *interpret* laws. But in practice these distinctions blur. There is a separation of powers, but there is also a blending or sharing of powers. Presidents, through the veto power, are a part of the legislative process. And as executives, presidents must interpret the laws they are to implement. If the lines of distinction are blurred, so too are the lines of authority. In practice, presidents execute, interpret, make, and implement the law. But just how independent and absolute is a president's authority to apply his or her understanding of the law to events?

There is no one, central authoritative center of power in the American system. There are three branches, three centers vying for political control.

All three branches have a vested interest (a self-interest) in determining what is and what is not constitutional. And who can say when and why one branch should willingly cede this important power to a rival branch? Thus, the president will assert a claim in determining precisely what the Constitution means, and because power can be bendable and fluid, the president's stake in establishing a constitutional territorial claim can have enormous consequences.

To the question "Should a president obey the law?" the presumptive answer must, of course, be "Yes." After all, the president takes an oath to do so. And yet, must presidents obey laws they deem unconstitutional or immoral? Can such laws be binding? And precisely whose view of law shall a president obey? The Constitution? Statutes passed by Congress? Interpretations of the Supreme Court? Does the separation-of-powers logic allow presidents room to dispute or even to violate laws of Congress and precedents of the Court?[10]

A president is no mere passive observer in this power struggle. A president has a constitutional stake in the outcome. And if the separation of powers divides, it also commingles. While each branch has a specific area of authority, no branch is completely autonomous of the other branches; that is to say, they are not "wholly unconnected with each other."[11] Because of this, conflict will arise. Each branch must attempt to protect its powers from the others, and there will be times when clashing interests lead to political conflict.

Presidents have asserted a broad power to disregard laws they believe to be infringements of their institutional authority, that they see as unconstitutional, or that they believe inhibit the ability of the government to respond to the needs of national security. This control over the interpretation of the law is a part of the rising influence of an administrative strategy presidents employ to gain leverage over policy.

THE PRESIDENT'S EMERGENCY POWER

Is a president ever justified in stretching the Constitution? And if so, who decides? While the word *emergency* does not appear in the Constitution, some founders envisioned the possibility of a president exercising "supraconstitutional powers" in time of national emergencies.[12]

Nowhere in the Constitution is it specified that a president will have additional powers in times of crisis. History, however, has shown us that in times of national emergency the powers of a president have greatly expanded, and while presidents have no explicitly implied powers which enable them to make or disregard laws, this is sometimes what presidents do.

During a crisis, presidents often assume extra constitutional powers. The branches which, under normal circumstances, check and balance a president will usually defer to the president in times of national crisis. A president's institutional position offers a vantage point from which he or she can more easily exert crisis leadership, and the Congress, Court, and public usually accept the president's judgments.

The idea that there might be a different set of legal and constitutional standards for normal conditions than for emergency conditions raises unsettling questions regarding democratic governments and constitutional systems. Can democratic regimes function in any but prosperous, peaceful circumstances? Or must the United States constantly rely upon the strength of a despot or "constitutional dictatorship" to save it from disaster? Are constitutional governments incapable of meeting the demands of crises?[13] The consequence of this view of an enlarged reservoir of presidential power in emergencies was characterized by constitutional scholar Edward S. Corwin as "constitutional relativity."[14] By this Corwin envisioned a constitution broad and flexible enough to meet the needs of an emergency situation as defined and measured by the Constitution. The Constitution can be adapted to meet the needs of the times.

PRESIDENTIAL ACTION IN TIMES OF EMERGENCY

In practice a president's emergency power has been great in comparison to powers under normal circumstances. When faced with a crisis situation, presidents have made exaggerated claims of power, have acted on these claims, and generally have gotten away with these excessive, and often extralegal, uses of power. History provides us with clear examples of the enormous power of a president in an emergency situation.

Presidents on occasion act with little regard for the wishes and dictates of the other branches. The necessity for quick, decisive, often extraconstitutional actions, which the crisis may demand, places a heavy burden upon the president. Being the only leader able to move quickly, the president must shoulder the burden of meeting the crisis. Yet, not everyone accepts that constitutional limits on a president should be loosened merely because of national security threats or emergencies.

For the crisis presidency to be seen as legitimate:

1. The president must face a genuine and a widely recognized emergency.
2. Congress and the public must, more or less, accept that the president should exercise supraconstitutional powers.
3. Congress may, if it chooses, override presidential acts.
4. The president's acts must be public so as to allow Congress and the public to judge them.
5. There must be no suspension of the next election.
6. The president should consult with Congress or its leaders where possible.

Lincoln and Roosevelt met (more or less) these requirements; Nixon, Reagan, and George W. Bush often did not. Clinton and Obama were mixed cases.[15]

Even when the preceding requirements are met, however, one should not be casual about presidential usurpations of power. Presidents must be held to account. As the Supreme Court reminded us in *Ex parte Milligan* (1866), "Wicked men, ambitious of power, with a hatred of liberty and contempt of law, may fill the place once occupied by Washington and Lincoln."

After the terrorism of 9/11 the public rallied behind George W. Bush in support of his efforts to battle the terrorist network responsible for the attack on the United States. While the president generally pursued his goals with reason and proportionality, some of the administration's actions proved controversial. The attorney general questioned the patriotism of anyone who objected to administration actions, and he ordered the detention, without being charged with a crime, without access to an attorney, and without recourse to judicial appeal, of several American citizens and numerous non-nationals.

Bush was able to get the Congress to quickly pass the U.S. Patriot Act into law. He orchestrated a war against Afghanistan, whose Taliban government had been harboring the terrorists of Al Qaeda. All of this was done either with the near-rubber stamp approval of Congress or on the president's own claimed authority, independent of congressional authorization.

COURT DECISIONS AND PRESIDENTIAL POWER

The Supreme Court rarely rules against a president. The two circumstances when the Court is most likely to decide against a sitting president are during times of intense political conflict and change (e.g., the Depression) or when partisan holdover majorities control the Court (in the Jefferson administration when the president faced a Court made up entirely of Justices appointed by Federalist presidents).

Five types of Supreme Court decisions are possible when presidential powers come into question (See Table 8.3). Most of the time, as noted, the Court approves or *expands* presidential authority. It often *legitimizes* presidential power. The Court can also duck the question on the grounds it is a political matter to be settled by Congress and the president. On rare occasions, a *two-sided decision* is possible, when the Court may restrict an individual president but add to the power of the office. The Nixon tapes decision in 1974 is illustrative of a two-sided ruling. The Court ordered Nixon to yield his tapes. The Court also, and for the first time, recognized executive privilege as having constitutional standing. Sometimes, of course, in a clash of views, the Supreme Court *restricts* or curbs a president and presidential powers.

When sensitive issues of national security arise, the Court often invokes what is commonly called the doctrine of "political questions" to avoid head-on collisions

Table 8.3 Types of Court Decisions Regarding Presidential Power

TYPE OF DECISION	DEFINITION	EXAMPLE
Expanding	Decision adding power to presidency.	*United States v. Curtiss-Wright Export Corp* (1936). Recognizes it as necessary for presidents to have more power in foreign than in domestic affairs.
Legitimizing	Decision giving Court approval for presidential activities that were questioned.	*Korematsu v. United States* (1944). Approved FDR and executive powers to intern Japanese American citizens in World War II.
Avoiding	Decisions the Court decided "not to decide"; avoids getting involved.	*Massachusetts v. Laird* (1970). Denied to hear a case that questioned the president's broad power in the Vietnam War, thus avoiding a decision on the war.
Two-Sided	Decisions going against a president yet adding power to institution of the presidency.	*U.S. v. Nixon* (1974). Nixon told to yield tapes, yet court recognizes "executive privilege" as valid in serious national security situations.
Restricting	Decisions curbing or even diminishing presidential power.	*Youngstown Sheet and Tube Co. v. Sawyer* (1952). Truman and his Secretary of Commerce told they had exceeded their power in seizing the nation's steel mills to prevent a strike. Truman based his action on general powers of his office. Court held he could take no such action without express authorization from Congress.

with the president. The doctrine rests on the separation-of-powers theory, namely that the Supreme Court exercises the judicial power and leaves policy or political questions to the president and Congress. Chief Justice John Marshall invented the "political question" doctrine as early as 1803 when he said that matters in their nature political are "not for this Court to resolve." He affirmed this later, as in 1829, when he refused to rule on a boundary dispute between the United States and Spain. The judiciary shall not, said Marshall, decide foreign policy. Questions such as foreign boundaries, he added, are more political than legal.

Expanding and legitimizing decisions are fairly common. They are much more likely than restricting decisions. Most analysts of Court–presidency relations emphasize the Court's role in the expansion of presidential powers. The Supreme Court has often supported the vigorous actions of our strong presidents. The Supreme Court has been and will likely continue to be a supportive ally in most potential showdowns, especially in the case of emergency or national security contexts.

Many of the cases cited here are cases in which the highest court essentially gave or approved of power that had been previously undefined or undetermined. The issue at stake is whether presidents are able to cite a law or precise wording in the Constitution, or whether their broad and vague "executive power" allows them to conduct certain activities.

The Prize Cases (1863) were not the first dealing with presidential power to come before the Court, yet they are the first dealing with extraordinary, independent actions taken during a crisis. The Supreme Court ruled 5-4 that Lincoln could wage war with the South, under his authority as commander-in-chief, without congressional declaration. Presidential discretion was deemed sufficient for exercising this power. Indeed it was deemed to be within the broad grant of executive power found in Article II of the Constitution. The maxim that "There are two Constitutions, one for peace, the other for war" has its roots in these Civil War decisions.[16]

Before 1863, under international law ships could be legally taken as prizes only when a conflict had been recognized as a war between two belligerent powers. Thus, if the Supreme Court said the South did not have belligerent status, it appeared the justices would have had to rule the blockade as illegal. They decided instead to give primacy to executive discretion.

Another pro-presidency landmark case, *In re Neagle* (1890),[17] dealt not with foreign affairs but rather with the domestic task of effectively carrying out the functions of government. David Neagle, deputy U.S. marshal in the San Francisco region, was assigned to travel with Supreme Court Justice Stephen J. Field. Field's life had been threatened by a Californian whom Field had sentenced to prison. The U.S. Attorney General assigned Neagle to help protect Field. In implementing his assignment Neagle had to shoot, fatally it turned out, the man who in fact did try to attack Field.

The central question involved in this case was whether a president has either the constitutional or the prerogative sources of power to execute orders of the kind assigning Neagle to his duties. Is a president limited to enforcing only acts of Congress?

Here again the Supreme Court ruled that the president had been granted broad executive powers which he must be able to use at his discretion in order to administer properly the laws of the land. The Court openly acknowledged it was interpreting the word *law* in a liberal manner, the only conceivable manner which would serve the interests of justice in this instance. The president's executive order was clearly constitutional under the "faithfully execute" clause of the Constitution. The president's duty to fulfill this clause is consequently not limited to the enforcement of acts of Congress, according to their express terms, "but includes also the rights, duties and obligations growing out of the Constitution itself, our international relations, and all the protection implied by the nature of the government under the Constitution."

This decision strengthened and expanded the powers of the presidency. This broad interpretation was underlined a few years later in a subsequent case that legitimized President Grover Cleveland's sending troops into the Chicago area to deal with a railroad strike. Workers at the Pullman railroad company in 1894 had gone out on strike over certain wage reductions. The American Railway Union carried out a secondary boycott against the Pullman Company, a boycott that eventually threatened violence. A federal court issued an order seeking to halt the boycott on the grounds that the strike crippled interstate commerce. Union President Eugene V. Debs and his aides ignored the court order, were arrested, convicted of contempt, and sentenced to prison. President Grover Cleveland had dispatched federal troops to Chicago and ordered the U.S. Attorney in Chicago to halt the strike. Debs not only ignored these federal initiatives but petitioned the Supreme Court for a writ of habeas corpus, challenging his detention as illegal. Writing for the Court in this famous *in re Debs* (1895) case, Justice David J. Brewer affirmed sweeping executive emergency powers.

In a 1926 landmark decision, *Myers v. The United States*, the Court in a 6–3 decision granted a president, and presumably the presidency, with further administrative power, authorizing presidents to remove governmental officials without obtaining the consent of Congress. Frank Myers, postmaster for Portland, Oregon, was removed by President Woodrow Wilson without Wilson's securing Senate consent. Myers brought suit for salary for the remainder of his term. Back in 1876 Congress had passed a law providing for Senate participation in the removal of postmasters. Thus the question at hand, in the 1920s, was: May Congress limit a president's removal power?

Here is a rare instance in which the Supreme Court went against the wishes of Congress, at least as represented by the old statute under which Myers claimed to have his job protected. As we have seen, the Court usually defers to congressional judgment when Congress has specifically addressed the issue at hand, yet in this case the Court did not. The majority in this case believed a strict separation of powers is necessary if the executive is to function effectively.

In the *United States v. Curtiss-Wright Export Corporation* (1936), the Court in a 7–1 decision chose to affirm the broad foreign powers held by the president. The executive, the Court said in an aside not directly relevant to the case, was the sole spokesman of the nation, not the Constitution, nor Congress. To many observers this expansive decision came close to saying the president was "the sovereign." Congress could delegate, or so it seemed, virtually any foreign policy authority to the White House.[18]

A year later, in *United States v. Belmont* (1937), a near unanimous Court ruled that the national executive has the sole right to enter into executive agreements with other nations. State laws or policies do not supersede presidentially arranged international agreements even if they are not precisely in treaty form requiring Senate approval. Implicitly, if not explicitly, the Court ruled that executive agreements had the binding force of treaties.[19]

In 1944, an even more decisive delegation of authority was added to the long list of pro-presidency precedents. The Court, in *Korematsu* and related cases, gave the president national security powers even when those powers extended primarily to domestic public policy considerations. On February 19, 1942, President Roosevelt issued an executive order empowering the secretary of war to clear the three West Coast states and parts of Arizona of all persons of Japanese descent, 70,000 of whom were American citizens, and place them in detention centers.

Fred T. Korematsu, an American-born citizen of Japanese descent, violated the civilian exclusion order, a part of the implementation of FDR's general order, and was given a suspended sentence of five years of probation by the federal court. He appealed his case and the Court began to consider his and similar cases in May 1943.

Lawyers for Mr. Korematsu in 1943 (and in later years when his conviction was overturned) said Roosevelt in effect was using his commander-in-chief authority to condemn a race to imprisonment. No charge had been issued; no trial conducted. With his action, FDR called into question several constitutional rights for all American citizens: personal security, the right to move about freely, and the right not to be deprived of those rights except on an individual basis after trial by jury. All these traditional rights were imperiled. The force of the Fifth Amendment that guaranteed equal treatment under the law and due process was weakened. The character of U.S. citizenship and the wartime powers of the military over citizenry were also called into question.

On December 18, 1944, the U.S. Supreme Court ruled against Korematsu, effectively legitimizing FDR's actions as constitutional. During the trial, no claim was made that Korematsu was a disloyal citizen. His "crime" consisted solely of refusing to leave the restricted West Coast region, in the state where he was a citizen near the house where he was born.

Korematsu is an example of the Supreme Court's reluctance to question and its readiness to affirm a president's determination of necessity under the conditions of wartime. In dissent, Justice Frank Murphy said the judicial test of whether the executive, on a plea of military necessity, can validly deprive an individual of his rights must be reasonably related to a public danger that is so immediate as not to admit of delay and not to permit the intervention of ordinary constitutional processes to alleviate the danger. He believed the situation did not warrant the conviction.

Scholars now regard the *Korematsu* decision as one of the Court's dismal blunders. Racism, hysteria, and misleading military judgments were at work. One legal scholar concludes:

> Given the tensions of the period after Pearl Harbor, one might charitably advance the excuse of wartime hysteria for the harried members of Congress and the executive branch who made the initial decisions. No such excuse can be entertained for the justices of the Supreme Court who abandoned their most sacred principles at the first whiff of grapeshot.[20]

One of the ironic expansions came about as a result of the *U.S. v. Nixon* case in 1974. The case involved an appeal made by the Nixon Administration to vacate an order by federal district court Judge John Sirica requiring Nixon to release tapes and transcripts of sixty-four White House conversations that had been subpoenaed by Watergate Special Prosecutor Leon Jaworski. The executive branch claimed that the president had the right under the doctrine or custom of "executive privilege" to withhold the tapes. It was essential, it claimed, for presidents to be able to speak freely with their advisors without fear that such conversations would be available for public consumption.

Although the Court, speaking through Chief Justice Warren Burger, held Nixon's claims erroneous, it also believed it was their duty to define executive privilege. The Court seemed to say national security considerations would weigh heavily in balancing executive privilege against a competing constitutional claim. In the case at hand, in the summer of 1974, national security was not being threatened, this was a criminal case, and hence Nixon had to yield the tapes. To be sure, then, the Court limited President Nixon's claims of executive privilege, yet only after acknowledging for the first time the constitutionality of executive privilege.

A divided Supreme Court in June of 1982 ruled 5–4 that a president enjoys absolute immunity from civil damage suits for official actions exercised while on duty in the White House. Toward the end of 1995, President Clinton, however, found himself facing charges of sexual harassment. Paula Corbin Jones accused the President of improperly approaching her while Clinton was governor of Arkansas. She was a state employee at the time. In 1997, the Supreme Court ruled unanimously that a sitting president is not immune from civil suits of this type, and the Paula Jones case was allowed to proceed. Eventually, a settlement was reached between the parties.

Several post-9/11 actions by President George W. Bush were litigated in the courts. The actions taken by the second Bush administration in response to the terrorist attack against the United States have some precedent in history, as do court decisions challenging the constitutionality of such acts. The courts were asked to adjudicate on a vexing set of concerns: does the *rule of law* apply in a crisis? What are the proper limits on a president acting without the consent of the Congress during a crisis? Must the United States, in order to defend itself, undermine the Constitution?[21]

A recent presidency-boosting case involved a passport dispute wherein Menachem Zivotofsky's parents applied for a passport for their young son who was born in Jerusalem in 2002. The parents, U.S. citizens, citing a 2002 law, asked the State Department to designate Jerusalem, Israel, as Menachem's place of birth. The State Department refused, explaining that, notwithstanding the law, the U.S. government did not recognize that Jerusalem—which was claimed by Israel and others—was officially a part of Israel, as the city's sovereignty was still in dispute. Both the Bush and Obama administrations sided with the State Department's decision.

Justice Anthony Kennedy, writing for the majority, argued that the Constitution—while not literally granting the authority—gave to the president the "sole power to negotiate treaties," was rooted in the text of the Constitution, and is supported by historical practice as well as "functional considerations." The Congress, he argued, has other tools—budgeting, for example—with which to confront a president.

In dissent, Chief Justice John G. Roberts noted that the decision was a first of its kind: "Never before has this court accepted a president's defiance of an act of Congress in the field of foreign affairs." But it is not quite that simple. President George W. Bush signed the Foreign Relations Authorization Act in 2002; he attached a *signing statement* in which he asserted that he would not follow the passport provision. Does a signing statement trump a law?

Also writing in dissent, Justice Antonin Scalia argued that "the tragedy of today's decision is not its result, but the principle that produces this result." Scalia argued that the framers' Constitution divided power between the executive and legislature in "foreign power policy and . . . for just about everything else." He concluded that this decision "will systematically favor the president at the expense of Congress."

Although FDR suffered some initial setbacks, he eventually got most of what he wanted from the Court and indeed shaped, with nine appointments, a decidedly pro-national government and pro-presidency Court. Nixon also suffered several setbacks. He lost a number of cases both in the Supreme Court and in lower federal courts. During the Clinton, George W. Bush, and Obama years, the courts decided several cases against the president.

PRESIDENTIAL LOSSES BEFORE THE SUPREME COURT

Presidents do lose some key Court decisions. The Court has taken decisive stands against presidents after the Civil War, during the first New Deal, briefly near the end of the Korean War, during the Watergate affair, in the second Clinton term, and against President Bush in the War on Terror. Moreover, these anti-presidency rulings were often tempered by the fact that they generally were not direct, independent, or confrontational challenges to a president. Thus the Court stood up to Lincoln only after his assassination. The Court backed off after its brief though significant foray against the early New Deal legislation, and it reacted to Watergate only after the press, the public, and Congress were already "up in arms." The Court, then, has not been a secure protector of individual rights and freedoms or the separation of powers during times of crisis.

Still, when presidents have acted against provisions of the Constitution or an explicit congressional directive, or both, the Court has been inclined to stop them from treading further. The Court, understandably enough, is usually a bit bolder in these assertions of its role when a president has suffered notable declines in public approval.

Because we have treated some of these cases earlier, especially in the discussions of Lincoln and FDR, and because the major pattern in the Court-presidency relationship has been in expanding presidential power, we shall just briefly discuss these restraining decisions. Note, however, that these counterpoint decisions are no less important; they are merely the exceptions to the pattern.

The first significant case arose in Jefferson's term when Chief Justice John Marshall, Jefferson's antagonist, explicated the doctrine of judicial review. The *Marbury v. Madison* (1803)[22] decision, while cleverly avoiding a direct confrontation with the president, gave the Court the means for serving as the primary interpreter of what laws or executive actions conform to the U.S. Constitution. In the process of handing down this decision, John Marshall also said President Jefferson and his Secretary of State, James Madison, acted improperly. More important, however, was the establishment of the Court and its authority to serve as a vital branch if not exactly a co-equal branch with the other two branches of government.

A year later the Court, in a unanimous decision, instructed executive branch officials to pay for damages in the seizure of a Danish vessel, a seizure the Court said took place because of improper or invalid presidential instructions. The *Little v. Bareme* case involved the following question: Can a naval captain be found civilly liable for following what the Court found to be an executive order that went beyond what Congress had authorized?[23]

Chief Justice John Marshall confessed that initially he believed that although President John Adams' instructions of 1799 could not give a right for the seizure, they might yet excuse the navy captain, Captain Little, from paying damages. He added, however, "I was mistaken." The instructions were invalid and therefore furnished no protection for the navy captain, who obeyed his president at his peril, because the congressional legislation in question authorized only the seizure of vessels proceeding to French ports. Executive instructions cannot, the Court ruled, ever change the nature of an administrative transaction or legalize an act which would have been a plain trespass. If the Congress had been silent on the matter, the president's general authority as commander-in-chief would probably have been sufficient, but once Congress had prescribed the manner in which the law was to be carried out the president and all other executive officials were obliged to respect the limitations imposed by congressional statute.

Another major case again arose during a military emergency (just as nearly all limiting or presidency-constraining decisions arose during unusual circumstances), the Civil War, during which Lincoln had suspended the writ of habeas corpus. Chief Justice Taney, acting in his additional role as a circuit court judge, ruled that Lincoln had no constitutional power to suspend the writ. Lincoln never complied with this order, and a major lesson was learned. Rarely again would the Court attempt to stop a presidential action while it was taking place. Presidents can seldom if ever be enjoined from taking an action, only reprimanded once they have taken it. Still, *Ex parte Merryman* (1861) was important in that a Supreme Court justice recognized limits to presidential power, even in wartime.

In *Ex parte Milligan* (1866), the Court did place clear limitations on the emergency powers of the president, limiting his military authority. Yet this happened after the fact, after the war was over, and after Lincoln had died. In the *Korematsu* case of 1944, when the danger to the Union was arguably non-existent, a different Court ignored this *Milligan* Civil War precedent and granted to the chief executive all the powers Lincoln had assumed and more. Thus, in many respects, these two Civil War limitations can be said to be of limited utility in the overall definition of presidential power, even as they are important because they were among the first weak attempts by the Supreme Court to recognize that individual rights deserve to be considered as important as a strong national executive.

Other clashes between the Court and the presidency arose once again in emergency circumstances, during the height of the Depression. Here again, the Court believed that the president lacked the constitutional authority to act alone in "saving the Union." Roosevelt's multiple plans to shore up the economy or regulate economic behavior met with Court disfavor. The Court's several rulings about the unconstitutionality of the early New Deal measures have been discussed. Congress, in one sense, had erred by giving Roosevelt too general a mandate. Had FDR been carrying out specific congressional plans, he would have probably won the Court's approval in most instances (although it is doubtful Congress could have agreed on specific plans for him to administer). These anti–New Deal Court rulings represented a distinction the Supreme Court has always made between foreign and domestic affairs. In foreign affairs, a president only needs a broad mandate from Congress. But domestic and economic affairs have usually required more detailed statutes.

This maxim was proved true once again in the 1935 case of *Humphrey's Executor v. United States*.[24] In this case, a congressional prescription for removing a Federal Trade Commission commissioner was violated by Franklin Roosevelt. The Court responded by narrowing and in some ways overturning the *Myers* decision it had made just nine years earlier. In this 1935 ruling, the Court acknowledged that Congress, in creating agencies to carry out judicial and legislative duties, could restrict a president's removal power in specified cases, and thus it overruled FDR. *Humphrey* became one of only a handful or so of the actual major precedents serving to limit presidential powers.

Another case in which a president was limited came during what most people might consider less than a national crisis, although President Truman apparently thought otherwise. This was the *Youngstown Sheet and Tube Co. v. Sawyer* (1952) case. Sawyer was Truman's secretary of commerce who was instructed by Truman to seize and operate certain steel mills that otherwise would have been shut down by union strikes (or, depending on your outlook, by the failure of the steel mill companies to improve pay and benefits).

Truman seized, through his secretary of commerce, all the steel mills affected by the strike. This accounted for eighty-six companies, over 200 steel mills, 600,000 workers, and 95 percent of the nation's steel production.

The seizure was implemented without much administrative trouble. Executive order number 10340 was issued, and all employees of these mills then worked for the U.S. government and did so at the same wages as before. Every company was ordered to fly the American flag above its mills. Everyone complied. Yet the steel companies didn't like it and filed suit in federal court.

Meanwhile Truman, his popularity already low, was attacked for being a bully, a usurper, a lawbreaker, and an architect of a labor dictatorship. "Newspapers, magazines, steel executives, business organizations, and Republicans [exceeded] their own performances of the Roosevelt years. They attacked Truman as a Caesar, an American Hitler or Mussolini, an author of evil. . . ."[25] Within days the Supreme Court responded and heard the case. The steel companies hammered away at the unconstitutionality of Truman's actions. He had, they said, acted without congressional approval and without constitutional justification.

Truman's Justice Department countered with every plausible precedent, especially from the Lincoln and FDR eras. It didn't work. Justice Hugo Black, speaking for a 6–3 majority, agreed with the steel companies. No clause in the Constitution justified Truman's action, nor had it been authorized by Congress.

The Court ruled that the Korean crisis was not a full-scale emergency justifying the full invocation and exercise of presidential war powers. Truman was furious about this decision, and also bitter toward his appointee and former Attorney General Tom Clark, who voted against him.

Other notable cases limiting executive power involve Nixon. Richard Nixon several times tested the limits of the office, sometimes succeeding in gaining power for the office and sometimes having his authority curbed. In the Pentagon Papers case, or *New York Times Co. v. United States* (1971),[26] the Supreme Court acted for the first time under wartime conditions since it had done so belatedly during the Civil War to protect institutional liberties against inroads from the executive branch. Vietnam was, however, an undeclared war, being waged with diminishing public and congressional support and by a somewhat unpopular president.

The Nixon administration attempted to halt publication in the *New York Times* and the *Washington Post* of a collection of classified but leaked essays and documents entitled "History of U.S. Decision-Making Process on Vietnam Policy." The real question, the only question on which, ultimately, this decision is based, is whether publication of these articles and documents would have yielded "direct, immediate, and irreparable damage to our nation and its people."

Nixon and the Justice Department said the publication of the so-called Pentagon Papers assaulted the principle of government control over classified documents. There are other parts of the Constitution that grant power and responsibilities to the president, they claimed, and the First Amendment was never intended to make it impossible for the president to function or to protect the security of the nation.

The Court was not persuaded. They ruled 6–3 in favor of the *New York Times* and permitted publication. The reasoning of the justices, however, is not simple to explain. There were six separate opinions for the majority and one for the three dissenters. The common bond linking the six majority judges was that the executive branch had simply failed to prove that the publication of these documents posed a major threat: "Any system of prior restraint of expression comes to this Court bearing a heavy presumption against its constitutional validity," the Court said. "The Government thus carries a heavy burden of showing justification for the enforcement of such a restraint."[27]

While the Supreme Court in this important case did not allow the Nixon Administration to run roughshod over the First Amendment, it left the door open for executive discretion. Several justices acknowledged that had the publication of the Pentagon Papers truly threatened national security, they might have allowed for prior restraint. The Court still would not put an absolute limit on executive authority.

A second decision that somewhat limited presidential power was a unanimous one in *United States v. U.S. District Court* in 1972.[28] Here the Supreme Court ruled that domestic surveillances required a warrant from the courts. And, in fact, a lower court extended this decision to foreign wiretaps (made for national security purposes).

Critics of Nixon and of the growing expansion of presidential power especially welcomed this decision. Clear limits, they believed, were placed on the executive through this opinion. Consequently the FBI had to disconnect several wiretaps.

There are indications, however, that the executive branch's compliance with this Court ruling has undermined its spirit. In practice, the executive branch wins regular approval through convenient procedures the Judiciary and the Justice Department subsequently established, for example making it easier for a president to gain Foreign Intelligence Surveillance Act (FISA) approvals.

In the end, the courts shrank the powers of the presidency in some key areas. In the Paula Jones lawsuit, the president's lawyers sought immunity from the suit while the president was in office, asking that the case be postponed until after Clinton left office. The Supreme Court eventually decided that the president enjoys no immunity, even temporary, from civil suits for unofficial acts.[29] This makes future presidents more open to court challenges and gives presidents somewhat less protection from lawsuits, frivolous and otherwise.

Presidents have long claimed that discussions with aides were privileged and could be kept from Congress. In past conflicts over such information, presidents usually struck a compromise with Congress. But during the Clinton years, all sides took an all-or-nothing approach. Thus, the courts were called to intervene. And in the end, the Court sided with Congress, leaving Clinton and future presidents more vulnerable and less protected. On the other hand, when the same courts were asked, in the early days of the presidency of George W. Bush, to force Vice President Dick Cheney to reveal with whom he had discussed a controversial energy policy, the courts sided with Cheney and against the Government Accountability Office, the investigatory arm of Congress.

In the aftermath of the September 11, 2001, terrorist attacks against the United States, President Bush's power increased. A rally-'round-the-flag effect lifted his popularity, the public demanded action, the Congress deferred to the president, and the courts waited silently in the wings. Not shy about using this power, Bush launched a war against terrorism and challenged the rule of law.

Many of these things were done solely on the orders of the President.[30] But did the President—acting alone, on his own claimed authority—truly have such discretionary powers? Had the United States come full circle from a revolution against the tyrannical power of a British King only to edge toward an elective version of monarchical authority in the president?

If Bush initially had a free hand, over time the president's policies, one-by-one, began to backfire and opposition began to build.[31]

Surprisingly, one of the first and most forceful rebuffs of the President and his policies came from the Republican-dominated Supreme Court. In a series of critical decisions, the Court—after standing alone in opposition to the President—rejected some of the key claims of independent authority that animated presidential actions, and trimmed the power-sails of the presidency.

In 2004, in *Rasul v. Bush*[32] the Court, in a 6–3 decision, ruled that those detained in Guantanamo Bay had a right to challenge their imprisonment in an American court. The Bush administration had maintained that these detainees had no such rights. The President was forced to back down, and established a three-person military panel to review the status of detainees.

Also in 2004, in *Hamdi v. Rumsfeld*[33] the Court reversed the dismissal of a *habeus corpus* petition brought by a U.S. citizen, Yaser Esam Hamdi, held as an "illegal enemy combatant." In this 8–1 decision, Justice Sandra Day O'Connor, writing for a plurality of four justices, denied the president powers to hold U.S. citizens without legal process, writing that "a state of war is not a blank check for the President," and that the commander-in-chief clause is not a license to "turn our system of checks and balances on its head."

In June 2006, in *Hamden v. Rumsfeld*,[34] the Court held that the military commissions set up by the Bush administration to try detainees should be halted because they violated the Uniform Code of Military Justice as well as four Geneva Conventions signed in 1949 by the United States. In a 5–3 ruling, the Court said the president did not have the inherent authority, absent the approval of Congress, to set up special military trials. Bush then went to the Congress, which authorized such trials and stripped detainees of certain rights and appeals.

But in 2008, in *Boumediene v. Bush*,[35] the Court, in a 5–4 ruling, held that foreign prisoners held at Guantanamo Bay did have a right to a hearing before a federal Judge. Writing for the majority, Justice Anthony Kennedy noted that "the laws and Constitution are designed to survive, and remain in force, in extraordinary times. Liberty and security can be reconciled; and in our system they are reconciled within the framework of the law."

In sum, Bush's overreaching claims of inherent, independent powers in wartime were modified by the Supreme Court. The Bush-Cheney quest for unilateral power met a Supreme Court intent on constitutionalizing the president's wartime powers. The rule of law and the separation of powers—battered, bruised, and challenged—emerged, viable if not fully intact.[36]

On several occasions, President Obama was rebuffed by the Supreme Court. Critics argued that Obama, facing a hostile Congress controlled by the opposition, resorted to executive overreach in attempting to achieve his policy goals. The Court agreed, and dealt several blows to Obama's discretionary decisions. In *NLRB v. Canning* (2014), the Court greatly limited President Obama's (and future presidents') use of recess appointments. And in 2016, in a 5–4 decision, the Court in *Virginia v. EPA* limited the president's ability to regulate coal emissions to combat global warming by issuing a stay of a Virginia Court's decision to halt Obama administration regulations. This marks the first time the Court granted a request to block a regulation before a final legal decision could be reached.

While, historically, the courts have been a bit reluctant to decide cases against presidents, that trend has reversed in recent years. Although President Obama won major court victories in health care, gay rights, and abortion, overall his record was poor.[37] This reflects a trend *away* from deference to presidents, signaling a more confrontation approach by the courts (see Figure 8.1).

On March 16, President Obama nominated Merrick Garland, 63, a fairly moderate chief judge of the United States Court of Appeals for the District of Columbia, the second most important court in the United States. Garland had an impeccable record and reputation. Denying him a hearing would be potentially risky, but that is precisely what the Republican-controlled Senate did. This left the court with eight members, and in a number of cases, 4–4 ties let lower court decisions stand, thereby taking the nation's highest court out of the process.

President Donald J. Trump was in office less than a month when he faced a court rebuke from the 9th Circuit Court of Appeals over his January 27 executive

President	Percentage of Wins
Ronald Reagan	75%
George H.W. Bush	70%
Bill Clinton	63%
George W. Bush	60%
Barack Obama	50.5%

Figure 8.1 Percentage of President's Wins in Supreme Court Cases[38]

order banning travel to the United States by people form seven predominantly Muslim countries. The court decision let stand a lower court ruling that halted the ban. The President, outraged, lashed out at the court via twitter, but in the end decided not to challenge the court but to rewrite the executive order taking into account the objections of the courts.

CONCLUSION

Supreme Court justices tend to share with presidents a similar national perspective and a common outlook about the national interest. However, they have different obligations and responsibilities and operate in a different political forum. More often than not, the Supreme Court and the lower federal courts have sided with presidents as new demands and emergencies encouraged presidents to stretch the formal powers of the office. This trend or pattern is now well established and is rooted in Sutherland's famed, if controversial, 1936 *Curtiss-Wright* decision. This judicial deference exists especially in wartime and when presidents enjoy high popularity. But such deference is not without its limits, as several recent presidents have discovered.

The Court appreciates that only the president is elected by the nation. Still it is a paramount function of the Court to insist that presidents do not go beyond what is necessary or to try to singularly embody the nation's sovereignty. No president should be allowed to make the law or disregard for long the general commands of the U.S. Constitution.

Strong presidents invariably look for ways to expand their prerogatives and authority. Often, of course, this may be due to the emergencies confronting the nation. Their public approval ratings can have an important bearing on whether they win victories in clashes with the Court. Strong presidents try to nominate new justices who will advance their policies and values. For several generations now it has become common practice for presidents to appoint justices with a sympathy to their policy leanings, and this will continue.

One of the strengths of the Supreme Court is its ability to function as an independent and at least a somewhat unpredictable institution. No president can shape it for long. As noted, members of the Court develop their own independent constitutional philosophies, the more so the longer they remain on the Court.

Courts are most likely to take on presidents who boldly make claims of independent power—Lincoln during the Civil War, FDR during the Great Depression, and George W. Bush during the War on Terror, for example. Even when these presidents are popular, presidents who push the envelope on presidential power too far may well face a Court willing to push back. Courts are more likely to defer to presidents in foreign affairs rather than domestic, during times of war or crisis rather than in normal times, and when the partisan majority on the Court is controlled by the party opposed to the president's party.

We cannot expect the Supreme Court to be the sole or even main accountability check on presidents. Our system functions best when Congress, the president, and the Court each energetically promote their own independent vision of good government. Preferring a strong presidency should not lead one to want a corresponding weakness in the other two branches, but rather a corresponding strength and assertiveness.

FURTHER READINGS

Abraham, Henry J. *Justices, Presidents, and Senators*, 5th ed. Lanham, Md.: Rowman & Littlefield, 2008.

Binder, Sarah, and Forrest Maltzman. *Advice & Dissent: The Struggle to Shape the Federal Judiciary*. Washington, D.C: Brookings Institution, 2009.

Novkov, Julie, *The Supreme Court and the Presidency: Struggle for Supremacy*. Washington, D.C.: CQ Press, 2013.

Sollenberger, Mitchel A. *Judicial Appointments and Democratic Controls*. Durham, N.C.: Carolina Academic Press, 2011.

CHAPTER 9

The Future of the American Presidency

The presidency changes from season to season, occupant to occupant, challenge to challenge—and this will continue. We have certainly seen this in the Obama and Trump years. We have had several effective presidents, many ineffective presidents, and still others judged as merely average. This trend, too, will continue.

Presidents bring different experiences, character, styles, goals, assets, and liabilities to the office. Each understands that while the American political experiment has been a path-breaking, ambitious, and noble experiment, it remains an unfinished endeavor. A major part of each new president's job is to promote policy initiatives that will achieve the shared aspirations of Americans.

Each president in the future, as in the past, will learn how challenging it is to provide leadership in a nation that celebrates liberty and rights over obligations, and individualism over communitarian values.

And every generation of Americans must learn again that strong presidents are undesirable—unless their policy objectives are fair and in service to the common good, and unless their political dealings are constitutional and democratic. "We honor the great presidents of the past not for their strength," presidential historian Clinton Rossiter reminded us, "but for the fact that they used it wisely to build a better America."[1]

Ours has been a political system that increasingly depends on strong, effective presidential leadership. Perhaps the only way to reduce this need for a strong presidency is to reduce America's role in the world and retreat from global leadership (which some people would like to see), and free our mixed economy from most regulations and controls (which, again, libertarians and some conservatives favor).

Future presidents will have to live with the following realities, most of which we have discussed in previous chapters:

- Trust in- government will continue to be low while expectations on presidents will continue to be high.

- The way we recruit and elect presidents will continue to be messy (as the 2016 election was)—overly long, expensive, and with a premium on negative ads as well as processes that discourage voter turnout.
- Hyper-partisanship and a variety of Madisonian checks and balances will make it difficult for presidents to initiate and enact significant policy reforms—except when the president's party enjoys majorities in both houses of Congress, or during times of crisis.
- Globalization and the development of new technologies (disruptive technologies for some) will make presidential leadership more important, but more challenging.
- Every president will be asked to enhance the nation's homeland security and help prevent terrorism and cyberattacks of all kinds yet not trample on our liberties.
- Every president will be challenged to help the nation create more jobs and economic growth while balancing the budget and protecting social security and health entitlements.
- Every president will have to work vigilantly with many others to promote greater equality and tolerance. And each should remember the maxim attributed to the great Supreme Court justice Louis Brandeis: "We can have concentrated wealth in the hands of a few, or we can have a democracy. But we can't have both."
- Americans will continue to be divided on what kind of presidential leadership they want, depending on their partisan loyalties as well as their views about stronger versus limited government and on the proper role of the United States in world affairs.
- In the future, as in the past, numerous reforms will be proposed, some of them amendments to the Constitution, aimed at making the presidency more effective or more accountable and democratic, and others will be aimed at improving the way we nominate and elect presidents. Most of these proposals, as we discuss in this chapter, will languish and not be approved.
- And there will always be conflicting expectations and paradoxes about presidential leadership. Can we rid the presidency of its paradoxes? We couldn't even if we wanted to. Contradictions and paradoxes are part of the nature of leadership in a democracy. And in our nation, formed of varied interests and backgrounds representing different constituencies, bringing people together will always be an exacting challenge. Effective presidents are aggregators, bringing groups together rather than splitting them apart.

We will continue to want a presidency grounded in the fundamental values set out by the nation's founders, yet we will need a presidency that can meet the challenges of the twenty-first century. An enduring paradox, and a central theme of this book, is that the same office that can nourish responsible, coherent leadership also offers the opportunity for toxic leadership. We may want a fearless "take charge" leader, especially in fearful times, but we never want that fearlessness to turn into recklessness.

One of the paradoxes of the American political experiment is that it took a *revolution* coupled with bold and sweeping constitutional inventions to create the American Republic, yet our values nowadays are rooted in a strong faith in social and political *gradualism* and a skepticism about any significant constitutional change. Part of the paradox is that people celebrate the Constitution as promoting democracy even though many aspects of it are undemocratic (e.g., the Senate, the Electoral College, life terms for justices, etc.). With perhaps the one exception of agreeing to get rid of the Electoral College, Americans are constitutional conservatives.

The role of the U.S. Constitution in American political culture is itself paradoxical. The U.S. Constitution, unlike the Declaration of Independence, is dry, legalistic, and wholly lacking in eloquence. Moreover, it is a document based on a skeptical view of the ability of people to govern themselves without multiple safeguards, shared arrangements, and checks and balances. "There is no visible 'democratic faith' in this constitution," wrote Irving Kristol, "and yet—and yet it is a founding document that is venerated" by the American people.[2] It is, most Americans believe, a glorious and sacred document and one of the reasons for the Republic's longevity and prosperity. This veneration borders on being a "cult of the Constitution" regardless of its being largely unread and often misunderstood.

But reverence for the Constitution has not deterred scores of lawyers, political scientists, and reformers (from a variety of persuasions) from proposing constitutional and political fixes for the American presidency.[3] These include calling for a parliamentary system; compulsory voting; a proportional voting system; direct one-person, one-vote election of presidents; presidential question hours in Congress; and a slew of additional "remedies." We devote most of this chapter to discussing and evaluating a representative sample of some of the most debated of these reforms.

MAKING THE PRESIDENCY MORE EFFECTIVE

The nation's founders would doubtless be pleased at how the American system of checks and balances has thwarted executive tyranny. However, they would be less pleased with the gridlock and dysfunctionality that often characterizes relations between the president and Congress.

Was the separation-of-powers shared leadership a curse or a blessing? To several presidents there were times where a parliamentary system or at least quasi-parliamentary features seemed attractive.

Woodrow Wilson, writing in 1884, long before he became president, saw the separation as creating a political escape clause for blame and responsibility. "Power and strict accountability for its use," Wilson wrote, "are the essential constituents of good government. . . ."

> It is, therefore, manifestly a radical defect in our federal system that it parcels out power and confuses responsibility as it does. The main purpose of the

> Convention of 1787 seems to have been to accomplish this grievous mistake. . . .
> Were it possible to call together the members of that wonderful Convention . . .
> they would be the first to admit that the only fruit of dividing power has been to
> make it irresponsible.[4]

Several others, agreeing with Wilson, have proposed ideas that would allow a
president to have greater sway with Congress. Some have proposed electing presidents and members of Congress as part of the same ticket and for similar four-year
terms. Others have recommended allowing members of Congress to serve in the
president's cabinet. Still others favor providing presidents an item veto and granting presidents an enhanced role as a legislator.

Many of these reformers are convinced that presidents are in a better position
than members of Congress to ascertain what is in the public interest. Presidents
therefore should have the means to help shape coherent national programs. The
idea is that more and more of our nation's problems are national or international
in scope and should be addressed by an official responsible to a national electorate
rather than by 535 members of Congress who are beholden to parochial interests.

Most of those advocating for a stronger presidency have simultaneously been
advocates of a stronger, bigger, and more progressive national government. They
want more comprehensive planning and coherent national policies. They point to
the Manhattan Project (that produced atomic weapons during World War II), the
Interstate Highway System, NASA, and the National Science Foundation as a few
examples where presidents took the lead to mobilize national resources to meet
demonstrable national needs.

The larger argument is that the Madisonian system of checks and balances,
combined with intense partisan polarization, the rise of the anti-government Tea
Party, and the rise of well-financed special interest groups and Super PACs have
all combined to create a "vetocracy," a situation in which it is easier to prevent the
national government from doing things than it is to encourage government to
promote the common good.[5]

There is little support in America for shifting to a parliamentary system (save
among some comparative politics scholars) or for a major overhaul of our presidential-congressional system by holding a second constitutional convention to
come up with something better.

We next discuss three representative examples of proposals to make the presidency more effective.

Presidential Item Veto?
The proposed item veto—sometimes called the "line-item veto"—would allow a
president to veto, delete, or send back to Congress any subsection or portion of
an appropriations bill passed by Congress. Proposed item veto measures typically
provide for a process by which Congress could override, by a two-thirds vote in
both houses.

Congress enacted a statutory provision giving presidents this type of veto
during the Bill Clinton presidency, but the U.S. Supreme Court (in *Clinton v. City*

of New York, 1998) rejected this delegation of power to presidents. The Court ruled it was a violation of the Constitution's Presentment Clause, as the power allowed the president to, in effect, rewrite the legislation presented to him by Congress. The Court's majority opinion made it clear this type of power could only by given to a president through the amendment procedures set forth in Article V of the Constitution.

Still, several presidents and many reformers advocate this idea as a means of giving presidents needed responsibility for controlling deficits and eliminating wasteful, so-called "earmarked spending." A proposed constitutional amendment providing for the item veto authority was approved by a bipartisan vote in the U.S. House of Representatives of 254–173 in 2012. But that's as far as it got then, or since.

Here, in brief, are the reasons for which advocates urge giving item veto authority to presidents:

- The item veto would help eliminate waste in the federal budget, such as the "Bridge to Nowhere" in Alaska, museums honoring members of Congress in their home districts or no-longer-needed weapons systems.
- The president's general veto has been subverted by various congressional practices of huge "overstuffed" appropriations, tax benefits, or bailouts presented to the White House—and the item veto would restore the intended objective of the presidential veto power.
- Most state governors have an item veto authority, and they like it because it gives them a tool for reminding legislators that economy in the public interest is just as important as spending in local district interests. Polls regularly show that majorities of business executives as well as the American public support this "reform."

Here, however, are the major reasons to oppose amending the Constitution to provide presidents with item veto authority:

- It would shift additional power away from Congress and doubtless expand the power of unelected aides at the White House and in the Office of Management and Budget.
- It could encourage further irresponsibility in congressional spending behavior and thereby weaken Congress as an institution for collective policymaking.
- The item veto could strengthen a president's hand in dealing with individual members of Congress, pressuring them to support presidential priorities or risk having their special projects item vetoed. In the hands of a big-spending president this might have the ironic effect of encouraging greater rather than smaller deficits.
- Both presidents and members of Congress already have procedures available to them to eliminate wasteful spending; they just have to have the will power to vote them down, or veto them down. Why not insist that Congress and presidents use the authority they already have?

- Studies show the item veto has had a limited effect on spending levels in those states which provide for it. It mainly changes the composition of the spending, often substituting a governor's priorities for those of state legislators.
- One Reagan Administration economist faulted George W. Bush's call for an item veto "as little more than smoke-and-mirrors—an effort to show that he is serious about out-of-control spending without actually doing anything to cut spending or even restrain its growth." Bruce Bartlett adds: "But no one should delude themselves into thinking that the lack of a presidential line-item veto is all that stands between us and a balanced budget."[6]

In recent years, some lawmakers have recommended what many are calling a modified item veto. This new proposal, called "expedited rescission," tries to get around the Supreme Court's ruling that said only a president may sign or veto a bill. Under this new modification—or limited item veto—Congress would pass an appropriations bill, send it to the White House, then a president could sign the bill but send one or two wasteful spending items back to Congress. Congress would then vote on these in both chambers within a specified time, such as forty-five days, with no possibility for amendments or, in the Senate, no filibuster allowed.

Most presidents would welcome this as a tool to go after wasteful "earmarking." But some critics think that even this watered down presidential item veto weakens Congress and is yet another example of delegating legislative authority to the White House. "It's a disgusting idea," said Louis Fisher, a respected scholar of Congress and constitutionalism. "It's a cheap and easy thing for members to do. But it weakens Congress. And to have this very romantic view of the president as better guardian of the Treasury, I just don't think that's the case."[7]

The most compelling reason to resist the item veto is that it would encourage yet another additional transfer of power from Congress to the presidency—a grant of authority that, yes, would strengthen the president's hand, yet would do so at the price of diminishing the capacity of Congress to function as a separate and vital branch of government.

The item-veto proposal has a certain amount of appeal and deserves periodic debates, yet we believe it illustrates once again journalist H. L. Mencken's theorem that for every difficult and complex problem, there is an obvious solution which is simple, easy, and wrong. In our view, the item veto authority would provide more power than an effective president needs, and more than a misguided or imperial president should have. The marginal benefits of trimming some "fat" from congressional spending and tax benefit measures would be outweighed by weakening of a Congress too inclined in recent generations to delegate away its constitutional power.

As noted, a strong presidency is desirable. However, constitutionally we also want a strong Congress and a strong federal judiciary to counterbalance a strong president. In the long run—the founders were right—the public and national interests will be best served when each of our branches is able and willing to exercise fully these individual as well as shared prerogatives.

"Fast Track" Legislative Authority?

Congress has sometimes granted presidents "fast track" authority to submit trade agreements with other nations. This "fast track" authority calls for an up-or-down majority vote in both chambers of Congress and bans amendments and a Senate filibuster. It also specifies a time period, such as 45 days, for hearings and debates.

Two political scientists, William Howell and Terry Moe, have proposed a constitutional amendment that would grant presidents general "fast-track" legislative authority—for major legislative proposals. A president, with this authority, would develop policy proposals on which Congress would have to vote without any amendments, and within a fixed two month- time period. Congress would retain the right to vote presidential proposals down, and they would likewise retain their existing authority to incubate and enact their own legislative measures.[8]

The rationale for the proposal is that Congress is too beholden to local, parochial interests and is rarely capable of providing the leadership needed to design and promote coherent policy solutions for the nation's most challenging economic and domestic problems.

The essence of the proposal is to strengthen the agenda-setting power of presidents, permitting them an enhanced legislative role akin to that of a prime minister under a parliamentary political system. "Presidents," Howell and Moe continue, "are the champions of coherence and effectiveness in a fragmented, parochial political world," and "Presidents have worked tirelessly to meet the expansive expectations that the American public has thrust upon them."[9]

Here are a few strengths of this proposal:

- There is the potential for it to help address and solve national problems in a better, more timely way. At the very least, it would require dissenting legislators to more fully justify why they voted against the president.
- We have seen some success in several international trade agreements and a similar process for closing some military bases. Moreover, the United States is one of a few nations that does not give its executive some power of mandating legislative initiation—and this proposal is merely a watered down version of that.
- Presidents enjoy greater informational expertise and planning resources than legislators or legislative committees. Presidentially designed policies may be better crafted, especially to meet the long-term interests of the nation.
- Fast-track authority would allow presidents to focus their power and resources on top policy priorities, and thereby might bypass the political polarization and stalemate that seems to define contemporary Washington, D.C.

However, Critics of the "fast-track" authority point to these weaknesses of this proposal:

- The modern presidency has grown, compared to the other branches or any other office, more powerful, and this would further strengthen the presidency at the expense of the other branches.
- The claim that presidents craft better policies and provide for coherent national solutions is at least partially weakened if not undermined by pointing

to major presidentially initiated policy failures such as Vietnam, Iraq, the Bay of Pigs invasion of Cuba, the costly and misguided War on Drugs," excessive tax cuts for the rich, Watergate, the Iran-Contra scandal, etc. We have learned, too often, that presidents are not infallible and they can be influenced by special interests and by so-called experts who "fix the facts."

- During times of unified government (where one party is in control of both Congress and the White House), it could allow majoritarian program initiatives to be pushed through Congress, without germane amendments, modifications, or adequate minority party input, and without proper time for cost-benefit analyses.

- It might not, in practice, make much of a difference. Our national government, in recent decades, has often been divided. It is unclear how, in a time of hyperpolarization, this proposal would succeed in its objectives. It seems likely that a Republican-controlled Congress would vote down most fast-track proposals of a Democratic president, and similarly a Democratically controlled Congress would withdraw majority support from most Republicans.

On balance, the "fast-track" legislative authority idea is a provocative one. It is something that has been tried. It is relatively low-risk. Congress still retains most of its legislative authority and the next president could reverse a policy enacted by "fast-track." Moreover, Congress does not need to consent to any presidential proposal.

Presidents of both parties, now and in the future, would love to have both the item-veto and "fast-track" powers. Both diminish the obstructionist tendencies of Congress, for example, House Rules Committee delays and filibustering in the Senate.

Your authors are conflicted with regard to both of these proposals. We confess that if we were president we would relish having these additional strategic resources. They both would provide the type of energy Alexander Hamilton famously described as essential for effective government. However, to institute these reforms would be to significantly shift many of Congress's constitutional powers to the president. Whether or not that shift would be for the best is not entirely clear, but it would change the American political landscape.

All reform proposals have side effects and unanticipated consequences that cannot be assessed ahead of time. And many believe that certain trade pacts such as the North American Free Trade Agreement (NAFTA), passed by "fast-track" authority, have sometimes favored corporate interests at the expense of working people.

Both of these proposed constitutional amendments deserve greater scrutiny. Both are legitimate ideas that could make the American presidency more effective, resilient, and relevant. Both would change business-as-usual in Washington. Both would also modify the eighteenth-century constitutional structure created by the founders, which would likely raise questions about whether other institutions, especially Congress and the federal judiciary, need to be reformed as well.

Repeal the Twenty-Second Amendment?

One of the frequently debated reforms of the American presidency is whether the Twenty-Second Amendment weakens or strengthens the office and whether it weakens or strengthens constitutionalism.[10]

Congress proposed the Twenty-Second Amendment in 1947. With 70 percent of those voting in Congress supporting it, it sailed through both houses and won ratification in 1951.

Advocates of repeal say this two-term limit violates the American citizen's right to decide who will be their leader. If the people want to vote for someone, especially an experienced veteran in the White House, there should be no rule telling them they do not have that choice. "It bespeaks a shocking lack of faith in the common sense and good judgment of the people,"[11] wrote political historian Clinton Rossiter.

Every president's sun now begins to set the day the second term begins—the "lame duck" syndrome.[12] We have, critics say, dealt the modern presidency a major blow by depriving second-term presidents of the political weapon of their availability to another term, which keeps both supporters and rivals guessing.

Proponents of a strong presidency fear that the Twenty-Second Amendment limitation weakens presidential independence and slopes the balance of power back too much in the direction of the Congress—a branch they fear is too unwieldy, risk averse, and "leaky" to provide the type of leadership we need in the twenty-first century.

The "fact remains that those who take pride in [this] amendment are Whigs, men who fear the presidency and put their final trust in Congress, and that those who propose to repeal it are Jacksonians, men who respect Congress but look for leadership to the presidency."[13]

Repeal advocates often also add that the one president who served for more then two terms, FDR, was an especially effective president whose presidential experience was critical in World War II.

Advocates of retaining the Twenty-Second Amendment say eight years is plenty. The notion of rotation in office is healthy and desirable, especially in a robust constitutional democracy. The two-term limit is invariably healthy in our two-party system. It helps prevent political stagnation. The two parties benefit and are rejuvenated by the challenge of recruiting and nominating a new team of leaders.

Most presidents burn out in their second terms. Eight years should be ample time to introduce one's and one's party's best ideas and to try to bring about necessary policy changes. If such changes are valid and valued, they will doubtless be continued by the next administration. Moreover, most Americans reject the idea that any political leader is indispensable.

Further, a long-term presidency would be able to pack the Supreme Court as well as the whole judiciary. A long-term executive was precisely the reason why we fought the Revolution. Finally, for a variety of understandable reasons, the presidency has become a far more powerful branch than ever imagined by the framers of our Constitution. Most of this cannot be reversed. But the Twenty-Second

Amendment is a practical new "auxiliary precaution" in Madison's sense of checks and balances.

A truly indispensable person could be kept on as a key presidential adviser or cabinet member to see us through some crisis. But surely in a nation 100 times larger than we were in 1788, we should have plenty of talented candidates for the office.

In short, Americans want an effective presidency, yet, as we have noted several times, they fear the arbitrary abuse of power and the potential of presidents who someday may delude themselves into believing they are indispensable.

The two-term limit allows an honored citizen to serve eight years in one of the world's most consequential positions, yet it protects the country from potential excesses of power that could come from prolonged tenure. On balance, although the Twenty-Second Amendment has its drawbacks, it is, for many (including two of your three authors), an acceptable, if imperfect, compromise. It does not hinder effective, responsible presidents, and it helps guarantee that a presidential dictatorship will not take root here.

MAKING THE PRESIDENCY MORE ACCOUNTABLE

Any discussion of presidential leadership and accountability must take into account the ever-present paradoxes of the presidency. Some part of us wants a larger-than-life, two-gun, charismatic Mount Rushmore leader. Harrison Ford in the movie *Air Force One* (1997), President Whitmore and a sidekick played by Will Smith in *Independence Day* (1996), and Whitmore again with new friends in *Independence Day: Resurgence* (2016) vivified this yearning. Still, there is also our remarkably enduring antigovernment, antileadership, chronic-complainer syndrome. We want strong, gutsy leadership to operate on alternate days with a "national city manager." We want presidents to have enough power to solve our problems, yet not so much that they can do damage.

Accountability implies not only responsiveness to majority desires and answerability for actions, but also taking the Constitution, plus the people and their views, into account. It also implies a performance guided by integrity and character. Accountability implies as well that important decisions could be explained to the people to allow them the opportunity to appraise how well a president is handling the responsibilities of the office.

To whom is accountability owed? No president, it would seem, can be more than partially accountable to the people, for each president will listen to some people and some points of view more than to others. If we have learned anything in recent years, however, it is that the doctrine of presidential infallibility has been rejected. Arbitrary rule by powerful executives has always been rejected here. But what should be done when there are sharp differences between experts or when expert opinion differs sharply from the preponderance of public opinion? How much accountability, and what kind, is desirable? Is it not possible that the quest for ultimate accountability will result in a presidency without the prerogatives and independent discretion necessary for creative leadership?

A too-strong presidency jeopardizes freedom. A too-weak president jeopardizes stability. An imperial presidency is not democracy, yet an imperiled presidency is equally troubling. The overriding challenge for any democracy is both to empower and to restrain those who govern.

The modern presidency, in fact, may be unaccountable because it is too strong and independent in certain areas and too weak and dependent in others. One of the perplexing circumstances characterizing the state of the modern presidency is that considerable restraints sometimes exist where restraints are least desirable and adequate restraints are not available where they are most needed. Also, presidential strength is no guarantee that a president will be responsive or answerable. Indeed, significant independent strength may encourage low answerability when it suits the president's short-term personal power goals.

How do you grant yet control power? Can the presidency be empowered yet also democratized?

These are classic questions our framers faced, and these have been central to debates in democratic political theory. Leadership implies influence; accountability implies limits. Contradictions aside, accountability is a fundamental piece of the democratic puzzle. In essence it denotes that public officials are answerable for their actions. But to whom? Within what limits? Through what means?

There are essentially three types of accountability: *ultimate accountability* (which the United States has via the impeachment process), *periodic accountability* (provided for by presidential as well as mid-term elections and occasional landmark Supreme Court decisions), and *daily accountability* (somewhat contained in the separation of powers). James Madison believed that, along with separation of powers, regular elections provided the "primary check on government." Others believe that public opinion is the main check on presidents, and in the long run, how a president will be judged by historians.

We may hold presidents accountable, but can they be made responsible? That is, can they muster enough power to govern? One means for improving accountability and also empowering leadership is to strengthen the party system in America. Our parties are, at least by European standards, weaker and decentralized. A stronger party system might possibly mobilize citizens, diminish the fragmentation of the separation of powers, and lessen the atomization of our citizenry—yet this seems unlikely to happen.

Here are three additional proposals, regularly proposed and debated, that purport to make presidents more accountable.

Limit Presidential War-Making Authority?

"Today I authorized the armed forces of the United States to begin a limited military action in Libya," said President Obama in 2011. *I* authorized? Shouldn't it be *we* (president and Congress) authorized?

The Constitution explicitly gives to the Congress the power to declare war. However, over past decades presidents have gradually usurped this power. James Madison called war "among the greatest of national calamities," and he and virtually all the other founders believed that only the representation of the collective wisdom of society—the Congress—should take the nation into war.

Madison feared a replay of the imperial prerogatives of a king, where one man could take the nation into war. "The Constitution supposes," he wrote, "what the History of all Govts demonstrates, that the Ex[ecutive] is the branch of power most interested in war, and most prone to it. It has accordingly, with studied care, vest the question of war in the legisl[ative]."[14]

In the modern world, where the United States is the globe's primary superpower, can the war power be tamed and brought back under congressional control? Should it? Given the importance of the decision to go to war, it makes good constitutional sense to put presidential decisions under closer scrutiny and tighter controls.

Immediately after the 9/11 attacks, citizens demanded a strong presidency. For a time, the public reacted favorably to a robust, even unilateral presidency. But as time passed, and problems—especially in Iraq, Afghanistan, Libya, and Syria—persisted, many Americans grew skeptical of a powerful executive. From the libertarian right and idealistic left, critics pointed to the dangers inherent in a strong presidency. Does the presidency pose a threat to constitutional government and democracy in America?

One of the major paradoxes of the modern presidency is that presidents have often decided which weapons to build (in secret, as was the case with the atomic bomb) and where to direct military operations and drone strikes with little or no congressional declarations of war or authorization. This is one of the most perplexing realities of the presidency.[15]

Presidents in the past have greatly aggrandized power, sometimes in clearly unconstitutional ways, but the powerful chief executives of yesteryear usually took pains to ground their power grabs in the patina of constitutionalism, always acknowledging that the Constitution was king. Lincoln during the Civil War, Wilson in World War I, and FDR in World War II used extraconstitutional authority to see the nation through crises. They acknowledged that while their actions may have exceeded normal practice, they were nonetheless bound to respect constitutional limits, especially as applied by the Congress.

After World War II, with the coming of the Cold War, presidents began to claim inherent, independent power, grounded either (mistakenly) in the Constitution or in the claimed authority of precedents from past presidents. During the Korean Conflict in the 1950s, President Truman claimed independent authority (as commander-in-chief) to commit U.S. troops to combat. This, of course, violated both the spirit and the letter of the Constitution, but in the atmosphere of Cold War hysteria, few had the political courage to challenge the president. And yet it is in just such times that the Constitution needs all the defenders it can muster.

From that point, presidents began to make grander claims of independent power, all of which led to the emergence of what in the 1970s historian Arthur M. Schlesinger, Jr., described as an imperial presidency. In effect, there has been a three-stage process in the aggrandizement of presidential war and foreign policy power. In stage 1, presidents sometimes acted unilaterally but always took great pains to pay deference to the constitutional limitations and role of Congress (even as they bypassed both); in stage 2, beginning with the Cold War and the Truman presidency, presidents began to claim—and the Congress and public were enablers in this—that they had constitutional powers as commander-in-chief, to send troops into war; in stage 3, the George W. Bush administration claimed that not only does the president have constitutional authority to commit the nation to war, but that such a power is nonreviewable by the other branches, a claim that, if true, places the presidency on the same plane as the English King we overthrew over two hundred and forty years ago. Today, amid a "permanent war" against terrorism, the Constitution faces strains as some people favor presidential powers that go beyond what most of us believe is constitutional.

Have we come full circle? The American presidency was invented in 1787 by men intent on rejecting the divine right of kings and rule by one man, who established a system with a limited government, under the rule of law, based on a Constitution that separated power within a regime of checks and balances in which the president was to preside as but one of three separate but connected branches. Has that presidency devolved into a presidential government that resembles the imperial government the framers rejected and overthrew? In short, have we come full circle from a hereditary monarchy to an elected monarchy with a presidency of imperial proportions?

In an age of terrorism we need an effective and influential presidency, and we will need one who occasionally bends, but does not break, the Constitution. But we most assuredly do not want one disembodied from the system of checks and balances that has served us so well for so many years. We want a powerful presidency that is also a constitutional presidency.

Are there "rules" that should guide us in our effort to attain a strong but accountable presidency in an age of terrorism and political cyberwars? While no firm, set rules can be stringently imposed, there are several features of accountability that must apply:

1. In a war or crisis, presidential power should expand to meet the demands of the times.
2. Added presidential power does not amount to a blank check for the president.
3. All presidential acts during an emergency are reviewable by Congress and the Courts.
4. Constitutional rights shall be enforced.
5. Where presidents believe they need to move beyond the law, they must consult with and get congressional approval (perhaps by a joint special committee of both Houses) prior to acting (except in response to an attack against the United States).

In sum, Congress already has the constitutional authority it needs to keep presidents accountable in wartime emergencies. Rewriting a strengthened War Powers Resolution (of 1973) might help some, yet there is no way to instill backbone into the Congress. If Congress wants to "chain the dog of war," it already has the necessary legislative and budgetary tools it needs at its disposal.

The American public has allowed presidents and their intelligence agencies rather broad national security and regime change and war-making authority. Some of this grew out of the unilateral and secret authority to build the atomic bomb during the Manhattan Project. The September 11, 2001, terrorist attacks on America, as noted, allowed presidents greater leeway in this area.

There was major public backlash to the Vietnam and Iraq wars. But the public has generally acquiesced in allowing a greater role for the president in war-making policy. When the public does not insist that Congress reclaim its war-declaring authority, it is rather unlikely Congress will do so on its own. But the public and vigilant watchdog groups should keep insisting that Congress and the judiciary compel presidents to heed the Constitution. For, as many have noted, the Constitution was written less for normal peacetime than for times of war and emergency.

Congressional Votes of No Confidence?

One of the responses to Watergate and the abuse of power by Richard Nixon was a proposed constitutional amendment providing for a vote by Congress of no confidence in the president.[16] The effect would be similar to the recall now provided for in about sixteen states.

How would a no-confidence amendment work? A three-fifths vote of the members of each House present and voting would be necessary. Such a resolution would take priority over any other pending issue before Congress. If adopted, Congress would fix a date, between 90 and 110 days, for a special election for the president and vice president as well as for members of Congress. If it occurs near the regular congressional election date, that date would be used. Note that under most such proposals, the incumbent president is eligible to stand for reelection even though he or she was the target of the no-confidence vote.

A reason put forward in defense of the no-confidence proposal is that the presidency in modern times has grown too powerful, especially in crisis contexts and in foreign affairs. Presidential power, it is argued, has risen above the level where the system of checks and balances can be effective in countering presidential actions. More bluntly, however, advocates of the no-confidence vote or similar national recall proposals believe that the four year fixed term is a liability if and when we have incompetent presidents who lose the confidence of the nation. Incompetence, they point out, is not an impeachable offense. A "no-confidence" vote might also be a way to replace a hopelessly failed administration.

A goal of the proposed vote of no confidence is to make future presidents more accountable to Congress as well as more accountable to the American people. But aren't modern presidents already accountable to Congress? Because Congress sometimes fails to do its constitutional job of keeping presidents accountable does not mean that the power is missing. A president, it is assumed, would realize that he or she is accountable for his or her actions, proposed programs, negotiations, policies, and decisions and would have to face up to criticisms by Congress.

The commission of high crimes or felonies would no longer be needed to justify a president's dismissal. Maintaining the confidence of Congress and the general public would be an ongoing necessity. Matters such as Vietnam or Iraq policy, for example, would have to be discussed in greater detail with congressional leaders to ensure that a president had the support of Congress. The vote of no confidence would be a means of retaliation against a president who too often worked behind the scenes or otherwise manipulated the spirit of checks and balances. Advocates reason that major decisions would have to be made by consultation, instead of by one person or a White House cabal. To some extent, then, this constitutional amendment would introduce a certain amount of plural or shared decision making in our national government. The fundamental dangers of decisions by a Lone Ranger president would be thereby reduced.

In a nutshell, the arguments in favor of the vote of no confidence are these:

- Impeachment is an inefficient check. At best it protects against gross criminal violations of the public trust but not against presidential incompetence.
- The president would be more disposed to working with Congress, explaining policies, and educating Congress and the general public about plans and conduct in office.
- This proposal would force more presidential consultation with Congress and the leaders of the major parties and should lessen the secrecy surrounding presidential policy making.
- The proposal does not take power away from the president; it only makes presidents more responsible for how they use their powers.

Critics, including your authors, view this reform as a prime example of "good intentions, bad policy." Congress, they point out, has plenty of resources with which to check a president if only they would use them. Further, even though presidents have become paramount in the conduct of foreign affairs, Congress has several means at its disposal to oversee this exercise of power.

In certain situations it would seem that a vote of no confidence would give Congress the power to continually frustrate a president with whom it disagreed. The alternatives are a government of continuous presidential elections and overall paralysis or a government in which president and Congress are so close as to defeat the basic concept of the separation of powers that is so fundamental to our system.

Moreover, the elections that would be the result of a vote of no confidence might well produce governmental instability and make the development and implementation of long-term programs very uncertain.

A vote-of-no-confidence arrangement might lead presidents to avoid making significant changes in policy that would antagonize Congress. Innovative leadership could be thwarted, as presidents might gear most of their actions to public opinion polls, to the wishes of the majority at the expense of minority rights, and to the short term at the expense of the longer term public interest. The proposal might lead a president to concentrate on short-term or immediately popular initiatives to "create" favorable public approval at the expense of long-term planning.

Our view is that this proposed cure is worse than the occasional ailment. The vote-of-no-confidence procedure would not necessarily improve the quality of presidential leadership, nor would it enhance accountability in any significant way. Presidents do not intentionally make poor decisions. What could result might be far worse than the rare arrogant president we have had to endure. This measure might make presidents too dependent on Congress, or make them conform too closely to popular opinion. This measure might even give us an endless line of unsuccessful short-term presidents and result in a paralyzed nation.

Campaign Finance Reform?

Running for president is obviously a costly enterprise (already discussed in Chapter 3). Candidates must raise large sums of money, and the sheer magnitude of this fund-raising poses serious questions for democratic accountability and integrity.

Advocates of campaign finance reform have been concerned about the large sums of money that have shaped presidential campaigns. Critics believe most of these donations come with "strings attached" and that the donors give because they favor certain government action or perhaps inaction. Most Americans believe that all politicians do favors for "fat cat" donors. A combination of failed reform efforts and court decisions have created an array of private political donor machines across the country, mostly on the right, but some on the left as well.

Some voters were attracted to Donald Trump's 2016 campaign precisely because his personal wealth allowed him to "self-fund" almost all of his campaign for the Republican nomination. Similarly, one of the appeals of the Bernie Sanders presidential campaign was his millions of contributors who averaged around $27 per donation. This allowed both of these men to boast that they were beholden to no special interests.

Those who favor campaign finance reform support much more aggressive and timely full-disclosure requirements so citizens will know who is donating how much to whom. Second, they favor strict restriction of how much can be given to a presidential candidate, or party, or political action committee. Many reformers would like a system of publicly funded campaigns. Reformers especially want the U.S. Supreme Court to overturn its 2016 *Citizens United v. Federal Election Commission* decision which allows for massive undisclosed "independent" campaign spending through parallel yet separate committees. This was, for example, in the 2016 Democratic Party platform.

The case for these reforms is based on this argument:

1. The dependence of most candidates on the largess of big donors raises the appearance, if not the reality, of undue influence if not a "pay-to-play," quid quo pro type of corruption.
2. Candidates must spend a large portion of their time raising vast sums of money—from rich or relatively rich people or organizations—and this raises serious questions about democratic accountability and integrity.

3. The candidate with the biggest war chest does not always win, yet the astounding amount of money involved in presidential campaigns gives the impression that the American presidency is for sale to the highest bidder—and this has led to two-thirds of the general public saying they oppose Citizens United.

The case for keeping the existing system for financing presidential campaigns is based on these principles:

1. Restricting how one spend one's money would be to deny a person their First Amendment rights of free speech. Thus a campaign donation should be unregulated just as a newspaper, book, or billboard ad should be unregulated.
2. Public financing of candidates and campaigns would undermine the initiative a candidate has to demonstrate as to their worthiness. If a candidate cannot attract funding because of his or her policy ideas and character, he or she shouldn't be subsidized by taxpayers' funds.
3. Corporations "are people," not legally created entities, and their money is speech, not property.
4. The constitutional principle of limited government is most clearly applied here with less regulation yet more efforts to increase transparency of the sources of campaign funding for political candidates. Such transparency will allow voting to evaluate whether candidates are unduly influenced by major campaign donors, and will do so more effectively than across-the-board limitations on campaign funding, which likely would spur strategies to work around such restrictions through independent groups and other efforts.

Our political process is awash in money, and it is likely to remain so for quite some time. We are mindful of the old saying that preventing money from being involved in politics is a lot like trying to prevent water from descending off of a mountain. We may be tilting at windmills, but some form of strict public funding of elections is imperative if we are to give back control of the government to citizens and not special or wealthy interests. Since television is the costliest campaign expenditure, one way to accomplish our goal is to require television and cable stations to—as a condition of getting a broadcast license—give free air time to candidates who rise above a certain threshold of public support.

Other steps we might take include requiring full and immediate disclosure of all money—even Super PACs—that is spent in the political process; or giving each voter a voucher with "X" dollars that citizens could give to any candidate(s) they wished, but only voucher money could be used in a campaign. Many support, and we agree, that the limits of how much one can donate to a candidate's campaign or to one's political party should be lifted to a higher level—in part to encourage stronger parties and in part to counteract the deep-pocketed Super PACs and so-called 527 groups that spend hundreds of millions of dollars and are less accountable than the political parties.

States and cities are currently experimenting with promising campaign-finance initiatives. Arizona, Connecticut, and Maine are experimenting with various limits. New York City matches small donations six-to-one for those candidates who agree to spending and contribution limits. Seattle is experimenting with providing voters four $25 "democracy vouchers" that can be donated to candidates willing to abide by spending limits. It may be that the best way for campaign finance reformers to reverse the *Citizens United* court ruling is to demonstrate successful models at the state and local levels. Both same-sex marriage activists and NRA gun rights activists eased the way for their desired changes by first bringing about legal changes at the state and local levels.[17]

OTHER GENERIC REFORMS

We now turn to four other regularly debated "remedies" that are proposed to improve the way we nominate and elect presidents.

A Third Party to the Rescue?

Critics and reformers from almost every viewpoint regularly propose that a creative, vital, new third party might be just what is needed to infuse more common sense and energy into our sometimes creaky political system.

"We usually have two parties bankrupting the country," says political scientist Larry Diamond. Indeed, "our two-party system is ossified, it lacks integrity and creativity and any sense of courage or high aspiration in confronting our problems."[18]

Others agree, saying we have been poorly served by an existing two-party duopoly. We need, writes *New York Times* columnist Tom Friedman, a rigorous third party that would propose serious education reform without worrying about the teachers unions; "financial reform without worrying about losing donations from Wall Street; corporate tax reductions to stimulate jobs without worrying about offending the left; energy and climate reform without worrying about offending the right and coal-state Democrats; and proper health care reform without worrying about offending insurers and drug companies."[19]

The point is, critics say, that the two main traditional parties are so tied to well-organized, well-financed, vested stakeholders that a paralyzing gridlock has made for a timid and virtually do-nothing government. It has also led to unreasonable and dangerous partisan brinkmanship.

Third party movements are hardly new. Teddy Roosevelt's Bull Moose Party transformed the 1912 election even though he came in second. Illinois Congressman John Anderson preached pragmatic centrist fiscal reform in 1980 when he challenged President Carter and Governor Ronald Reagan. Texas businessman Ross Perot won nearly 19 percent of the popular vote in 1992 as he tried then, and again in 1996, to build a new "Reform Party" dedicated to balancing the budget. Consumer advocate Ralph Nader tried on several occasions to build a third party comprised of environmental and anti-globalization activists. Libertarians of the Ron Paul and Gary Johnson (2012 and 2016) stripe have regularly run. Green Party candidate Jill Stein developed a small following in 2016. Nearly seven million voices voted for a "third party" team in 2016.

Such parties raise instructive issues and occasionally force the two main parties to explain their politics. But our entrenched two major parties and our election laws have made it difficult for a third party to become a major party. The last time a third party won the presidency was in 1860 when the nation was sharply divided over the issue of slavery.

State requirements for third-party candidates to get on the ballot are often very restrictive. In addition, our Electoral College system, as currently implemented, means that even if a new party can win millions of votes in scores of states, it still might wind up with few if any of the 270 electoral votes needed to win the presidency.

Americans may be frustrated with our existing parties, yet about 60 percent of Americans are registered or affiliated with these parties. And another 20 percent or more regularly vote with the party they "lean" toward.

The Democrats and Republicans are usually joined by the media in predicting that a vote for a third party is either a wasted vote or one, such as a vote for Ralph Nader in 2000, that probably was a "spoiler" vote, costing one of the two major party candidates the presidency.

"Like fast-food giants McDonalds and Burger King, the GOP and the Democratic Party are," writes political scientist Ross K. Baker, "a known quantity and somewhat reassuring for their very familiarity. A third party is a mystery burger."[20]

The political reality is that third parties have limited prospects in the near term. When third parties occasionally generate popular and constructive ideas, one of the major parties almost always gradually modifies and adopts these ideas into their own platform, sometimes as soon as the next election. Nixon did this with some of George Wallace's ideas. Republicans and Democrats did this with a few of Ross Perot's ideas.

Our two-party system needs to be challenged. A vigorous multiparty system in America might well stir people to participate more in the political process. If we so value competition in the marketplace, wouldn't it also be good for our seemingly sclerotic political system?

Still, in its defense, the two-party system has served this sprawling, decentralized country reasonably well. The history of the last three or four generations suggests that presidents are relatively successful in either enacting their policy goals or at least helping to advance their ideas so that at a later time they will be embraced. The Marshall Plan, the GI Bill, the Interstate Highway System, Civil and Voting Rights, Clear Air and Water Acts, economic stimulus initiatives, along with much more, has been achieved even if these accomplishments often took years of collaborative, bipartisan, and multibranch negotiations.

Ours is an often slow and messy system, yet it is representative and deliberative even if privileged interests admittedly have the loudest voice.

It is unlikely, we believe, that a magical third party is the answer to our modern political problems, yet the threat of possible third parties and especially their creative proposals is certainly a healthy situation, and at the very least reminds major party candidates that they are not the only choices.

Note that there is one much discussed election process reform that might stimulate greater third-party voting. This is instant runoff voting, a system in which voters rank presidential candidates in order of their preference. In the case where one candidate wins more than half the first-preference votes, she or he wins and the election is over. If no one wins a majority, the candidate with the least votes is eliminated (or perhaps all of those with less than 20 percent), and the ballots are re-tabulated. If a voter's first-choice candidate is eliminated, their second-choice preference gets their vote. Runoffs can be held until a candidate earns the needed majority.

This process may complicate and prolong the general election process, yet its appeal is that it lets voters register their preferences without having to worry that they may be wasting their vote or even having their vote actually help the least favored candidate win the election.

This reform could be used with or without the Electoral College, but even though we admire this voting process change, we doubt America is likely to move in this direction anytime soon.

In sum, we think third parties are less the answer to America's political problems than lessening some of the pernicious effects of money in politics, and finding incentives (such as fewer gerrymandered districts) for politicians in our main political parties to collaborate on vital national interests.

One-Day National Primary?

Most people are frustrated or even upset at the long "nobody's-in-charge" presidential nominating process that begins with Iowa's caucus and New Hampshire's statewide primary. The complaints are many. It takes too long, especially compared to parliamentary systems which take just a few weeks. These contests begin before most voters have really had a chance to understand the candidates and issues. The length, the cost, and the "demolition derby" charades of the process doubtless deter many would-be quality candidates who might run if the process could be shortened.

Many people complained of the undemocratic aspect of the Democratic Party having so many elitist "superdelegates." Both Donald Trump and Senator Sanders called the existing system "rigged" by their party's establishment.

The idea of a one-day national primary, which would probably be scheduled on a Tuesday in August or early September, would allow many more people to participate and do so at a time where the issues and candidates have received more adequate scrutiny. Most advocates of this reform add that this system would provide for a run-off election between the top two finishers—a system already widely used in mayoral elections in the United States.

It is hardly a new idea. Both Theodore Roosevelt and Woodrow Wilson promoted this reform more than a century ago.

Those who favor this one-day national primary do so for these reasons:

- Every vote would count equally.
- A national primary would shift focus from regional and parochial issues (such as ethanol in Iowa) to vexing national issues.

- Public opinion polls regularly indicate popular support for this reform.
- Moving the national presidential nominating process to mid-August or early September would also "mean that people would be asked to vote when they are paying attention to the election, not before—another spur not just to higher turnout, but also to a more informed electorate."[21]

Those who oppose this proposed way of nominating presidents counter with these concerns:

- This arrangement, even more than the current one, advantages celebrity and wealthy candidates at the expense of more representative Americans.
- A well-known wealthy or big-donor-backed candidate might skip whatever debates take place that Spring and Summer and enter as a surprise candidate at the last moment—thereby evading the normal, if harsh, vetting most candidates have to face.
- In a one-day national contest candidates would have had to amass huge amounts of money up front. Underdog or "dark horse" candidates such as Obama and Sanders would not be as successful—because they raised much of their money after they had fared reasonably well in some early contests.
- This proposal would eliminate most face-to-face retail politics in favor of "tarmac campaigns" where candidates fly from one metropolitan airport to the next, all the while relying mostly on expensive, negative television ads aimed at denigrating their chief rivals.

Thus the unanticipated consequences of the one day national primary may make us miss our current crazy-quilt system or even the earlier method which was party elites making the selection in a smoke-filled room at the national convention.

Your authors acknowledge the simplicity and seductive appeal, as well as the egalitarian elements, of the proposal, yet we view it as an idea whose time has not arrived. There are, we believe, several ways the major parties could reform the existing system (e.g., by shortening the process, eliminating caucuses, lessening the number and influence of "superdelegates," and providing for proportional delegation selection, etc.) rather than adopt what we view as the more radical one-day primary proposal.

A Six-Year Term Limit?

One of the more curious proposals to reform the presidency is the idea of a single six-year presidential term. It has been proposed hundreds of times and supported by at least ten presidents.

The idea behind the reform is to try to remove a president as much as is possible from what are considered the negative aspects of partisan politics. The assumption is that, once elected to a single, nonrenewable term, a president would cast aside partisan calculation and act on behalf of all the people.

The case in favor of the single six-year term is based on these assumptions:

- It would liberate a president from the worries and indignations of running for reelection and prevent Watergate-type scandals.

- It would provide more time for an administration to concentrate on coherent policy planning and program implementation.
- It would eliminate the advantages of incumbency from presidential elections.
- It would lessen the temptation to make decisions based on political expediency or the influence of large campaign donations.
- It might encourage more compromise and centrism, which could lessen gridlock.

The single-term proposal has a comforting ring of good government and nonpartisanship to it. But it has not, and almost surely will not, be adopted for the following reasons:

- Four years is just about the right amount of time for a president to set the agenda, craft a few national budgets and be appropriately judged as to whether or not he or she is worthy of another four years.
- A six-year term would give us two long and probably painful years of the "clunkers" and two years less of the effective presidents who are doing, or attempting, the great work of reform and governing in the public interest.
- Most effective presidents have been skilled politicians. They knew how to stretch the limited resources of the office, liked politics, and enjoyed the responsibility of party leadership. They welcomed the challenge of reelection.
- The single-term advocates are trying, wrongly, to take the politics out of national leadership. Yet it is impossible and undesirable to take the politics out of constitutional democracy. An apolitical president, disinterested in reelection, motivated mainly by personal objectives or moralistic abstractions, and aloof from the concerns of our political parties could become a highly irresponsible president.
- What probably dooms the prospect of this proposed reform is that if we elect a really ineffective or bad president, we would be stuck for two years more than under the present four-year term system. Waiting out four years, we believe, is plenty long enough.

Abolish the Electoral College?

This is unlikely to happen, event if it is the most debated aspect of the American presidency. It is unlikely to happen because small states get an extra bonus in the way electoral votes are allocated. Minority populations in several of the large state believe, probably correctly, that they have a greater influence through the Electoral College, especially if they vote in blocks. There are also those devoted to federalism who dislike the idea of a national versus state-by-state election. Then there are those, like Trump and his supporters, who because they won due to the Electoral College arrangements, became enthusiastic fans of its continuation. Four of the last four candidates who lost the popular vote but won the presidency have been Republicans.

Since we discussed the pros and cons of this debate in Chapter 3, we'll merely summarize the two sides here.

Those who favor abolishing the Electoral College—and polls show that a majority do—favor it because:

1. A direct one person, one vote system is the way we elect virtually every other leader in our country.
2. The popular winner can lose under the existing system.
3. The Electoral College system discourages people from voting in noncompetitive, non–battle ground states.
4. The runoff system, if no one wins a majority of Electoral College votes, is wholly undemocratic and antiquated.

Those who favor retaining the Electoral College do so because:

1. They believe, rightly or wrongly, that it helps us retain the generally moderate two-party system and prevents more extremist parties from gaining the White House.
2. The Electoral College is part of the complicated federalist structure of our political system, and abolishing it would weaken federalism.
3. Direct election might lead to encouraging splinter political parties and force contingency runoff elections.
4. It would necessitate national control of every aspect of the electoral process.

Two of your authors believe that it is time to abolish the Electoral College. The third favors mending the process by a constitutional amendment that would retain the state election process yet abolish the existing runoff system by providing for a runoff among the top three candidates in a one-off contingency election with the candidate getting 45 percent declared the legitimate winner. But most important, we would grow the Electoral College by adding 102 bonus votes (added up nationally in a national poll) to the national vote winner. This 102 symbolically matches the two existing electoral bonus votes given to each of the fifty states and to Washington, D.C., and, mathematically, it virtually guarantees that the national-vote winner wins. This would ensure that the popular-vote winner wins, and because of the national bonus vote competition it would motivate voters to turn out even in very red and very blue states. This innovation would improve fairness and an enhanced public acceptance of the electoral process without being a radical restructuring.

This plan, referred to as the National Bonus Plan, is merely one of several alternatives that might be considered—but one thing we all can be sure of is that the debate over the Electoral College will continue.

GIVING UP ON POLITICS IS NOT AN OPTION

Politician bashing is a favorite American pastime: "Don't vote—it only encourages them!" "If God wanted us to vote, He or She would have given us candidates!" "A politician is someone who answers every question with an open mouth!"

But thank goodness Washington, Madison, Jefferson, Lincoln, the Roosevelts, Kennedy, Reagan, and Obama were skilled professional politicians. Our American experiment in constitutional democracy depends on political discussion and on the hard work of bargaining and mediating agreements that make it possible for us to live together in a civilized way.

America has always had politiphobes—people who are convinced that politicians are crooks and politics is dirty, distasteful, and unnecessary. Such people have a right to their opinions, yet they are mostly wrong. Politics is inevitable, necessary, and desirable. A country that dismisses and denigrates politics will not long survive as a democracy.

In our democracy, there is a continuing tension between competing truths, between cherished values and conflicting American Dreams. That's part of free speech and liberty. It is the job of politicians to help us reconcile and balance these contending aspirations—freedom and equality, individualism and community, idealism and pragmatism, capitalism and communitarian compassion.

It isn't always pretty, but politicians are the indispensable horse traders, coalition builders, agreement negotiators, and paradox navigators we employ to keep our diverse pluralistic society going. Political leaders help create options and opportunities and, at their best, help inspire people to imagine the possibilities of a better world. The ability to debate and disagree civilly is absolutely essential to the functioning of a constitutional democracy.

Not giving up on politics means being willing to confront the paradoxes that are inherent in our system. We need effective politicians able to recognize these contradictions, see various sides, and understand how there are competing claims to the American Dream. To face these paradoxes is to recognize that the competition of ideas and opinions—what we call politics—is a good thing.

One lesson is that it helps for people in politics to have a high threshold for ambiguity and paradox. U.S. Senator Lindsey Graham explains this flexibility in discussing his operational style in his dealings with the Obama White House: "That's the way life is. You kick their ass one day and you'll work with them the next. If you can't do two things at once, don't go into politics."

Giving up on politics often means being unwilling to see the other side. How many of us can't stand to listen to a politician with whom we disagree? But politics is a two-way street—abdicating from politics simply gives others more control over your life.

The resilience of our republic depends on both the quality of the leaders we elect and the character of the people. Judge Learned Hand, a highly regarded federal judge, was right when he wrote that liberty lies in the hearts of men and women; "when it dies there, no constitution, no law, no court can even do much to help it." He added:

> The spirit of liberty is the spirit which is not too sure that it is right; the spirit of liberty is the spirit which seeks to understand the minds of other men and women; the spirit of liberty is the spirit which weighs their interests alongside its own without bias.[22]

Sure, in our system of elections, politicians need to be ambitious and calculating—calculating how they might win, as well as how they can advance the public good. Candidates have to have enormous self-confidence to get up on the public stage and try to get our attention. Of course, some of what they do in a campaign is stagecraft and posturing. Our process essentially demands this. Representative politics is always an admixture of personal striving and substantive policy differences.

U.S. Senator Daniel Patrick Moynihan liked to say that "elections are not our finest hour." What he meant is that the claims and counterclaims in a campaign are too often oversimplifications of complex political choices. He knew that serious policy answers seldom fit on a bumper sticker, that charges and countercharges escalate, and that going negative becomes an irresistible temptation in campaigns.

But you can't have a representational republic without politics. Politics means politicians and voters debating contending ideas, forming coalitions, expressing their opinions in campaigns, and voting in elections. Yet the policies and programs that are enacted after an election are still only an imperfect attempt to solve the contradictions and paradoxes of our democracy.

Too many of us get too pious when politicians change their positions. We often charge them with flip-flopping and calculating their positions based solely on political expediency.

Candidates sometimes change their minds because circumstances have changed. Sometimes, too, they change because they have learned new facts or understand new realities. Sure, they sometimes change because of political expediency. But it is only the stubborn, rigid, overly self-confident and politically deaf leader who is unwilling to compromise and change course when this is sensible.

Consistency can be good; yet creative, adaptive compromising is sometimes appropriate. Lincoln, thankfully, changed his mind about deporting slaves to Africa and about emancipation. FDR changed his mind on neutrality in World War II. Nixon changed his mind about dealing with China. Reagan evolved on how best to relate to the Soviets. In short, politicians occasionally flip-flop or evolve because it makes sense or perhaps because we the people had also evolved.

The best democratic leaders are teachers, reminding us about the promise and mission of America, encouraging the best in us. As Franklin Roosevelt once said, the presidency is "pre-eminently a place of moral leadership." What he meant was that presidents should use their office to appeal to our better instincts, and lead democratically. It was through politics and government that the nation's progressive social movements helped move us toward greater racial and gender equality, devised policies to expand education and opportunities to a wider segment of the population, attempted to protect and expand the rights of citizens. These battles are far from over. As a nation, we have a long way to go before we can truly grant the blessings of liberty and prosperity to all citizens, yet it is through politics—and primarily through politics—that we can achieve these goals.

Distrust in government and political leaders is as old as the Republic. That's why the founders spread out the power among branches and levels of government. Yet if we want the blessing of liberty and prosperity, we need to be willing to confront the paradoxes of our system, to debate conflicting values, to acknowledge competing claims about what our nation should be, and to try to recognize not only what our leaders can offer but what we must contribute as well.

Giving up on politics is not an option—not for presidents, not for citizens. Politics is the indispensible heart of a representative republic. It is to democracy what the experimental method is to physics, what melody is to music, what imagination is to poetry.

FURTHER READINGS

Cronin, Thomas E. *Imagining a Great Republic: Celebrated Political Novelists and the Idea of America.* Lanham, MD: Rowman and Littlefield, 2018.

Ellis, Richard J., and Michael Nelson, ed. *Debating the Presidency*, 4th ed. Thousand Oaks, Calif.: CQ Press, 2018.

Hacker, Jacob, and Paul Pierson. *American Amnesia: How the War on Government Led Us to Forget What Made America Prosper.* New York: Simon and Schuster, 2016.

Howell, William, and Terry Moe. *Relic: How Our Constitution Undermines Effective Government and Why We Need a More Powerful Presidency.* New York: Basic, 2016.

Levinson, Sanford. *Our Undemocratic Constitution.* New York: Oxford University Press, 2006.

Sabato, Larry. *A More Perfect Constitution.* New York: Walker, 2008.

Savage, Charlie. *Power Wars.* New York: Little, Brown, 2016.

Selected Bibliography

REFERENCE WORKS ON THE PRESIDENCY

Bose, Meena. *The New York Times on the Presidency, 1853–2008*. Washington, DC: CQ Press, 2008.

Edwards, George C., and William G. Howell, eds. *The Oxford Handbook of the American Presidency*. New York: Oxford University Press, 2009.

Genovese, Michael A., and Alison Howard, eds. *The Encyclopedia of the American Presidency*. 3d ed. New York: Facts-on-File, 2017.

Goldsmith, William M. *The Growth of Presidential Power: A Documented History*. 3 vols. New York: Chelsea House, 1974.

Graff, Henry F., ed. *The Presidents: A Reference History*. New York: Scribner's, 1984.

Leuchtenburg, William E. *The American President: From Teddy Roosevelt to Bill Clinton*. New York: Oxford University Press, 2015.

Levy, Leonard W., and Louis Fisher, eds. *Encyclopedia of the American Presidency*. 4 vols. New York: Simon & Schuster, 1994.

Nelson, Michael, ed. *Guide to the Presidency*. Washington, DC: CQ Press, 1989.

Shane, Peter M., and Harold H. Bruff, eds. *The Law of Presidential Power*. Durham, NC: Carolina Academic Press, 1988.

IMPORTANT WORKS

Abraham, Henry J. *Justices, Presidents and Senators*. 5th ed. Lanham, MD: Rowman and Littlefield, 2008.

Abrams, Herbert L. *"The President Has Been Shot": Confusion, Disability and the 25th Amendment*. Stanford, CA: Stanford University Press, 1994.

Adler, David Gray, and Michael A. Genovese, eds. *The Presidency and the Law: The Clinton Legacy*. Lawrence: University Press of Kansas, 2002.

——, and Larry N. George, eds. *The Constitution and the Conduct of Foreign Policy*. Lawrence: University Press of Kansas, 1996.

Alterman, Eric. *When Presidents Lie: A History of Official Deception and Its Consequences*. New York: Viking, 2004.

Arnold, Peri. E. *Making the Managerial Presidency*. Princeton, NJ: Princeton University Press, 1986.

Barber, James David. *The Presidential Character: Predicting Performance in the White House*. 4th ed. Englewood Cliffs, NJ: Prentice-Hall, 1992.

Baumgartner, Jody C. *The American Vice Presidency Reconsidered*. Westport, CT: Praeger, 2006.

Beckmann, Matthew N. *Pushing the Agenda: Presidential Leadership in U.S. Lawmaking, 1953–2004*. New York: Cambridge University Press, 2010.

Bessette, Joseph M., and Jeffrey Tulis, eds. *The Presidency in the Constitutional Order*. Baton Rouge: Louisiana State University Press, 1984.

Binder, Sarah, and Forrest Maltzman. *Advice and Dissent: The Struggle to Shape the Judiciary*. Washington, DC: Brookings Institution, 2009.

Borrelli, MaryAnne. *The President's Cabinet: Gender, Power, and Representation*. Boulder, CO: Rienner, 2002.

Bose, Meena. *Shaping and Signaling Presidential Policy: The National Security Decision Making of Eisenhower and Kennedy*. College Station, TX: Texas A&M University Press, 1998.

Brown, Lara M. *Jockeying for the American Presidency: The Political Opportunism of Presidents*. Amherst, NY: Cambria, 2010.

Burke, John P. *The Institutional Presidency*. Baltimore: Johns Hopkins University Press, 1992.

Burns, James MacGregor. *Roosevelt: The Lion and the Fox*. New York: Harcourt, 1956.

———. *Deadlock of Democracy*. Englewood Cliffs, NJ: Prentice-Hall, 1963.

———. *Presidential Government: The Crucible of Leadership*. Boston: Houghton Mifflin, 1965.

———. *Roosevelt: Soldier of Freedom*. New York: Harcourt Brace, Javanovich, 1970.

———. *Leadership*. New York: HarperCollins, 1978.

Calabresi, Steven G., and Christopher S. Yoo. *The Unitary Executive: Presidential Power From Washington to Bush*. New Haven, CT: Yale University Press, 2008.

Cameron, Charles M. *Veto Bargaining: Presidents and the Politics of Negative Power*. New York: Cambridge University Press, 2000.

Canes-Wrone, Brandice. *Who Leads Whom? Presidents, Policy and the Public*. Chicago: University of Chicago Press, 2006.

Cannon, Lou. *President Reagan: The Role of a Lifetime*. New York: Touchstone 1991.

Carter, Stephen L. *The Confirmation Mess: Cleaning Up the Federal Appointments Process*. New York: Basic, 1994.

Ceasar, James W. *Presidential Selection*. Princeton, NJ: Princeton University Press, 1979.

Clinton, Bill. *My Life*. New York: Knopf, 2004.

Cole, David, and James X. Dempsey. *Terrorism and the Constitution*. 3d ed. New York: New Press, 2006.

Conley, Richard S. *Presidential Relations with Congress*. New Brunswick, NJ: Transaction 2017.

Cooper, Philip J. *By Order of the President: The Use and Abuse of Executive Direct Action*. Lawrence: University Press of Kansas, 2002.

Corwin, Edward S. *Total War and the Constitution*. Westminster, MD: Knopf, 1947.

———. *The President: Office and Powers, 1978–1984*. 5th ed. New York: New York University Press, 1984.

Crenson, Matthew, and Benjamin Ginsberg. *Presidential Power: Unchecked and Unbalanced*. New York: Norton, 2007.

Cronin, Thomas E., *The State of the Presidency*. 2d ed. Boston: Little, Brown, 1980.

——. ed. *Inventing the American Presidency*. Lawrence: University Press of Kansas, 1989.

——. *On the Presidency*. Boulder, CO: Paradigm, 2009.

——, and Michael A. Genovese. *Leadership Matters: Unleashing the Power of Paradox*. Boulder: Paradigm, 2012.

——, and Sanford Greenberg, eds. *The Presidential Advisory System*. New York: Harper & Row, 1969.

——, and Rexford Tugwell, eds., *The Presidency Reappraised*. New York: Praeger, 1977.

Crouch, Jeffrey. *The Presidential Pardon Power*. Lawrence: University Press of Kansas, 2009.

Donald, David H. *Lincoln*. New York: Simon & Schuster, 1995.

Eastland, Terry. *Energy in the Executive: The Case for the Strong Presidency*. New York: Free Press, 1992.

Edwards, George C. *At the Margins: Presidential Leadership in Congress*. New Haven, CT: Yale, 1989.

——. *On Deaf Ears: The Limits of the Bully Pulpit*. New Haven, CT: Yale University Press, 2003.

——. *Why the Electoral College Is Bad for America*. New Haven, CT: Yale University Press, 2004.

——. *Predicting the Presidency: The Potential for Persuasion Leadership*. Princeton: Princeton University Press, 2016.

Farnsworth, Stephen J. *Spinner-in-Chief: How Presidents Sell Their Policies and Themselves*. Boulder, CO: Paradigm, 2009.

——, and S. Robert Lichter. *The Nightly News Nightmare: Media Coverage of U.S. Presidential Elections 1988–2008*. Lanham, MD: Roman and Littlefield, 2010.

Felzenberg, Alvin S. *The Leaders We Deserve*. New York: Basic, 2008.

Fisher, Louis. *The Constitution Between Friends*. New York: St. Martin's Press, 1978.

——. *Presidential War Power*. Lawrence: University of Kansas Press, 1995.

——. *The Politics of Shared Power: Congress and the Executive*. 4th ed. College Station: Texas A&M University Press, 1998.

——. *The Constitution and 9/11: Recurring Threats to America's Freedoms*. Lawrence: University of Kansas Press, 2008.

Genovese, Michael A. *The Supreme Court, the Constitution, and Presidential Power*. Landham, MD: University Press of America, 1980.

——. *The Nixon Presidency: Power and Politics in Turbulent Times*. Westport, CT: Greenwood, 1990.

——. *The Presidency in an Age of Limits*. Westport, CT: Greenwood, 1993.

——. *Contending Approaches to the American Presidency*. Washington, DC: CQ Press, 2012.

——. *The Power of the American Presidency, 1787–2000*. New York: Oxford University Press: 2001.

——. *The Presidential Dilemma: Leadership in the American System*. 2d ed. New York: Longman, 2002.

——. *Memo to a New President*. New York: Oxford, 2008.

Gergen, David. *Eyewitness to Power*. New York: Simon & Schuster, 2000.

Gerhardt, Michael J. *The Federal Appointment Process: A Constitutional History*. Durham, NC: Duke University Press, 2003.

Goldsmith, Jack. *The Terror Presidency: Law and Judgment in the Bush Administration*. New York: Norton, 2007.

Goldstein, Joel K. *The Modern American Vice Presidency: The Transformation of a Political Institution*. Princeton, NJ: Princeton, 1982.

Goodwin, Doris Kearns. *Team of Rivals*. New York: Simon & Schuster, 2005.

Greenstein, Fred. *The Hidden-Hand Presidency: Eisenhower and Leader*. New York: Free Press, 2004.

——. *The Presidential Difference: Leadership Style from FDR to George W. Bush*. Rev. ed. New York: Free Press, 2004.

Gregg, Gary L. *The Presidential Republic: Executive Representation and Deliberative Democracy*. Lanham, MD: Rowland & Littlefield, 1997.

Hamilton, Alexander, James Madison, and John Jay. *Federalist Papers*. New York: New American Library, 1961.

Han, Lori Cox. *Governing from Center Stage: White House Communication Strategies during the Television Age of Politics*. Cresskill, NJ: Hampton, 2001.

Harriger, Katy J. *Independent Justice: The Federal Special Prosecutor in American Politics*. Lawrence: University Press of Kansas, 1998.

Healy, Gene. *The Cult of the Presidency: America's Dangerous Devotion to Executive Power*. Washington, DC: Cato Institute, 2008.

Hess, Stephen. *Organizing the Presidency*. Washington, DC: Brookings Institution, 1976.

——. *What Do We Do Now? A Workbook for the President Elect*. Washington, DC: Brookings, 2008.

Howell, William G. *Power without Persuasion: The Politics of Direct Presidential Action*. Princeton, NJ: Princeton University Press, 2003.

——, and Jon C. Peverhouse. *While Dangers Gather: Congressional Checks on Presidential War Powers*. Princeton, NJ: Princeton University Press, 2007.

Jacobson, Gary C. *A Divider Not a Uniter*. New York: Pearson, 2007.

Jamieson, Kathleen Hall. *Packaging the Presidency*. New York: Oxford, 1996.

Johnson, Loch K. *U.S. Intelligence Agencies in a Hostile World*. New Haven, CT: Yale University Press, 1996.

——. *Fateful Decisions: Inside the National Security Council*. New York: Oxford University Press, 2003.

Jones, Charles A. *The Presidency in a Separated System*. Washington, DC: Brookings Institution, 1994.

Kamarck, Elaine C. *Why Presidents Fail And How They Can Succeed*. Washington, DC: Brookings Institution, 2016.

Kernell, Samuel M. *Going Public: New Strategies of Presidential Leadership*. 4th ed. Washington, DC: CQ Press, 2006.

——, and Samuel Popkin, eds. *Chief of Staff*. Berkeley: University of California Press, 1986.

Kessel, John H. *Presidents, the Presidency and the Political Environment*. Washington, DC: CQ Press, 2001.

Kein, Joe. *The Natural: The Misunderstood Presidency of Bill Clinton*. New York: Doubleday, 2002.

Kleinerman, Benjamin A. *The Discretionary President: The Promise and Peril of Executive Power*. Lawrence: University Press of Kansas, 2009.

Koh, Harold Kongju. *The National Security Constitution: Sharing Power After the Iran–Contra Affair*. New Haven, CT: Yale University Pres, 1990.

Krehbiel, Keith. *Pivotal Politics: A Theory of U.S. Lawmaking*. Chicago: University of Chicago Press, 1998.

Kumar, Martha Joynt. *Managing the President's Message*. Baltimore, MD: Johns Hopkins University Press, 2007.

Lammers, William W. *Presidential Politics: Patterns and Prospects*. New York: HarperCollins, 1976.

Landy, Marc, and Sidney M. Milkis. *Presidential Greatness*. Lawrence: University Press of Kansas, 2001.

Laski, Harold. *The American Presidency: An Interpretation*. New York: Harper & Brothers, 1940.

Leuchtenburg, William E. *In the Shadow of FDR: From Harry Truman to Ronald Reagan*. Ithaca, NY: Cornell University Press, 1983.

Lewis, David E. *The Politics of Presidential Appointments: Political Control and Bureaucratic Performance*. Princeton, NJ: Princeton University Press, 2008.

Light, Paul C. *Vice Presidential Power: Advice and Influence in the White House*. Baltimore: Johns Hopkins University Press, 1984.

———. *The President's Agenda*. 3d ed. Baltimore, MD: Johns Hopkins University Press, 1998.

Lowi, Theodore J. *The Personal President: Power Invested, Promise Unfulfilled*. Ithaca, NY: Cornell University Press, 1985.

Mackenzie, G. Calvin, ed. *Innocent Until Nominated: The Breakdown of the Presidential Appointments Process*. Washington, DC: Brookings Institution, 2001.

Maltese, John. *Spin Control: The White House Office of Communications and the Management of Presidential News*. Chapel Hill: University of North Carolina Press, 1992.

Martin, Janet M. *The Presidency and Women: Promise, Performance, and Illusion*. College Station: Texas A&M University Press, 2003.

Mayer, Jane. *The Dark Side: The Inside Story of How the War on Terror Turned into a War on American Ideals*. New York: Doubleday, 2008.

Mayer, Kenneth R. *With the Stroke of a Pen: Executive Orders and Presidential Power*. Princeton, NJ: Princeton University Press, 2001.

Mayhew, David. *Divided We Govern*. New Haven, CT: Yale University Press, 1991.

Mearsheimer, John J. *Why Leaders Lie*. New York: Oxford University Press, 2011.

Miroff, Bruce. *Pragmatic Illusions: The Presidential Politics of John F. Kennedy*. New York: McKay, 1976.

———. *Icons of Democracy*. New York: Basic Books, 1993.

Murray, Robert K., and Tim H. Blessing. *Greatness in the White House: Rating the Presidents, Washington through Reagan*. University Park: Pennsylvania State University Press, 1994.

Nathan, Richard *The Administrative Presidency*. New York: Wiley, 1983.

Nelson, Michael. ed. *The Evolving Presidency: Landmark Documents*. 3d ed. Washington, DC: CQ Press, 2008.

Nemacheck, Christine L. *Strategic Selection: Presidential Nomination of Supreme Court Justices from Herbert Hoover through George W. Bush*. Charlottesville: University of Virginia Press, 2007.

Neustadt, Richard E. *Presidential Power and the Modern Presidents*. New York: Free Press, 1990.

Novokov, Julie. *The Supreme Court and the Presidency*. Washington DC: CQ Press, 2013.

Nye, Joseph S. Jr. *The Powers to Lead*. New York: Oxford University Press, 2008.

Obama, Barack. *The Audacity of Hope: Thoughts on Reclaiming the American Dream*. New York: Crown, 2006.

Patterson, Bradley H., Jr. *The White House Staff: Inside the West Wing and Beyond*. Washington, DC: Brookings Institution, 2000.

————. *To Serve the President: Continuity and Innovation in the White House Staff*. Washington, DC: Brookings Institution, 2008.

Pfiffner, James P., ed. *The Strategic Presidency: Hitting the Ground Running*. 2d ed. Lawrence: University Press of Kansas, 1996.

————. *The Managerial Presidency*. 2d ed. College Station: Texas A&M University Press, 1999.

————. *Character and the Modern Presidency*. Washington, DC: Brookings Institution, 2001.

Phelps, Glenn A. *George Washington and the American Constitutionalism*. Lawrence: University Press of Kansas, 1994.

Pious, Richard M. *Why Presidents Fail: White House Decision Making from Eisenhower to Bush II*. Lanham, MD: Rowman and Littlefield, 2008.

Poser, Eric A., and Adrian Vermeule. *The Executive Unbound: After the Madisonian Republic*. New York: Oxford University Press, 2010.

Rapoport, Ronald B., and Walter J. Stone. *Three's a Crowd: The Dynamics of Third Parties, Ross Perot, and Republican Resurgence*. Ann Arbor: University of Michigan Press, 2008.

Renshon, Stanley A. *Presidential Success: A Practical Guide*. New Brunswick: Transaction, 2017.

Robinson, Donald L. *"To the Best of My Ability": The Presidency and the Constitution*. New York: Norton, 1987.

Rockman, Bert. *The Leadership Question: The Presidency and the American System*. New York: Praeger, 1984.

Rossiter, Clinton. *Constitutional Dictatorship: Crisis Government in the Modern Democracy*. Princeton, NJ: Princeton University Press, 1948.

————. *The American Presidency*. New York: Harcourt, Brace and World, 1956.

Rozell, Mark J. *Executive Privilege: Presidential Power, Secrecy, and Accountability*. 2d ed. rev. Lawrence: University Press of Kansas, 2002.

Rudalevige, Andrew. *Managing the President's Program: Presidential Leadership and Legislative Policy Formulation*. Princeton, NJ: Princeton University Press, 2002.

————. *The New Imperial Presidency*. Ann Arbor: University of Michigan Press, 2005.

Savage, Charlie. *Takeover: The Return of the Imperial Presidency and the Subversion of American Democracy*. Boston: Little, Brown, 2007.

Schlesinger, Arthur M., Jr. *The Imperial Presidency*. Boston: Houghton Mifflin, 1973.

————. *War and the American Presidency*. New York: Norton, 2005.

Shane, Peter M. *Madison's Nightmare: How Executive Power Threatens America's Democracy*. Chicago: University of Chicago Press, 2009.

Simonton, Dean Keith. *Why Presidents Succeed*. New Haven, CT: Yale University Press, 1987.

Skowronek, Stephen. *The Politics Presidents Make*. Cambridge, MA: Belknap, 1993.

————. *Presidential Leadership in Political Time*. Lawrence: University Press of Kansas, 2007.

Sollenberger, Mitchel A. *Judicial Appointments and Democratic Controls*. Durham, NC: Carolina Academic, 2011.

————. *Executive Branch Czars and the Erosion of Democratic Accountability*. Lawrence: University Press of Kansas, 2012.

Spitzer, Robert J. *The Presidential Veto: Touchstone of the American Presidency*. Albany: State University of New York Press, 1988.

————. *President and Congress: Executive Hegemony at the Crossroads of American Government*. New York: McGraw-Hill, 1993.

Sundquist, James L. *Constitutional Reform and Effective Government.* Washington, DC: Brookings Institution, 1986.

———. *Dynamics of the Party System.* Rev. ed. Washington, DC: Brookings Institution, 1993.

Thomas, Helen. *Watchdogs of Democracy? The Waning Washington Press Corps and How It Has Failed the Public.* New York: Scribner, 2007.

Thurber, James A., ed. *Rivals for Power: Presidential–Congressional Relations.* 3d ed. Lanham, MD: Rowman and Littlefield, 2005.

Tulis, Jeffrey K. *The Rhetorical Presidency.* Princeton, NJ: Princeton University Press, 1987.

Warber, Adam L. *Executive Orders and the Modern Presidency.* Boulder, CO: Lynne Rienner, 2006.

Warshaw, Shirley Anne. *Powersharing: White House–Cabinet Relations in the Modern Presidency.* Albany: State University of New York Press, 1996.

Wayne, Stephen J. *Is This Any Way to Run a Democratic Election?* 3d ed. Washington, DC: CQ Press, 2007.

Weko, Thomas J. *The Politicizing Presidency: The White House Personnel Office, 1948–1994.* Lawrence: University Press of Kansas, 1995.

Wittes, Benjamin. *Law and the Long War: The Future of Justice in the Age of Terror.* New York: Penguin, 2008.

Yoo, John. *The Power of War and Peace.* Chicago: University of Chicago Press, 2005.

———. *War by Other Means.* New York: Atlantic Monthly Press, 2006.

———. *Crisis and Command.* New York: Kaplan, 2009.

Notes

CHAPTER 1

1. We are grateful for this insight to George R. Goethals. See his *Presidential Leadership and African Americans* (New York: Routledge, 2015), p. 4.
2. Andrew Rudalevige, *The New American Presidency* (Ann Arbor: University of Michigan Press, 2006), p. 259. See also Garry Wills, *Bomb Power: The Modern Presidency and the National Security State* (New York: Penguin, 2010).
3. Benjamin A. Kleinerman, *The Discretionary President: The Promise and Peril of Executive Power* (Lawrence: University Press of Kansas, 2009), p. xi.
4. Woodrow Wilson, *Mere Literature and Other Essays* (New York: Grosset and Dunlap, 1896), p. 207.
5. Alan Ehrenholt, "The Paradox of Corrupt Yet Effective Leadership," *New York Times* (Sept. 30, 2002).
6. A call for a more powerful presidency is forcefully made in William G. Howell and Terry M. Moe, *Relic: How Our Constitution Undermines Effective Government and Why We Need a More Powerful Presidency* (New York: Basic Books, 2016).
7. James MacGregor Burns, *Leadership* (New York: Harper & Row, 1978).
8. William Davison Johnston, *TR, Champion of the Strenuous Life* (Oyster Bay, N.Y.: Theodore Roosevelt Association, 1958), p. 95.
9. We are indebted to Steven Ortéga for ideas here. For examples of negative consequences of presidential boldness, see Steven Kinzer, *Overthrow* (New York: Times Books, 2006).
10. Obama in an interview with Jeffrey Goldberg, "The Obama Doctrine," *The Atlantic* (April, 2016): p. 78.
11. Stephen Skowronek, *The Politics Presidents Make: Leadership from John Adams to George Bush* (Cambridge, Mass.: Belknap, 1993), and his *Presidential Leadership in Political Time: Reprise and Reappraisal* (Lawrence: University Press of Kansas, 2008).
12. Stephen Skowronek, *Presidential Leadership in Political Time* (Lawrence: University Press of Kansas, 2008), p. 95.
13. Reagan, in 1989, quoted in Skowronek, *Presidential Leadership*, p. 95.
14. Skowronek, ibid, p. 78.
15. See Roger Draper, *Dead Certain* (New York: Free Press, 2007); Stephen Kinzer, *Overthrow: America's Century of Regime Change* (New York Times Books, 2006). But

for a defense of Bush and Dick Cheney, see Dick Cheney and Liz Cheney, *Exceptional: Why the World Needs a Powerful America* (New York: Threshold Editions, 2015).

16. Quoted in Robert A. Caro, *Lyndon Johnson and the Passage of Power* (New York: Knopf, 2012), p. xv.

17. John Keegan, *The Mask of Command* (New York: Penguin Books, 1987).

18. Robert S. McNamara, *In Retrospect* (New York: Random House, 1995), p. 333; see also "The Fog of War" (Errol Morris, Director, 2003), the award-winning documentary that interviews McNamara.

19. David Brooks, "The Bush Paradox," *New York Times* (June 24, 2008): A23.

20. Paraphrased ideas from William E. Leuchtenburg, *The American President* (New York: Oxford University Press, 2015), p. 812.

21. Kenneth M. Duberstein, quoted in Kenneth T. Walsh, "When It's Gut-Check Time in the Oval Offices," *U.S. News and World Report* (Nov. 3, 2008): 32.

22. *Boston Globe* (Jan. 7, 1976).

23. This is how one of our students aptly put it in a class discussion a few years ago.

24. George C. Edwards, On Deaf Ears: *The Limits of the Bully Pulpit* (New Haven, Conn.: Yale University Press, 2003), p. 247. See also Brendan Doherty, *The Rise of the President's Permanent Campaign* (Lawrence: University Press of Kansas, 2012).

25. Howard Gardner, *Five Minds for the Future* (Boston: Harvard Business Press, 2008), p. xiii.

CHAPTER 2

1. See, for example, Edward S. Corwin, *The President: Office and Powers* (New York: New York University Press, 1957); Arthur M. Schlesinger, Jr., *The Imperial Presidency* (Boston: Houghton Mifflin Company, 1973); Andrew Rudalevige, *The New Imperial Presidency* (Ann Arbor: University of Michigan Press, 2006); and James P. Pfiffner, *Power Play* (Washington, DC: The Brookings Institution, 2008).

2. Walter Berns, "The American Presidency: Statesmanship and Constitutionalism in Balance," *Imprimis* (January 1983): 3.

3. Jon Meacham, *American Lion: Andrew Jackson in the White House* (New York: Random House, 2008), p. 211.

4. See David H. Donald, *Lincoln* (New York: Simon & Schuster, 1995), pp. 128–29. See also James M. McPherson, *Tried by War: Abraham Lincoln as Commander-in-Chief* (New York: Penguin, 2008).

5. Pew Research Center, "Beyond Distrust: How American's View Their Government," November 23 2015.

6. Lyn Ragsdale, *Presidential Politics* (Boston: Houghton Mifflin, 1993), p. 143.

7. Gary King and Lyn Ragsdale, *The Elusive Executive* (Washington, DC: Congressional Quarterly Press, 1988), p. 290.

8. George Edwards, *The Public Presidency* (New York: St. Martin's Press, 1983), p. 233.

9. See Richard Waterman, Carol Silva and Hank Jenkins-Smith, *The Presidential Expectations Gap: Public Attitudes Concerning the Presidency* (Ann Arbor, MI: University of Michigan Press, 2014).

10. For instructive analysis of presidential fiascoes, see Richard M. Pious, *Why Presidents Fail* (Lanham, Md.: Rowman and Littlefield, 2008).

11. Jeffrey E. Cohen, *Presidential Leadership in Public Opinion: Causes and Consequences* (New York: Cambridge University Press, 2015).

12. Samuel Kernell, *Going Public: New Strategies of Presidential Leadership*, 4th ed. (Washington, D.C.: Congressional Quarterly Press, 2006).

13. George C. Edwards III, *On Deaf Ears: The Limits of the Bully Pulpit* (New Haven, Conn.: Yale University Press, 2003), Brandice Canes-Wrone, *Who Leads Whom? Presidents, Policy and the Public* (Chicago, Ill.: University of Chicago Press, 2006).

14. Todd L. Belt, *"Leading the Public/Following the Public,"* in Michael A. Genovese, ed., *The Quest for Leadership* (Amherst, N.Y.: Cambria, 2015); See Jeffrey E. Cohen, *The Presidency in the Era of 24-Hour News* (Princeton, N.J.: Princeton University Press, 2008).

15. Stephen Farnsworth, *Spinner in Chief* (Boulder, Colo.: Paradigm, 2009).

16. Jeffery E. Cohen, *The Presidency in the Era of 24-Hour News* (Princeton, N.J.: Princeton University Press, 2008).

17. George C. Edwards, III, *On Deaf Ears: The Limits of the Bully Pulpit* (New Haven, Conn.: Yale University Press, 2003). See also Edwards, *The Strategic Presidency* (Princeton, N.J.: Princeton University Press, 2009).

18. Edwards, *On Deaf Ears*, p. 254.

19. Quoted in George C. Edwards and Stephen Wayne, *Presidential Leadership*, 3rd ed. (New York: St. Martin's Press, 1994), p. 90.

20. Arthur M. Schlesinger, Jr., "The Ultimate Approval Rating," *New York Times Magazine* (December 15, 1996): 51.

21. Drew Westen, *The Political Brain* (New York: Public Affairs, 2007), p. 310.

CHAPTER 3

1. Michael S. Lewis-Beck et al., *The American Voter Revisited* (Ann Arbor: University of Michigan Press, 2008); Richard R. Lau and David Redlawsk, *How Voters Decided* (New York: Cambridge University Press, 2006); and Bryan Caplan, *The Myth of the Rational Voter* (Princeton, N.J.: Princeton University Press, 2008).

2. James P. Pfiffner, *The Character Factor* (College Station: Texas A&M University Press, 2004).

3. Martin Walker, book review of Robert Wilson's *Character Above All* in *The Washington Monthly* (April 1996): 54; Robert A. Wilson, ed., *Character Above All* (New York: Simon and Schuster, 1995).

4. Jane Mayer, *Dark Money: The Hidden History of the Billionaires Behind the Rise of the Radical Right* (New York: Doubleday, 2016).

5. John Nichols and Robert W. McChesney, *Dollarocracy* (New York: Nation Books, 2013); and Kenneth P. Vogel, *Big Money* (New York: Public Affairs, 2014).

6 Quoted in *New York Times*, October 19, 1974, p. E18.

7. Anthony Gierzynski, *Money Rules* (Boulder: Westview, 2000).

8. 494 U.S. 652. (1990).

9. 540 U.S. 93 (2003).

10. Nicholas Confessore, Sarah Cohen, and Karen Yourish, "Small Pod of Rich Donors Dominates Election," *New York Times*, August 1, 2015.

11. See Wesley Lowery, "91% of the Time the Better-Financed Candidate Wins. Don't Act Surprsied," *Washington Post*, Updated, April 4, 2014.

12. Quoted in Jasper B. Shannon, *Money and Politics* (New York: Random House, 1959), p. 35.

13. Richard L. Fox and Jennifer M. Ramos, *iPolitics: Citizens, Elections, and Governing in the New Media Era* (New York: Cambridge University Press, 2012).

14. See Markus Prior, *Post-Broadcast Democracy* (New York: Cambridge University Press, 2007).

15. Adam Nagourney, "The '08 Campaign: Sea Change for Politics as We Know It," *New York Times* (November 3, 2008): 1.

16. Ibid.

17. See Christopher Hall, *Grassroot Rules: How the Iowa Caucus Helps Elect American Presidents* (Palo Alto: Stanford Law and Politics, 2007).

18. H. L. Mencken and Alistair Cooke, The Vintage Mencken: The Finest and Fiercest Essays of the Great Literary Inconoclast, New York: Vintage Reissue edition, 1990.

19. Laura R. Olson and John C. Green, *Beyond Red State, Blue State: Electoral Gaps in the Twenty-First Century American Electorate* (Upper Saddle River, N.J.: Pearson, 2008); see also the splendid essays in Jody C. Baumgartner and Peter Francia, *Conventional Wisdom and American Elections 2nd edition* (Lanham, Md.: Rowman and Littlefield, 2012).

20. Robert A. Dahl, "Myth of the Presidential Mandate," *Political Science Quarterly* 105 (Fall 1990), pp. 335–72; Patricia H. Conley, *Presidential Mandates: How Elections Shape the Natural Agenda* (Chicago: University of Chicago Press, 2001).

21. See Mark Weston, *The Runner-Up Presidency: The Election That Defied America's Public Will* (New York: Lyons Press, 2016).

22. Norman Ornstein, "No Need to Repeal the Electoral College," *State Legislators Magazine* (February, 2001).

23. George Will, "Forward," in Tara Ross, *Enlightened Democracy: The Case for the Electoral College* (Dallas: Colonial Press, 2004), p. xi.

24. Tara Ross, ibid, pp. 34-59, 172.

25. Arthur Schlesinger, Jr., "The Electoral College Conundrum," *Wall Street Journal* (April 4, 1977). See also his "It's a Mess, but We've Been Through It Before," *Time* (November 20, 2000), p. 64.

26. See *Electing the President: A Report of the Commission on Electoral College Reform* (Chicago: American Bar Association, 1967).

27. Editorial, "Flunking the Electoral College," *New York Times* (November 20, 2008), p. A32.

28. George Edwards, *Why the Electoral College Is Bad for America* (New Haven: Yale University Press, 2011), p. 39.

29. Such a system was supported by a group called the Center for Voting and Democracy, as well as by the Ralph Nader–inspired Public Interest Research Group. See www.votersdecide.com. Australia uses a similar system for its parliamentary elections, and Ireland uses it to elect their president, the ceremonial head of state.

30. William Poundstone, *Gaming the Vote: Why Elections Aren't Fair and What We Can Do About It* (New York: Hill and Wang, 2008).

CHAPTER 4

1. Pew Research Center, "Trust in Government: 1958–2015," November 23, 2015.

2. Samuel P. Huntington, *American Politics: The Promise of Disharmony* (Cambridge, Mass.: Harvard University Press, 1981), pp. 4, 33.

3. Clinton Rossiter, *Conservatism in America* (New York: Vintage, 1962), p.72.

4. George W. Bush, Address to Airline Employees, O'Hare International Airport, Chicago, Illinois. September 27, 2001; available at The American Presidency Project, http://www.presidency.ucsb.edu/ws/?pid=65084.

5. George W. Bush, *Decision Points* (New York: Crown Publishing, 2010), p. 444.

6. President Donald J. Trump, "Inaugural Address," 20 January 2017. Available at www.whitehouse.gov.

7. Stephen Skowronek, *The Politics Presidents Make* (Cambridge, Mass.: Belknap Press, 1993).

8. Arthur M. Schlesinger, Jr., *The Cycles of American History* (Boston: Houghton Mifflin, 1986), pp. 22–27.

9. Jacob S. Hacker and Paul Pierson, *American Amnesia: How the War on Government Led Us to Forget What Made America Prosper* (New York: Basic Books, 2016), p. 7.

10. The original publication was Richard E. Neustadt, *Presidential Power: The Politics of Leadership* (New York: John Wiley & Sons, 1960). The last edition, *Presidential Power and the Modern Presidents: The Politics of Leadership* (New York: Free Press, 1990), includes commentary up to and including the Reagan presidency. See also John P. Burke, *Presidential Power: Theories and Dilemmas* (Boulder, Colo.: Westview Press, 2016).

11. Niccolo Machiavelli, *The Prince* (New Haven, Conn.: Yale University Press, 1997), Chapter XVII.

12. Garry Wills, *Nixon Agonistes: The Crisis of the Self-Made Man* (Boston: Houghton Mifflin, 1970; reprint ed. 2002), p. 221.

13. L. Gordon Corvitz and Jeremy A. Rabkin, eds., *The Fettered Presidency: Legal Constraints on the Executive Branch* (Washington, D.C.: American Enterprise Institute, 1989). See also the helpful revisionist commentary on Neustadt's analysis by Fred Greenstein, *The Presidential Difference: Leadership Style from FDR to Barack Obama*, 3rd ed. (Princeton, N.J.: Princeton University Press, 2009), pp. 292–94.

14. James P. Pfiffner, *The Strategic Presidency: Hitting the Ground Running*, 2nd ed., rev. (Lawrence: University Press of Kansas, 1996); George C. Edwards, *The Strategic President: Persuasion and Opportunity in Presidential Leadership* (Princeton, N.J.: Princeton University Press, 2009).

15. Jeffrey K. Tulis, *The Rhetorical Presidency*, rev. ed. (Princeton, N.J.: Princeton University Press, 1988); Samuel Kernell, *Going Public: New Strategies of Presidential Leadership*, 4th ed. (Washington, D.C.: CQ Press, 2006).

16. George C. Edwards III, *On Deaf Ears: The Limits of the Bully Pulpit* (New Haven: Yale University Press, 2003).

17. Pfiffner, *The Strategic Presidency*, p. 3.

18. William G. Howell and Terry M. Moe, *Relic: How Our Constitution Undermines Effective Government—And Why We Need a More Powerful Presidency* (New York: Basic Books, 2016).

19. Gene Healy, *The Cult of the Presidency* (Washington, D.C.: Cato Institute), p. 3.

20. Louis Fisher, "Teaching the Presidency: Idealizing a Constitutional Office," *PS* (January, 2012): 17–31.

CHAPTER 5

1. James Madison, *Federalist* No. 51, "The Structure of the Government Must Furnish the Proper Checks and Balances Between the Different Departments," *New York Packet*, 8 February 1788.

2. James Madison, *Federalist* No. 45, "The Alleged Danger from the Powers of the Union to the State Governments Considered," *Independent Journal*, date not available; and Alexander Hamilton, *Federalist* No. 70, "The Executive Department Further Considered," *New York Packet*, 18 March 1788.

3. Glenn A. Phelps, *George Washington and American Constitutionalism* (Lawrence: University Press of Kansas, 1993).

4. Herman Belz, *Lincoln and the Constitution: The Dictatorship Question Reconsidered* (Fort Wayne, Ind.: Louis A. Warren Lincoln Library and Museum, 1984); James G. Randall, *Constitutional Problems under Lincoln*, rev. ed. (Urbana: University of Illinois Press, 1951); David Donald, *Lincoln* (New York: Simon & Schuster, 1995).

5. Jeffrey K. Tulis, *The Rhetorical Presidency* (Princeton, N.J.: Princeton University Press, 1987).

6. Theodore Roosevelt, *The Autobiography of Theodore Roosevelt* (New York: Charles Scribner's Sons, 1941), p. 197–98; Doris Kearns Goodwin, *The Bully Pulpit: Theodore Roosevelt, William Howard Taft, and the Golden Age of Journalism* (New York: Simon & Schuster, 2013).

7. William E. Leuchtenburg, *In the Shadow of FDR: From Harry Truman to Ronald Reagan* (Ithaca, N.Y.: Cornell University Press, 1983).

8. Fred I. Greenstein, *The Hidden-Hand Presidency: Eisenhower as Leader* (New York: Basic Books, 1982).

9. Larry Berman, *Lyndon Johnson's War* (New York: Norton, 1989).

10. John F. Kennedy, quoted in Richard Nixon, *RN: Memoirs of Richard Nixon* (New York: Grosset & Dunlap, 1978), p. 235.

11. Richard Nixon, quoted in Theodore White, *The Making of the President 1968* (New York: Atheneum, 1969), p. 147.

12. Louis Fisher, *Presidential War Power*, 3rd ed. rev. (Lawrence: University Press of Kansas, 2013).

13. See, for example, Jeffrey Goldberg, "The Obama Doctrine: How He's Shaped the World," *The Atlantic* (April 2016): 70–90.

14. One such critique is Dick Cheney and Liz Cheney, *Exceptional: Why the World Needs a Powerful America* (New York: Simon & Schuster, 2015), chs. 4–7.

15. See, for example, John Hudak, *Presidential Pork: White House Influence over the Distribution of Federal Grants* (Washington, D.C.: Brookings Institution Press, 2014).

16. George W. Bush, *Decision Points* (New York: Crown Publishing, 2010), p. 440.

17. Iwan Morgan, *The Age of Deficits: Presidents and Unbalanced Budgets from Jimmy Carter to George W. Bush* (Lawrence: University Press of Kansas, 2009); Steven E. Schier, ed., *Transforming America: Barack Obama in the White House* (New York: Rowman & Littlefield, 2011).

18. George W. Bush, *Decision Points* (New York: Crown Publishers, 2010), p. 330.

19. Jonathan Alter, *The Promise: President Obama's First Year* (New York: Simon and Schuster, 2010).

20. Marc J. Hetherington and Thomas J. Rudolph, *Why Washington Won't Work: Polarization, Political Trust, and the Governing Crisis* (Chicago, IL: University of Chicago Press, 2015).

21. Jacob S. Hacker and Paul Pierson, *American Amnesia: How the War on Government Led Us to Forget What Made America Prosper* (New York: Simon & Schuster, 2016).

CHAPTER 6

1. James S. Young, *The Washington Community, 1800–1828* (New York: Columbia University Press, 1966), pp. 75–76.

2. Emmet John Hughes, *The Living Presidency* (New York: Coward, McCann & Geoghegan, 1973), p. 208.

3. See Gary Andres and Patrick J. Griffin, "Successful Influence: Managing Legislative Affairs in the Twenty-First Century," in *Rivals for Power: Presidential-Congressional*

Relations, 2nd ed., ed. James A. Thurber (New York: Rowman & Littlefield, 2002), p. 144.

4. As *Federalist* No. 47 reminds us, "The executive magistrate forms an integral part of the legislative authority."

5. Clinton Rossiter, *The American Presidency* (New York: Harcourt, Brace & World, Inc., 1980), p. 26.

6. George C. Edwards III, *At The Margins: Presidential Leadership of Congress* (New Haven: Yale University Press, 1989).

7. *Youngstown Sheet and Tube Co. v. Sawyer,* 343 US 579, 635 (1952).

8. Keith Krehbiel, *Pivotal Politics: A Theory of U.S. Lawmaking* (Chicago: University of Chicago Press, 1998).

9. Samuel Kernell, *Going Public: Strategies in Presidential Leadership* (Washington, D.C.: CQ Press, 1986; 4th ed. 2006).

10. George C. Edwards, III, *On Deaf Ears: The Limits of the Bully Pulpit* (New Haven: Yale University Press, 2003).

11. Brandice Canes-Wrone, "The President's Legislative Influence from Public Opinion," *American Journal of Political Science* 45, no. 2 (2001):313–329. See also M. Eshbaugh-Soha and J. Peake, "Presidential Influence over the Systemic Agenda," *Congress and the Presidency* 31 (2004): 181–201; and Andrew W. Barrett, "Gone Public: The Impact of Going Public on Presidential Legislative Success," *American Politics Research* 32, no. 3 (May 2004): 338–370.

12. Andrew Rudalevige, *Managing the President's Program: Presidential Leadership and Legislative Policy Formation* (Princeton, N.J.: Princeton University Press, 2002).

13. Matthew N. Beckmann, *Pushing the Agenda: Presidential Leadership in U.S. Lawmaking: 1953-2004* (New York: Cambridge University Press, 2010); Jasmine Farrier, *Passing the Buck: Congress, the President, and Deficits* (Lexington: University Press of Kentucky, 2004).

14. Robert Spitzer, *The Presidential Veto* (Albany: State University of New York Press, 1988).

15. Charles M. Cameron, *Veto Bargaining: Presidents and the Politics of Negative Power* (New York: Cambridge University Press, 2000).

16. Robert V. Remini "The Emergence of Political Parties and Their Effect on the Presidency," in Philip C. Dolce and George H. Skau, eds., *Power and the Presidency* (New York: Columbia University Press, 1959), pp. 24–34.

17. Quoted in Arthur B. Tourtellot, *The Presidents on the Presidency* (New York: Doubleday, 1964), p. 387.

18. Ibid., p. 5

19. Leonard W. Levy, *Original Intent and the Framers' Constitution* (New York: Macmillan, 1988), p. 30.

20. Arthur M. Schlesinger, Jr., *The Imperial Presidency* (Boston, Mass.: Houghton Mifflin, 1973).

21. President Barack Obama, report to Congress, "United States Activities in Libya," June 15, 2011.

22. William G. Howell and John C. Penthouse, *While Dangers Gather: Congressional Checks on Presidential War Powers* (Princeton: Princeton University Press, 2007). See also Andrew Rudalevige, *The New Imperial Presidency* (Ann Arbor: The University of Michigan Press, 2005); and James P. Pfiffner, *Power Play: The Bush Presidency and the Constitution* (Washington, D.C.: Brookings, 2008).

23. Michael J. Gerhardt, *The Federal Appointment Process: A Constitutional History* (Durham, N.C.: Duke University Press, 2003); G. Calvin Mackenzie, ed., *Innocent Until*

Nominated: The Breakdown of the Presidential Appointment Process (Washington, D.C.: Brookings Institution Press, 2001).

24. John Massaro, *Supremely Political: The Role of Ideology and Presidential Management in Unsuccessful Supreme Court Nominations* (Albany: State University of New York Press, 1990); Christine L. Nemacheck, *Strategic Selection: Presidential Nominations of Supreme Court Justices from Herbert Hoover through George W. Bush* (Charlottesville: University of Virginia Press, 2007).

25. The case for strong presidential leadership is made in William G. Howell and Terry M. Moe, *Relic: How Our Institutions Undermine Effective Government—And Why We Need a More Powerful Presidency* (New York: Basic Books, 2016); and in Jacob S. Hacker and Paul Pierson, *American Amnesia: How the War on Government Led Us to Forget What Made America Prosper* (New York: Simon & Schuster, 2016).

CHAPTER 7

1. See MaryAnne Borrelli, *The President's Cabinet: Gender, Power, and Representation* (Boulder, Colo.: Lynne Rienner, 2002); Shirley Anne Warshaw, *Powersharing: White House–Cabinet Relations in the Modern Presidency* (Albany: State University of New York, 1996); and Anthony J. Bennett, *The American President's Cabinet: From Kennedy to Bush* (New York: St. Martin's, 1996). Finally, see Robert B. Reich's curious memoir from the Bill Clinton years, *Locked in the Cabinet* (New York: Knopf, 1997).

2. Jimmy Carter, *Keeping Faith: Memoirs of a President* (New York: Bantam, 1982), p. 60.

3. Henry Learned, *The President's Cabinet: Studies in the Origin, Formation, and Structure of an American Institution* (New Haven, Conn.: Burt Franklin, 1912, reissued in 1972), p. 119. See also Mary L. Hinsdale, *A History of the President's Cabinet* (Ann Arbor: University of Michigan Press, 1911). The best study of the cabinet in the mid-twentieth century was Richard Fenno, *The President's Cabinet* (New York: Vintage, 1959).

4. Robert B. Reich, *Locked in the Cabinet* (New York: Knopf, 1997), pp. 51–52.

5. McGeorge Bundy, *The Strength of Government* (Cambridge, Mass.: Harvard University Press, 1968), p. 39.

6. Bradley H. Patterson Jr., *The President's Cabinet: Issues and Questions* (Washington, D.C.: American Society for Public Administration, 1976), pp. 17–18. See also his *The White House Staff: Inside the West Wing and Beyond* (Washington, D.C.: The Brookings Institution, 2000).

7. Charles Dawes, quoted in Kermit Gordon, "Reflections on Spending," in J. D. Montgomery and Arthur Smithies, eds., *Public Policy* (Cambridge, Mass.: Harvard University Press, 1966), p. 15.

8. Walter J. Hickel's letter to President Nixon, May 6, 1970, quoted in *New York Times* (May 7, 1970): C18.

9. Quoted in *U.S. News and World Report* (March 29, 1982): 28. For a Reagan cabinet member's perspective, see the instructive memoir by Secretary of Education "Ted" Bell, who served from 1981 to 1985, when he was unceremoniously let go; Terrel H. Bell, *The Thirteenth Man: A Reagan Cabinet Member* (New York: Free Press, 1988).

10. Kenneth Mayer, *With the Stroke of a Pen: Executive Orders and Presidential Power* (Princeton, N.J.: Princeton University Press, 2001), and Phillip Cooper, *By Order of the President: The Use and Abuse of Executive Direct Action* (Lawrence: University Press of Kansas, 2002).

11. See *Jenkins v. Collard*, 1891, 145 U.S. 546.

12. See, for example, Charlie Savage, *Power Wars: Inside Obama's Post-9/11 Presidency* (New York: Little, Brown and Co., 2015).

13. James P. Pfiffner, "The President's Chief of Staff: Lessons Learned," Working Paper 92, Institute of Public Policy, George Mason University, October 1992, p. 19.

14. Summarizing interviews with White House aides Charles E. Walcott, Shirley Anna Warshaw, and Stephen Wayne, "The Office of Chief of Staff," in Martha Joynt Kumar and Terry Sullivan, eds., *The White House World* (College Station, Tex.: Texas A&M University, 2003), p. 136.

15. Quoted in David Axelrod, *Believer: My Forty Years in Politics* (New York: Penguin, 2015), p. 430.

16. Helen Thomas, *Watchdogs of Democracy* (New York: Scribner, 2006), p. 36.

17. See Jules Witcover, *The American Vice Presidency: From Irrelevance to Power* (Washington, D.C.: Smithsonian Books, 2014), and Paul C. Light, *Vice Presidential Power: Advice and Influence in the White House* (Baltimore, Md.: Johns Hopkins University Press, 1984), p. 1. See also Jody C. Baumgartner, *The American Vice Presidency Reconsidered* (Westport, Conn.: Praeger, 2006).

18. Allan P. Sindler, *Unchosen Presidents: The Vice-President and Other Frustrations of Presidential Succession* (Berkeley: University of California Press, 1976).

19. See his memoir, Dick Cheney, *In My Time* (New York: Threshold, 2011).

20. David Bromwich, "The Co-President at Work," *New York Review of Books* (Nov. 20, 2008): 33.

21. David Plouffe, *The Audacity to Win: The Inside Story and Lessons of Barack Obama's Historic Victory* (New York: Viking, 2009), p. 289.

22. Peter Baker, "Finding Voice Again, Biden Sees Time Left to Make a Difference," *New York Times* (Dec. 10, 2015): A28.

23. Fred I. Greenstein, *The Presidential Difference* (New York: Free Press, 2000), p. 195.

24. See Alexander L. George and Eric K. Stern, "Harnessing Conflict in Foreign Policy Making: From Devil's to Multiple Advocacy," *Presidential Studies Quarterly* (September 2002): 484–508. See David Gergen, *Eyewitness to Power: The Essence of Leadership from Nixon to Clinton* (New York: Simon & Schuster, 2000). See also Richard M. Pious, *Why Presidents Fail* (Lanham, Md.: Rowman and Littlefield, 2008), chaps. 10 and 11.

25. Chu quoted in John M. Broder, "Energy Secretary's Challenge" *New York Times* (March 23, 2009): A13.

CHAPTER 8

1. Terry Eastland, *Energy in the Executive: The Case for the Strong Presidency* (New York: Free Press, 1992), p. 235.

2. Selections from the *Correspondence of Theodore Roosevelt and Henry Cabot Lodge, 1884–1918* (New York: Charles Scribner's Sons, 1925), Vol. II, p. 519. For a good study of President Harding's appointment of a Supreme Court Justice, see David J. Danelski, *A Supreme Court Justice Is Appointed* (New York: Random House, 1964).

3. Lees Epstein and Eric A. Posner, "Supreme Court Justices' Loyalty to the President," *Journal of Legal Studies* 45 (June 2016): 406.

4. Michael Comiskey, *Seeking Justices: The Judging of Supreme Court Nominees* (Lawrence: University Press of Kansas, 2016).

5. Stephen L. Carter, *The Confirmation Mess* (New York: Basic Books, 1994).

6. Jane Mayer and Jill Abramson, *Strange Justice: The Selling of Clarence Thomas* (New York: Houghton Mifflin, 1994); John C. Danforth, *Resurrection: The Confirmation of Clarence Thomas* (New York: Viking, 1994). For a reaction to both the Bork and Thomas nominations, see Stephen L. Carter, *The Confirmation Mess* (New York: Basic Books, 1994).

7. James Gerstenzang, "Bush Urges Judicial Process Changes," *Los Angeles Times* (October 31, 2002): A10.

8. Robert Scigliano, *The Supreme Court and the Presidency* (New York: The Free Press, 1971), pp. 146–147. Another study concludes that most presidents by and large do rather well in appointing individuals who will be supportive of the administration which supports them, at least during their first few years on the Court. "After that initial period, there is an apparent falling off." See Roger Handberg and Harold F. Hill, Jr., "Predicting the Judicial Performance of Presidential Appointments to the United States Supreme Court," *Presidential Studies Quarterly* (Fall, 1984): 538–547.

9. Scigliano, *The Supreme Court and the Presidency*, p. 159. This view is also echoed in David M. O'Brien, *Storm Center: The Supreme Court in American Politics* (New York: Norton, 1986), Ch. 2.

10. Frederick Schauer, "Should Presidents Obey the Law?" in Terry L. Price and J. Thomas Wren, eds., *The Values of Presidential Leadership* (New York: Palgrave MacMillan, 2007).

11. See Hamilton, Madison, and Jay, *The Federalist Papers*, No. 48. (New York: New American Library, 1961) p. 316

12. Daniel P. Franklin, *Extraordinary Measures: The Exercise of Prerogative Powers in the United States* (Pittsburgh: University of Pittsburgh Press, 1991).

13. See Richard A. Posner, *Not a Suicide Pact: The Constitution in a Time of National Emergency* (New York: Oxford University Press, 2006).

14. Edward S. Corwin, *Total War and the Constitution* (Westminster, Md: Knopf, 1947), p. 80.

15. Ryan C. Hendrickson, *The Clinton Wars: The Constitution, Congress, and War Power* (Nashville, Tenn.: Vanderbilt University Press, 2002); Louis Fisher, "The Law: Legal Disputes in the Clinton Years," *Presidential Studies Quarterly* (September 1999);

16. *The Prize Cases*, 67 U.S. (2 Black) 635 (1863).

17. *In re Neagle*, 135 U.S. 1 (1890).

18. *United States v. Curtiss-Wright Export Corporation* 299 U.S. 304 (1936).

19. *United States v. Belmont* 301 U.S. 324 (1937).

20. Eugene V. Rostow, book review, *Washington Post National Weekly Edition* (January 2, 1984): 34. See also Peter Irons, *Justice at War: The Story of the Japanese American Internment Cases* (New York: Oxford University Press, 1983).

21. William H. Rehnquist, *All the Laws but One: Civil Liberties in Wartime* (New York: Knopf, 2001).

22. *Marbury v. Madison*, 1 Cranch, 137, 2 L. Ed. 60 (1803).

23. *Little v. Bareme*, 2 Cranch 170 (1804).

24. *Humphrey's Executor v. United States*, 295 U.S. 602, 628 (1935).

25. Robert J. Donovan, *Tumultuous Years* (New York: Norton, 1982), p. 387.

26. *New York Times Co. v. United States* 403 U.S. 712 (1971).

27. Ibid.

28. *United States v. U.S. District Court*, 407 U.S. 297 (1972).

29. *Clinton v. Jones*, 520 U.S. 681 (1977).

30. Jack Goldsmith, *The Terror Presidency: Law and Judgment Inside the Bush Administration* (New York: Norton, 2007); Jane Meyer, *The Dark Side* (New York: Doubleday, 2008).

31. Allan A. Ryan, *The 9/11 Terror Cases* (Lawrence: University Press of Kansas, 2015).
32. *Rasul v. Bush*, 542 U.S. 466, 2004.
33. *Hamdi v. Ramsfield*, 542 U.S. 507, 2004.
34. *Hamden v. Rumsfeld*, 548 U.S. 557, 2006.
35. *Boumediene v. Bush*, 553 U.S. 723, 2008.
36. Jonathan Mahler, *The Challenge:* Hamden v. Rumsfeld *and the Fight over Presidential Power* (New York: Farrar, Straus, and Giroux, 2008); Benjamin Wittles, *Law and the Long War: The Future of Justice in the Age of Terror* (New York: The Penguin Press, 2008).
37. Adam Liptak, "Some Big Wins in Court, But Weak Record Overall," *New York Times* (Jan. 24, 2017): A12.
38. Eric Posner and Lee Epstein, "Supreme Court Justices' Loyalty to the President," *Journal of Legal Studies*, 401 (2016).

CHAPTER 9

1. Clinton Rossiter, *The American Presidency* (New York: Harcourt, Brace, 1956), p. 257.
2. Irving Kristol, "The Spirit of '87," *The Public Interest* (Winter, 1987): 3.
3. A few examples of these reform proposals are found in Richard J. Ellis and Michael Nelson, eds., *Debating the Presidency*, 4th ed. (Thousand Oaks, CA: CQ Press, 2018); Sanford Levinson, *Our Undemocratic Constitution* (New York: Oxford University Press, 2006); and Larry Sabato, *A More Perfect Constitution* (New York: Walker, 2008).
4. Wilson, quoted in Larry Berman, *The New American Presidency* (Boston: Little, Brown, 1987), p. 117.
5. See Francis Fukuyama, "American Political Decay or Renewal?" *Foreign Affairs* (July/August, 2016): 58; and Jacob Hacker and Paul Peirson, *American Amnesia: How the War on Government Led Us to Forget What Made America Prosper* (New York: Simon and Schuster, 2016).
6. Bruce Bartlett, http://bartlett.blogs.nytimes.com (accessed March 15, 2006).
7. Fisher, quoted in Gregory Korte, "Lawmakers Modify Idea of Line-Item Veto," *USA Today* (December 9, 2011): 6A.
8. William Howell and Terry Moe, *Relic* (New York: Basic Books, 2016).
9. Ibid., p. 151.
10. Michael J. Korzi, *Presidential Term Limits in American History: Power, Principles and Politics* (College Station: Texas A&M University Press, 2011).
11. Clinton Rossiter, *The American Presidency* (New York: Harcourt, Brace, and World, 1960), p. 232.
12. James R. Hedtke, *Lame Duck Presidents: Myth or Reality?* (Lewiston, N.Y.: Edwin Mellen Press, 2002).
13. Ibid., p. 236.
14. Quotation from Gaillard Hunt, ed., *The Writings of James Madison*, vol. 6 (New York: G. P. Putnam's Sons, 1900–1910), pp. 312–314.
15. See Garry Wills, *Bomb Power: The Modern Presidency and the National Security State* (New York: Penguin, 2010); and Charlie Savage, *Power Wars* (New York: Little, Brown, 2016).
16. See *George Washington Law Review*, which contained a symposium on the no-confidence proposal (January 1975): 328–500.

17. David Cole, "How to Reverse *Citizens United*," *The Atlantic* (April, 2016): 13–15.

18. Diamond, quoted in Thomas L. Friedman, "Third Party Rising," *New York Times* (October 3, 2010): 8, Sunday Opinion.

19. Friedman, ibid., p. 8.

20. Ross K. Baker, "Third Party in 2012? Forget About It," *USA Today* (December 7, 2012).

21. Michael Nelson, writing in defense of the idea, in Richard J. Ellis and Michael Nelson, eds., *Debating the Presidency* 3rd edition, (Thousand Oaks, Calif.: CQ Press, 2015), p. 45.

22. Learned Hand, "The Spirit of Liberty," a speech in 1944.

Presidential Election Results, 1789–2016

Presidential Election Results, 1789–2016

YEAR	PRESIDENTS/VICE-PRESIDENTS/OTHER CANDIDATES	PARTY	POPULAR VOTE	ELECTORAL VOTE
1789	George Washington			69
	John Adams			
	John Adams			34
	Others			35
1793	George Washington			132
	John Adams			
	John Adams			77
	George Clinton			50
	Others			5
1796	John Adams	Federalist		71
	Thomas Jefferson			
	Thomas Jefferson	Democratic-Republican		68
	Thomas Pinckney	Federalist		59
	Aaron Burr	Democratic-Republican		30
	Others			48
1800	Thomas Jefferson	Democratic-Republican		73
	Aaron Burr			
	Aaron Burr	Democratic-Republican		73
	John Adams	Federalist		65
	Charles C. Pinckney	Federalist		64
1804	Thomas Jefferson	Democratic-Republican		162
	George Clinton			
	Charles C. Pinckney	Federalist		14
1808	James Madison	Democratic-Republican		122
	George Clinton			
	Charles C. Pinckney	Federalist		47
	George Clinton	Independent-Republican		6
1812	James Madison	Democratic-Republican		128
	Elbridge Gerry			
	DeWitt Clinton	Federalist		89

Presidential Election Results, 1789–2016

YEAR	PRESIDENTS/VICE-PRESIDENTS/OTHER CANDIDATES	PARTY	POPULAR VOTE	ELECTORAL VOTE
1816	James Monroe	Democratic-Republican		183
	Daniel D. Tompkins			
	Rufus King	Federalist		34
1820	James Monroe	Democratic-Republican		231
	Daniel D. Tompkins			
	John Quincy Adams	Independent-Republican		1
1824	John Quincy Adams	Democratic-Republican	108,740(30.5%)	84
	John C. Calhoun			
	Andrew Jackson	Democratic-Republican	153,544(43.1%)	99
	Henry Clay	Democratic-Republican	47,136(13.2%)	37
	William H. Crawford	Democratic-Republican	46,618(13.1%)	41
1828	Andrew Jackson	Democratic	647,231(56.0%)	178
	John C. Calhoun			
	John Quincy Adams	National Republican	509,097(44.0%)	83
1832	Andrew Jackson	Democratic	687,502(55.0%)	219
	Martin Van Buren			
	Henry Clay	National Republican	530,189(42.4%)	49
	William Wirt	Anti-Masonic		7
	John Floyd	National Republican	33,108(2.6%)	11
1836	Martin Van Buren	Democratic	761,549(50.9%)	170
	Richard M. Johnson			
	William H. Harrison	Whig	549,567(36.7%)	73
	Hugh L. White	Whig	145,396(9.7%)	26
	Daniel Webster	Whig	41,287(2.7%)	14
1840	William H. Harrison	Whig	1,275,017(53.1%)	234
	John Tyler			
	Martin Van Buren	Democratic	1,128,702(46.9%)	60
1844	James K. Polk	Democratic	1,337,243(49.6%)	170
	George M. Dallas			
	Henry Clay	Whig	1,299,068(48.1%)	105
	James G. Birney	Liberty	63,300(2.3%)	
1848	Zachary Taylor	Whig	1,360,101(47.4%)	163
	Millard Fillmore			
	Lewis Cass	Democratic	1,220,544(42.5%)	127
	Martin Van Buren	Free Soil	291,163(10.1%)	
1852	Franklin Pierce	Democratic	1,601,474(50.9%)	254
	William R. King			
	Winfield Scott	Whig	1,386,578(44.1%)	42
1856	James Buchanan	Democratic	1,838,169(45.4%)	174
	John C. Breckinridge			
	John C. Fremont	Republican	1,335,264(33.0%)	114
	Millard Fillmore	American	874,534(21.6%)	8
1860	Abraham Lincoln	Republican	1,865,593(39.8%)	180
	Hannibal Hamlin			
	Stephen A. Douglas	Democratic	1,381,713(29.5%)	12
	John C. Breckinridge	Democratic	848,356(18.1%)	72
	John Bell	Constitutional Union	592,906(12.6%)	79
1864	Abraham Lincoln	Republican	2,206,938(55.0%)	212

Presidential Election Results, 1789–2016

YEAR	PRESIDENTS/VICE-PRESIDENTS/OTHER CANDIDATES	PARTY	POPULAR VOTE	ELECTORAL VOTE
	Andrew Johnson			
	George B. McClellan	Democratic	1,803,787(45.0%)	21
1868	Ulysses S. Grant	Republican	3,013,421(52.7%)	214
	Schuyler Colfax			
	Horatio Seymour	Democratic	2,706,829(47.3%)	80
1872	Ulysses S. Grant	Republican	3,596,745(55.6%)	286
	Henry Wilson			
	Horace Greeley	Democratic	2,843,446(43.9%)	66
1876	Rutherford B. Hayes	Republican	4,036,571(48.0%)	185
	William A. Wheeler			
	Samuel J. Tilden	Democratic	4,284,020(51.0%)	184
1880	James A. Garfield	Republican	4,449,053(48.3%)	214
	Chester A. Arthur			
	Winfield S. Hancock	Democratic	4,442,035(48.2%)	155
	James B. Weaver	Greenback-Labor	308,578(3.4%)	
1884	Grover Cleveland	Democratic	4,874,986(48.5%)	219
	T. A. Hendricks			
	James G. Blaine	Republican	4,851,931(48.2%)	182
	Benjamin F. Butler	Greenback-Labor	175,370(1.8%)	
1888	Benjamin Harrison	Republican	5,444,337(47.8%)	233
	Levi P. Morton			
	Grover Cleveland	Democratic	5,540,050(48.6%)	168
1892	Grover Cleveland	Democratic	5,554,414(46.0%)	277
	Adlai E. Stevenson			
	Benjamin Harrison	Republican	5,190,802(43.0%)	145
	James B. Weaver	Peoples	1,027,329(8.5%)	22
1896	Wiliam McKinley	Republican	7,035,638(50.8%)	271
	Garret A. Hobart			
	William J. Bryan	Democratic; Populist	6,467,946(46.7%)	176
1900	William McKinley	Republican	7,219,530(51.7%)	292
	Theodore Roosevelt			
	William J. Bryan	Democratic; Populist	6,356,734(45.5%)	155
1904	Theodore Roosevelt	Republican	7,628,834(56.4%)	336
	Charles Fairbanks			
	Alton B. Parker	Democratic	5,084,401(37.6%)	140
	Eugene V. Debs	Socialist	402,460(3.0%)	0
1908	William H. Taft	Republican	7,679,006(51.6%)	321
	James S. Sherman			
	William J. Bryan	Democratic	6,409,106(43.1%)	162
	Eugene V. Debs	Socialist	420,820(2.8%)	0
1912	Woodrow Wilson	Democratic	6,286,820(41.8%)	435
	Thomas R. Marshall			
	Theodore Roosevelt	Progressive	4,126,020(27.4%)	88
	William H. Taft	Republican	3,483,922(23.2%)	8
1916	Woodrow Wilson	Democratic	9,129,606(49.3%)	277
	Thomas R. Marshall			
	Charles E. Hughes	Republican	8,538,211(46.1%)	254
1920	Warren G. Harding	Republican	16,152,200(61.0%)	404

Presidential Election Results, 1789–2016

YEAR	PRESIDENTS/VICE-PRESIDENTS/OTHER CANDIDATES	PARTY	POPULAR VOTE	ELECTORAL VOTE
	Calvin Coolidge			
	James M. Cox	Democratic	9,147,353(34.6%)	127
	Eugene V. Debs	Socialist	919,799(3.5%)	0
1924	Calvin Coolidge	Republican	15,725,016(54.1%)	382
	Charles G. Dawes			
	John W. Davis	Democratic	8,385,586(28.8%)	136
	Robert M. La Follette	Progressive	4,822,856(16.6%)	13
1928	Herbert C. Hoover	Republican	21,392,190(58.2%)	444
	Charles Curtis			
	Alfred E. Smith	Democratic	15,016,443(40.8%)	87
1932	Franklin D. Roosevelt	Democratic	22,809,638(57.3%)	472
	John Nance Garner			
	Herbert C. Hoover	Republican	15,758,901(39.6%)	59
	Norman Thomas	Socialist	881,951(2.2%)	0
1936	Franklin D. Roosevelt	Democratic	27,751,612(60.7%)	523
	John Nance Garner			
	Alfred M. Landon	Republican	16,681,913(36.4%)	8
	William Lemke	Union	891,858(1.9%)	0
1940	Franklin D. Roosevelt	Democratic	27,243,466(54.7%)	449
	Henry A. Wallace			
	Wendell L. Wilkie	Republican	22,304,755(44.8%)	82
1944	Franklin D. Roosevelt	Democratic	25,602,505(52.8%)	432
	Harry S. Truman			
	Thomas E. Dewey	Republican	22,006,278(44.5%)	99
1948	Harry S. Truman	Democratic	24,105,812(49.5%)	303
	Alben W. Barkley			
	Thomas E. Dewey	Republican	21,970,065(45.1%)	189
	J. Strom Thurmond	States' Rights	1,169,063(2.4%)	39
	Henry A. Wallace	Progressive	1,157,172(2.4%)	0
1952	Dwight D. Eisenhower	Republican	33,936,234(55.2%)	442
	Richard M. Nixon			
	Adlai E. Stevenson	Democratic	27,314,992(44.5%)	89
1956	Dwight D. Eisenhower	Republican	35,590,472(57.4%)	457
	Richard M. Nixon			
	Adlai E. Stevenson	Democratic	26,022,752(42.0%)	73
1960	John F. Kennedy	Democratic	34,227,096(49.9%)	303
	Lyndon B. Johnson			
	Richard M. Nixon	Republican	34,108,546(49.6%)	219
1964	Lyndon B. Johnson	Democratic	43,126,233(61.1%)	486
	Hubert H. Humphrey			
	Barry Goldwater	Republican	27,174,989(38.5%)	52
1968	Richard M. Nixon	Republican	31,783,783(43.4%)	301
	Spiro T. Agnew			
	Hubert H. Humphrey	Democratic	31,271,839(42.7%)	191
	George C. Wallace	American Independent	9,899,557(13.5%)	46
1972	Richard M. Nixon	Republican	46,632,189(61.3%)	520
	Spiro T. Agnew			
	George McGovern	Democratic	28,422,015(37.3%)	17

Presidential Election Results, 1789–2016

YEAR	PRESIDENTS/VICE-PRESIDENTS/OTHER CANDIDATES	PARTY	POPULAR VOTE	ELECTORAL VOTE
1976	Jimmy Carter	Democratic	40,828,587(50.1%)	297
	Walter F. Mondale			
	Gerald R. Ford	Republican	39,147,613(48.0%)	240
1980	Ronald Reagan	Republican	42,941,145(51.0%)	489
	George H. W. Bush			
	Jimmy Carter	Democratic	34,663,037(41.0%)	49
	John B. Anderson	Independent	5,551,551(6.6%)	0
1984	Ronald Reagan	Republican	53,428,357(59%)	525
	George H. W. Bush			
	Walter F. Mondale	Democratic	36,930,923(41%)	13
1988	George Bush	Republican	48,881,011(53%)	426
	James D. Quayle III			
	Michael Dukakis	Democratic	41,828,350(46%)	111
1992	Bill Clinton	Democratic	38,394,210(43%)	370
	Albert Gore			
	George Bush	Republican	33,974,386(38%)	168
	H. Ross Perot	Independent	16,573,465(19%)	0
1996	Bill Clinton	Democratic	45,628,667(49%)	379
	Albert Gore			
	Bob Dole	Republican	37,869,435(41%)	159
	H. Ross Perot	Reform	7,874,283(8%)	0
2000	George W. Bush	Republican	50,456,169(48%)	271
	Richard Cheney			
	Al Gore	Democrat	50,996,116(48%)	266
2004	George W. Bush	Republican	60,040,610 (50.73%)	286
	Richard Cheney			
	John Kerry	Democrat	59,028,439 (48.27%)	251
2008	Barack Obama	Democrat	69,499,428 (52.8%)	365
	Joseph Biden			
	John McCain	Republican	59,950,323 (45.6%)	173
2012	Barack Obama	Democrat	62,610,003 (50.6%)	332
	Joseph Biden			
	Mitt Romney	Republican	59,133,398 (47.8%)	206
2016	Donald Trump	Republican	62,979,636 (46.1%)	304
	Mike Pence			
	Hillary Clinton	Democrat	65,844,610 (48.2%)	227

Index

CPSIA information can be obtained
at www.ICGtesting.com
Printed in the USA
JSHW021546031019
1763JS00003B/11